Criminal Justice
Recent Scholarship

Edited by
Marilyn McShane and Frank P. Williams III

A Series from LFB Scholarly

Policing Cyberspace
A Structural and Cultural Analysis

Johnny Nhan

LFB Scholarly Publishing LLC
El Paso 2010

Copyright © 2010 by LFB Scholarly Publishing LLC

All rights reserved.

Library of Congress Cataloging-in-Publication Data

Nhan, Johnny, 1977-
  Policing cyberspace : a structural and cultural analysis / Johnny Nhan.
    p. cm. -- (Criminal justice)
  Includes bibliographical references and index.
  ISBN 978-1-59332-398-1 (hardcover : alk. paper)
  1. Computer crimes. 2. Cyberspace. I. Title.

HV6773.N53 2010
363.25'968--dc22
                            2010010236

ISBN 978-1-59332-398-1

Printed on acid-free 250-year-life paper.

Manufactured in the United States of America.

Table of Contents

Acknowledgements vii

CHAPTER ONE
Introduction 1

CHAPTER TWO
Police Reform and the Nodal Governance 15

CHAPTER THREE
Methods of Inquiry 33

CHAPTER FOUR
The Formation, Expansion, and Function of Nodal Networks 59

CHAPTER FIVE
Theoretical Mapping of Key Security Stakeholders 75

CHAPTER SIX
Compatibility of Desirable Outcomes 107

CHAPTER SEVEN:
Public Buy-In as Security Stakeholders 137

CHAPTER EIGHT
Concluding Thoughts and Policy Implications 167

References 181

Index 207

Acknowledgments

This book is dedicated to my support team that carried me through years of data collection and writing. First, I would like to thank my family and friends for their love and support, including my late grandfather who passed away during the time of this project.

I also wish to express my gratitude to the intellects and role models of my life. Dr. John Dombrink, my friend and colleague, was instrumental in helping me complete this research. Dr. Paul Jesilow, whose wisdom and guidance were invaluable during the writing process. Dr. Henry Pontell, who I admire and respect and who has opened more doors than I could have ever imagined. Dr. Laura Huey, an amazing scholar and writer from the University of Western Ontario, who I was fortunate to receive guidance from. To the many other professors and graduate students from UC Irvine that shared ideas and helped me, I am forever grateful.

I would also like to express my appreciation to a special "big guy" who granted me access to virtually everything law enforcement and helped out in every way possible.

I owe a great deal of gratitude to every person who participated in this research.

CHAPTER ONE:
Introduction

Cybercrime is no longer an emerging crime envisioned in the 1980s science fiction movie *WarGames*, but it is a clear and present threat. In a 60-Minutes special aired on November 8, 2009,[1] host Steve Kroft declared that the next big war will be waged in cyberspace.[2] According to one cyber security expert interviewed, terabytes of sensitive government information were stolen by a serious hacker attack in 2007 and in 2008, U.S. Central Command computers were compromised for several days by an attacker. These critical events have prompted the Obama administration declared the nation's cyber infrastructure a critical asset just four months after taking office, stating, "It's now clear this cyber threat is one of the most serious economic and national security challenges we face as a nation" (Baldor, 2009). As of the time of this writing, there are 18 cyber-related bills active in congress (Chun, 2009). These present dangers can be traced back to the origins of the computer revolution and the Internet, when crime and security was not a concern for its founding architects.

Over the last few decades, computer technology has evolved from centralized mainframe computing to a decentralized "network of networks," known as the World Wide Web or Internet (Tanenbaum, 2003). This technological shift has both social and commercial ramifications. Inexpensive personal computers and devices are now ubiquitously interconnected, allowing the masses access to technology and information once reserved exclusively for scientists. Furthermore, the Internet's permeation into areas of modern life has resulted in

---

[1] Messic, G. "Sabotaging the System." 60 Minutes aired on November 8, 2009. Columbia Broadcasting System (CBS).
[2] "Cyberspace" is a term coined by American-Canadian novelist William Gibson in his 1984 science fiction novel *Neuromancer*.

unprecedented economic growth and communications that has been the driving force in developing a global economy and community in the 21st century. The adaptation of the Internet for commerce has vastly expanded the global capitalist marketplace, allowing more access to once restricted markets. The Internet expands the sale of goods and services to many developing countries, adding value to both businesses and consumers (Kshetri, 2007). Moreover, the Internet has become extremely valuable to businesses by driving demand for information and "immaterial products" that virtually eliminates transportation costs and minimizes distances (Leamer & Storper, 2001). However, the Internet environment must be secure to allow for sustained growth and expansion of the marketplace.

The rate of adoption of electronic commerce (ecommerce) by the general public has paralleled developments in securing the online environment. Despite the Internet's exponential growth in the 1990s (Coffman & Odlyzko, 2001), online retailers during this period overestimated the public's trust of the Internet, which resulted in lower than expected sales. Early consumers who were attracted to the convenience and prices of online shopping were wary of giving personal information.[3] By the holiday shopping season of 2004, however, improved Internet security technology contributed to increased consumer confidence, resulting in a 25% or $4.7 billion increase in online spending compared to 2003.[4] Despite improvements in security, the Internet remains a largely insecure environment.

The open and insecure nature of the Internet has made it an attractive medium for crime. The expanded marketplace has given more groups access and opportunities to commit crimes online (Maclean, 2005). The Internet was designed for flexibility and openness, not security (Dekker, 1997). The increasing complexity of the Internet, with its backbone of billions of lines of computer code, contains countless software bugs that can potentially be exploited by attackers. University of Washington computer security expert Tadayoshi Kohno explains that without a native security infrastructure, *ad hoc* security measures will remain insufficient. He states, "…[I]t is

---

[3] *See* www.sunriseecommerce.com/ecommerce_facts.htm.
[4] According to research by Goldman Sachs, Harris Interactive and Nielson/Netratings (ibid footnote 3).

Introduction

incredibly challenging, if not impossible, to retrofit the existing Internet infrastructure to meet all of today's security goals" (Leggett, 2009). Today, an insecure Internet environment does not simply result in less company sales, but can have national security implications. Critical national infrastructures, ranging from vital emergency communications channels to electrical grids, are at risk of large-scale cyber attacks and has drawn the attention of the U.S. federal government ("The National Strategy to Secure Cyberspace," 2003). According to a 2007 congressional committee report, the U.S. is "paying enormous costs for relying on such an insecure infrastructure" in terms of risk of a major disaster ("Toward a Safer and More Secure Cyberspace," 2007). The report draws attention to the "ominous" and constant threat created by the open environment, stating, "Cyberspace in general, and the Internet in particular, are notoriously vulnerable to a frightening and expanding range of accidents and attacks by a spectrum of hackers, criminals, terrorists and state actors who have been empowered by unprecedented access to more people and organizations than has ever been the case with any infrastructure in history." The result has been a dramatic rise in computer and Internet related offenses since the 1990s, [5] indicating that various control mechanisms have failed to keep pace. These mechanisms are not limited to purely technologically deterministic.

Securing and policing cyberspace requires human and social control considerations. Princeton University researcher Edward Felton explains, "A lot of the problems and issues have to do with interactions between users and computers – it's the human interface that is problematic," adding, "I'm skeptical about what you can do at the core of the technology" (Riordan, 2008). Computer security expert Bruce Schneier echoes this emphasis on the human vulnerabilities in security. Using passwords as an example, he states, "Left to themselves, people don't choose strong passwords. If they're forced to use strong passwords, they can't remember them," adding, "The classic example

---

[5] The FBI's Internet Crime Complaint Center (IC3) shows a dramatic rise in reported complaints from less than 25,000 in 2000 to over 200,000 in 2006, with the average cost in dollars lost from 17.8 million in 2000 to 198.4 million in 2006. *See* Internet Crime Report: January 1, 2006 – December 31, 2006 at http://www.ic3.gov/media/annualreport/2006_IC3Report.pdf.

of this is the user who gives his password to his co-workers so they can fix some problem when he's out of the office."[6] However, social control is very difficult to establish in the expansive and complex environment.

DEFINING CYBERCRIME

Computer crimes have been embodied in the catchphrase "cybercrime," but not without a bit of controversy. The term has been used to describe highly variable orientations, ranging from technical computer intrusions and viruses to more conventional street crimes that use computer technology as a medium, such as child pornography and fraud. Without a set definition, criminal justice, legal, and research inconsistencies which often serve as red herrings for meaningful theoretical and policy discussions and development in academic spheres. This substantive problem is similar to that of white-collar crime, whose definition has been debated for decades (Nhan & Bachmann, 2010). Consequently, white-collar crime and cybercrime, is often marginalized as a niche area of study.

Many individuals and groups have attempted to define cybercrime. Grabosky (2007: 11) loosely categorizes computer crimes as being: (1) The *instrument* used to commit the crime, (2) *target* of the offense, or (3) *incidental* to the offense. Other definitions are derived from the legal components of cybercrime, comparing its actions and motives to traditional crimes (Brenner 2001; 2001b; 2004). Rosoff, Pontell, and Tillman (2007; 1998: 365) classify cybercrime as an evolved form of white-collar crime, stating, "In short, white-collar crime has entered the computer age." Computer networks researcher Steven Furnell (2001) takes a more structured approach to defining cybercrime by categorizing cybercrime into *computer assisted* crimes, where computers are used to support crimes that can be accomplished without them, and *computer-focused crimes*, where computers have generated a new form of crime. In addition, he draws distinctions between "human oriented" crimes, such as hacking and misuse of computer systems, and "malware," such as computer viruses. Furnell concludes that "without a clear and standardized nomenclature, the

---

[6] *See* www.schneier.com/essay-028.html

Introduction 5

cybercrime issue risks being clouded by misunderstanding" (Furnell, 2001: 34). This book uses a variable definition of cybercrime defined by each security actor, or organization or group that participates in security formally or informally. Security stakeholders used for this study will include law enforcement, private companies, government agencies, and the general public. The important commonality is that an element of the Internet is used to facilitate the crime. From this orientation, the exact definition of cybercrime is not important, but rather its impact to each respective security actor and their response. Each actor will be disproportionately impacted by a certain type of cybercrime and will respond differently. The differences each actor responds to a particular type of Internet-enabled crime will give better understanding to structural and cultural variables that affect policing. This will be covered in more depth in the subsequent chapters.

A GROWING PROBLEM

Information is being converted and stored digitally at an exponential rate. In 2006 alone, an estimated 161 exabytes (billion gigabytes) of digital information was created, equivalent to three million times the information in all books ever written (Gantz, et al., 2007). That figure is expected to increase six-fold by 2010 and threatens to outpace data storage technology.

The large amount of information has been distributed with increasingly faster high-speed Internet services. The adaption of broadband Internet access has increased rapidly in the U.S. and globally. For example, broadband penetration in the U.S. is currently estimated at 74.1%, U.K. at 79.8%, and Japan at 74%.[7] Developing and lower income regions have also increased broadband adoption steadily, such as Vietnam (24.3%) and India (7%).

Digital information has also increased in value, making it a more attractive target of crime. Laptop computers and portable devices storing information are increasingly stolen not only for the value of reselling the item, but the information they contain as well. A recent theft of a Nashville, Tennessee county laptop computer contained the personal information of 337,000 registered voters, potentially costing

---

[7] *See* www.internetworldstats.com/list2.htm

$1 million in damages from loss of personal information (McMillan, 2008). Comparatively, the average loss from a bank robbery in the U.S. is $10,000 according to FBI statistics.[8]

The attractiveness of the high value of digital information coupled with the Internet's inherent lack of security and enforcement has facilitated very high rates of crime. According to a 2006 regional cybercrime survey in California, 81% of business respondents experienced a computer security incident.[9] The same survey found a 50% increase of unauthorized access to computer systems by both outside sources and company employees. In addition to network intrusions, Internet movie piracy has also been increasing, with the movie industry estimating $2.3 billion in losses in 2005 with a nearly 93% piracy rate in China (Siwek, 2006).

The motivation behind cyber crime has evolved over the years from mischievous acts towards utilitarian and destructive purposes. Originally, computer hackers were considered harmless curious teenager interested in the technical challenges of accessing computer systems, and even admired pioneers of the computer revolution (Hafner & Markoff, 1991; Hoath & Mulhall, 1998). Many malicious hackers today, drawn to the increasingly valuable information, are attacking financial and commercial institutions in what is described as a "multi-billion dollar industry" ("High Tech-Crime," 2007).

Internet malefactors today include highly organized and structured groups that operate piracy rings, identity theft rings, and organize coordinated attacks against computer systems. For example, malicious coders often create and distribute software (called Trojan viruses) that virally infects computer systems. Once infected, "zombie" computers known as "bots" function together in a "botnet" controlled by a remote source. Botnets are designed to overwhelm computer networks and have been used to gain access to information for the purpose of gaining unauthorized access to company data to extortion. Computer security experts describe this problem as "gigantic," with some researchers estimating that as many as 1.1 billion infected computer systems are available in the bot pool (Bort, 2007).

---

[8] *See* www.fbi.gov/publications/bcs/bcs2006/bank_crime_2006.htm
[9] It was requested that the title of the document was not provided due to the sensitive nature of the agency involved and research participants.

Introduction

High rates of cybercrime are indicative of a security deficit given the increased opportunities for crime. Cyber criminals are largely motivated by large rewards with relatively low risk of apprehension. Institutional indicators that are positively associated with reducing cybercrime are related to the proportion of crimes investigated, arrests made, and severity of punishment for convicted criminals (Kshetri, 2005: 557). One obvious solution is to increase the number of investigations. However, the capacity of law enforcement and the criminal justice system is challenged by the resource-intensive and abstract nature of cyberspace (Huey, 2002).

The Internet space challenges the traditional nature of policing which has been tied to spatial arrangements, making policing cyberspace less desirable (Huey, 2002). Law enforcement has historically enforced territorial borders through physical boundaries. Social control implemented by policing has meant maintaining order by enforcement of territorial boundaries. The lack of understanding highly complex and abstract computer and communications technologies has resulted in a police propensity to avoid cybercrime (Huey, 2002). Law enforcement, however, is a geographically-oriented organization that is historically resistant to change. Law enforcement's delay in recognizing the new crime medium and its continued emphasis on street crime has rendered it largely ill-equipped and ill-trained to police cyberspace (Muncaster, 2005). While law enforcement has successfully adopted technologies to further its crime control agenda, the abstract nature of decentralized digital information conflicts with its spatial-geographic orientation (Huey, 2002).

TOWARDS A NEW MODEL OF POLICING

Increased victimization and growing demands for policing services by both industry and the general public have served as the impetus for law enforcement to police cyberspace. According to IBM, the cost of cybercrime has overtaken the cost of physical crime for U.S. businesses.[10] A 2006 industry poll shows that 97% of the Americans sampled considered identity theft to be a serious problem and want

---

[10] See www-03.ibm.com/industries/financialservices/doc/content/news/ pressrelease/1563048103.html?g_type=rssfeed_leaf.

congress to take a larger, more active role in protecting them online.[11] Not surprisingly, police have been called upon to deal with this growing issue.

Police have historically established itself as the *de facto* entity for dealing with all forms of crime. Specifically, police have expanded their role to become a panacea-like agency for social control through professionalization. The police professionalization movement resulted in the image of the "expert crime-fighter," utilizing superior crime knowledge and advanced technology (Vollmer & Schneider, 1917; Bopp, 1977; Uchida, 2004). As a result, the general public has turned to police to deal with a variety of issues ranging from dealing with crime to order-maintenance duties. In essence, the public has to a large part relinquished its role in policing duties that was once prevalent in the night-watchmen (political) era of policing, where officers enforced community norms and relied heavily on community support (Kelling & Moore, 2005).

The increased crime fighting capacity and role came at the cost of severed community relations by a realignment of loyalties from community members to fellow officers. Officers today must have complete trust in other officers. As a result, a strong subculture has developed in the last few decades, characterized by a deep rooted cynicism towards the public and strong group introversion (Van Maanen, 1975; Skolnick & Fyfe, 1993). This subculture has served to insulate police from the public.

The "us versus them" subculture can be detrimental for enforcing the complex cyberspace environment, which often requires collaborative policing efforts and flexibility. In its current form, police simply do not outsource investigatory duties or allow the public to be active participants in the law enforcement process. Instead, the public is asked to give input and report crime to the police. The police subculture and group introversion is further solidified by a rigid paramilitary bureaucratic command structure. This structural rigidity has made it difficult for police to adapt quickly to changes in society and crime.

---

[11] Cyber Security Industry Alliance (CSIA) Spring 2006 Digital Confidence Survey. *See* www.csialliance.org/publications/publications/surveys_and_polls/dci_survey_May2006/index.html.

Law enforcement personnel find themselves in a predicament: professionalization has led to the exclusivity of police as "expert crime-fighters" while at the same time, the development of a strong subculture and organizational structure makes it relatively inflexible in allowing non-police entities to share in policing duties. However, demands for policing services have overwhelmed this monolithic model of law enforcement. As a result, police have turned to more efficient models in dealing with more and more sophisticated crime. Social changes brought upon by modernity require the policing paradigm to evolve from the professional model of monopolistic crime suppression to one of information-based risk management (Ericson & Haggerty, 1997). Police must process and use growing amounts of information to fight crime efficiently. Law enforcement, a slow-moving organization, has become overwhelmed by organizational pressures and the sheer volume of external demands (ibid: 295). Consequently, police no longer have the capacity to unilaterally control crime and must "govern" security by sharing risk and expertise with non-law enforcement institutional security stakeholders, or 'nodes' (Burris, Drahos & Shearing, 2005; Castells, 1996; Dupont, 2006).

A community model of policing is conceptualized in the *nodal governance* theoretical framework, based on a non-hierarchical social network of nodes that pool resources (capital) (Burris, Drahos, & Shearing, 2005; Castells, 1996; Dupont, 2006; and others). Sharing security, which ranges from technology to expertise and manpower, expands the scope and capacity of law enforcement in this model. Furthermore, it allows for increased flexibility in dealing with emergent crimes, such as cybercrime. The arrangement of these interrelationships and nature of shared security capital is the primary theoretical unit of analysis used in this book.

Nodal governance is a model of security based on social networks. In the context of nodal governance, social networks are complex sets of relationships between institutional nodes that function in governing security. In the traditional hierarchical model, police have exclusive power to establish security through crime control. In contrast, security is derived from shared power between police and a decentralized network of interconnected nodes in the nodal governance model. In addition, security resources such as manpower and technologies are shared between nodes. This model is often manifested in police task forces and collaborative efforts.

Complex crimes require new policing strategies based on industry-police collaborations. This framework has traditionally been operationalized using the task force model, formed on an *ad hoc* basis. Task forces have been used successfully in white-collar crime cases, such as the Justice Department's Enron task force, which combined the knowledge and resources of experienced prosecutors with federal agents (Johnson, 2004). It is important that police collaborations include non-police entities. Community policing, for example, functions by utilizing community-police "working partnerships" (Moore & Trojanowicz, 1989). Police rely heavily on social institutions such as schools, churches, and non-law enforcement governmental organizations in this model.

The evolution towards an information-based society brings forth two issues for law enforcement: (1) progressively, crimes will have some form of computer or digital element, and (2) the amount of information created will make forensics work more difficult and time consuming. Moreover, there is a growing need for a new model of policing and security that is flexible and robust enough to deal with increasingly sophisticated malefactors that are using countermeasures to mask criminal activities to prevent apprehension. This book uses this new model of policing as a framework to holistically examine the capacity of law enforcement in cyberspace. Exploring new models of policing and social control on the Internet is the focus of this research.

RESEARCH PURPOSE

This research applies the nodal governance security theoretical framework using Wood's (2006) empirical mapping guidelines applied to the cyber-security network in California. This mapping method identifies key stakeholders in cyber security and their relationships to each other. Wood's mapping technique, which stresses functional relations over physical geography, is ideal for mapping the "borderless" Internet environment. Assessing relational gaps between nodes or *nodal cluster*'s (sets of institutional actors with parallel functions and cultures that are identified as a single entity) can help to identify and extract structural, socio-political, legal, and cultural variables that affect inter-nodal relations.

In addition to examining inter-nodal collaboration and friction, this research considers key stakeholders and security assets shared in a network. The nature of and degree to which security capital is shared will be a key factor in the size and strength of the cyber security network in California. Some companies, for example, will find law enforcement's ability to conduct computer forensic investigations very useful. As a result, these companies often form stronger partnerships with police investigators compared to companies who have less utility for digital forensics capabilities.

Four key nodal clusters have been selected for assessment in this research: (1) law enforcement, (2) state government, (3) private industry, and (4) the general public. First, law enforcement was chosen for its role as the default formal social control agent and entry way to the criminal justice system. This research focuses specifically on law enforcement bodies assigned to high-tech and computer crimes. In California, this consists of a network of five regional high-tech crimes task forces. Second, state government was selected for its role in setting public policy, drafting legislation, and managing funding for law enforcement operations. This cluster is represented by the California state Office of Emergency Services (OES), which directly governs and funds cyber and high tech enforcement. Third, private industry was chosen for its historic role in regulating cyberspace using proprietary technologies and information security staffs. Fourth, the general public is considered for being the largest stakeholder in computer crime by sheer number; being potential victims, criminals, and social control agents. Since it was not feasible to interview or poll the public directly, existing published research were used to assess this nodal cluster. One issue of using "private industry" as a unit of analysis is it is simply too broad.

To narrow the scope of the private industry category, this research focuses on two industries that have historically been considered key stakeholders at the forefront of cyber security: the technology sector and film industry. These two nodal clusters were selected to compare and contrast one stakeholder that has traditionally been known to avoid law enforcement (tech sector), and one that has a working partnership with law enforcement (film). Both industries, however, have been active in employing technological and legal means to protect data ranging from financial information to intellectual property. In the past decade, these industries have increasingly turned to law enforcement for assistant. This help, however, has remained limited due in large part to the limitations of law enforcement in dealing with cybercrime.

The capacity of the criminal justice system may be a limiting factor in policing cybercrime. Henry Pontell's (1982, 1984) *system capacity theory* argues that the overall capacity of the criminal justice system to mete out justice is limited by points of inefficiency. For example, one systemic bottleneck that reduces the overall policing effectiveness is at the prosecutorial level. In Chapter six, we discuss the important role of prosecutors, who often have incentives to utilize plea bargain strategies or avoid cases altogether (Smith, Grabosky, & Urbas, 2004; Nhan, 2008). These findings were similar to Benson, Maakestad, Cullen, and Geis' (1988) study on prosecutorial gatekeeping functions in white-collar and corporate fraud cases.

This research will draw comparisons with white-collar crime research. Complex white-collar crime cases shares similar problems of enforcement, prosecution, victimization, and legal reform. For example, the fallout of large financial scandals early in the millennium, such as Enron and WorldCom, drew public attention to the real harm of victimization and social impact of white-collar crime (Kane & Wall, 2006).[12] As a result, major reforms have been implemented to regulate business practices, such as requiring greater scrutiny and new legislation[13] standardizing ethical accounting procedures in public companies. Despite these major reforms, the attention of the general public and mass media have continued to center on street crimes; a problem faced by a greater extent by cybercrime.

Large cyber attacks on online retailers have drawn the general public's attention for the first time but resulted in little support for cybercrime enforcement and legislation. In 2001, hackers gaining access to 98,000 Amazon.com customer accounts including credit card information for nearly four months (Greene, 2001). As recently as

---

[12] A 2006 National White Collar Crime Center (NW3C) poll shows 32.6% of respondents strongly disagreed that government devotes enough resources to combat white-collar crime. However, crimes involving physical harm are perceived as significantly more serious than those involving only monetary losses. *See* www.nw3c.org/ research/docs/national_public_household_survey.pdf

[13] Sarbanes-Oxley Act of 2002 (Pub. L. No. 107-204, 116 Stat. 745). The Public Company Accounting Reform and Investor Protection Act of 2002. *See* http://frwebgate.access.gpo.gov/cgi-bin/getdoc.cgi? dbname=107_cong_bills&docid=f:h3763enr.tst.pdf.

Introduction 13

December 23, 2009, Amazon, Wal-Mart and several other major online retailers were attacked by *distributed denial-of-service* (DDoS)[14] attacks which interrupted service during the busy holiday shopping season (Krazit, 2009). Despite similar widespread victimization, cybercrime have yet to gain public and legislative support to the degree received even by white-collar crime. Consequently, funds allocated towards high-tech law enforcement have been very minimal.

This research will contribute to the existing literature on policing and legal issues in cyberspace. Brenner (2007) found the fit between trans-border cybercrime and the localized crime scenes of the current model of law enforcement problematic from a legal perspective. Furthermore, legal complications arise when security participation is extended to non-law enforcement actors. Similarly, Wall (2007) found difficulties situating localized law enforcement within the global context of cyberspace, calling for a "transformation" of the policing paradigm built on forming networked relations. This research will attempt to compliment and validate these findings using empirical data and to further develop the nodal governance framework.

This research contributes to the nodal governance model using empirical data from California. The goal is threefold: (1) to identify the stakeholders in California cyber-security social network for the purpose of understanding how cyberspace is policed, (2) to examine each stakeholder's respective formal, social, and legal control mechanisms that govern each their behavior and how they interface with other security actors, and (3) how the Internet impacts these institutions and relationships. The interaction between actors in the context of cyberspace will give insight to the capacity and complex nature of security in this environment. This is achieved by empirically mapping California's security network using Wood's (2006) guidelines. The qualitative design of this research will provide empirical depth necessary to draw out these mapping variables.

The following chapter will review the nodal governance and system capacity theoretical models in the context of white-collar crime and policing. Chapter three will discuss the methods of inquiry. Chapter four will discuss the formation, expansion, and function of nodal networks, paying particular attention to California's cyber

---

[14] A denial-of-service attack is the deliberate or unintentional disruption of legitimate web services. A common method is "flooding" or overwhelming a network with information from multiple sources.

security network in the context of system capacity and the Internet geography. Chapter five will introduce and map the key stakeholders in the security network: law enforcement, government, private industry (represented by the film industry and the tech sector), and the general public. Using this information, Chapter six will analyze points of collaboration and friction between security actors to extract structural, cultural, and legal variables. Chapter seven will examine the relationships between law enforcement and private industry with the general public and consider the possibility of establishing collective efficacy in a virtual environment. Finally, chapter eight will discuss initial findings and policy implications.

Identify practical solutions to reduce structural blockades between security stakeholders and considering new collaborative policing models is one primary goal of this research. A heuristic model of applying ecological *defensible spaces* (Newman, 1973) to cyberspace is considered. Virtual or "*digital* defensible spaces" are secure online environments using the collective efficacy of online communities (Nhan & Huey, 2008). This may aid in finding more effective policing models to address a complex problem.

A final aim of this research is to draw more attention to cybercrime in the subfield of criminology, or cyber criminology. Computer-enabled crimes have long been categorized as a separate type of crime, often marginalized and labeled as "cybercrime" and given low priority by law enforcement (Young, 2007). Similarly, many scholars have questioned whether crimes utilizing computer and network technology are merely old forms of crimes in a new medium, warranting extra attention (Brenner, 2001; 2004a); the proverbial "old wine in new bottles" (Grabosky, 2001). Consequently, much of cybercrime research has been conducted by industry trade groups interested in commercial solutions and by the computer sciences that focus mainly on technological solutions. This study aims to build a better understanding of cybercrime from a criminological and policing perspective as foundations for future research considerations.

CHAPTER TWO:
Police Reform and the Nodal Governance Theoretical Framework

This chapter presents the theoretical tools used to assess cyber security in California. It will draw upon two bodies of work: the Nodal Governance theoretical model derived from urban sociologist Manuel Castell's (1977) research on social networks, and Henry Pontell's (1982, 1984) System Capacity model. The nodal governance framework identifies security stakeholders, their roles, and interactions for the purpose of identifying variables that contribute to or hinder cyber security. The nodal framework explains that there is not a single entity, such as law enforcement, is exclusively responsible for securing cyberspace. Instead, security is derived from a collaborative network of nodal clusters (Nhan & Huey, 2008). Specifically, security requires a combination of technologies, companies, government agencies, and online social communities working in tandem. Security stakeholders collectively detect and respond to malicious or deviant activities online. System capacity will be introduced in the context of white-collar crime to show that in complex crimes, each security actor's limitations can potentially limit the overall policing effectiveness in cyberspace.

To introduce these theoretical models into policing cybercrime, the development and integration of information technology in society will first be analyzed. Next, the historic adoption of technology will be explored. This will show a growing shift towards decentralized models of security, highlighting the changes in policing from a command-control model to one of risk management that has led to the development of nodal governance. Next, the nodal governance model of security will be explained in greater detail and examined in the context of cyber security. Finally, similarities will be drawn with policing strategies used in white-collar crime in the context of Pontell's

(1982; 1984) system capacity theoretical model to show how complex crimes can limit police and criminal justice ability to mete out justice.

DEVELOPMENTS IN TECHNOLOGY, SOCIETY, AND POLICING

The "information revolution" that originated in the 1970s from Silicon Valley has changed the modes of production and human relationships on a global scale. Major advancements in communications technology allowed a free flow of information which has influenced international politics and economies. The technological revolution ultimately altered modes of production, communications, and living (Castells, 1996). Emerging from this techno era was the Internet, an open information channel considered to be a "utopian, communal" space with "libertarian undercurrents" (ibid: 357). The permeation of the Internet throughout the masses has facilitated a fundamental change in the work/worker/firm relationship, allowing more flexibility while diminishing time and place. The Internet has expanded capitalism on a global scale, allowing more populations to participate in the marketplace. The result is a dynamic flow of power in a "culture of endless deconstruction and reconstruction" (ibid: 471).

The expanded marketplace can grant access to once closed markets for companies, but at the same time it opens up vulnerabilities through impoverished groups using crime as a legitimate means of income. For example, some residents in the depressed Nigerian economy have turned to advance-fee or 419 scams,[15] commonly known as "spam," to earn a living. These fraudulent schemes deceive victims into paying small fees in order to "free up" larger financial rewards. The Federal Trade Commission has described the Internet as facilitating Nigerian email scams to reach "epidemic proportions" with over 1.5 million complaints in the U.S. costing victims $437 billion in 2003 (Airoldi & Malin, 2004). Adomi and Igun (2008) have identified economic conditions and inadequate law enforcement in Nigeria as major contributing factors in the proliferation of spam.

While the global use of the Internet creates new markets for crime and criminal activity, it can also expand the capacity of law enforcement. The implementation of crime databases allows for

---

[15] 419 is the Nigerian penal code section for fraud.

efficient management and instant access to large amounts of information. Information technology (IT), for example, is valued by law enforcement for its ability to improve response times, increase officer safety, aide in catching criminals, as well as increase administrative efficiency and lower costs (Chu, 2001). This technology was touted by one police chief and head of the International Association of Chiefs of Police as "the greatest redirection, reorganization, and modification of policing since Sir Robert Peel and the Metropolitan Police" (ibid: 3).[16]

Despite the seemingly perfect fit between police and the benefits of using information technology to provide security in the information society, reliance solely on technological means to fight crime has diminishing returns. An over-dependence on technology by police has been described as a "technofallacy" that undermines their overall effectiveness (Corbett & Marx, 1991). For example, electronic monitoring devices that were engineered and deployed for crime prevention, "soft control," and non-human surveillance, ultimately undermined public trust and privacy (ibid: 401). Law enforcement's professionalization and increased efficiency in crime-fighting has eroded relations with communities. Police have sought to ameliorate this strained relationship in the last few decades during the community era.

POLICE DEVELOPMENT AND RISK

The professional era of policing was part of a progressive reform movement from approximately the 1930s to 1980s, which emphasized detangling of citizen and political influences to ameliorate corruption prevalent during the political era of policing. Police corruption was largely eradicated by standardized academy training and an emphasis on *scientific* crime-fighting (Kelling & Moore, 1988; 2005). In addition, the adoption of a rigid paramilitary command structure served to further insulate police from the public. However, an unforeseen consequence of group isolation was a breakdown in community relations which sparked urban violence during the 1960s. These

---

[16] 19th century English police reformer Sir Robert Peel stressed that police should be an integral part of the community and public agency to prevent crime and disorder (Allen, 1947; Plummer, 1999).

severed relations lead to the *community problem-solving era* marked by a return to external relationships with citizens (ibid). Violent skirmishes between police and community members have sparked political and public pressure for police reform. In the 1960s, it was clear that police-community relations were strained. These strained relations climaxed in 1965 with the arrest of an African American driver by a white motorcycle officer in Los Angeles which sparked the Watts riots (McCone, et al., 1965). An antagonistic "us versus them" mentality of police towards the public contributed to racial tensions and strain of poor social conditions in Los Angeles. Ironically, the Watts riots occurred during the LAPD Chief William Parker era, which was a national model for police innovation and professionalism during that time (Uchida, 2004). By the 1990s, strict professionalism was blamed for creating and perpetuating a strong police subculture, which was identified as a leading cause of the 1991 Los Angeles riots sparked by the beating of Rodney King by the Warren Christopher Commission (Report of the Independent Commission on the Los Angeles Police Department, 1991; Bobb, Epstein, Miller, & Abascal, 1996).

Ironically, police reform in the United States in recent decades has been characterized by undoing many negative repercussions of professionalism and returning to a community model that was once blamed for corruption. This does not imply the elimination of professionalism and its core principles, such as the bureaucratic command structure and statistical measures of success, but the new community policing paradigm seeks to re-establish severed community ties. One way to build relations, for example, is a focus on proactive crime prevention strategies based on close police-citizen relations tailored to regional crime problems. In contrast, stoic officers akin to Joe Friday in Dragnet, and statistics-based performance measures such as the Uniform Crime Reports, were the cornerstones of August Vollmer's student, O.W. Wilson's, professionalization.

The recognition of community agency during the reform period gave rise to *Community Policing*. The core principle of community policing is to co-produce security outcomes using a trust network of active participants, such as local government, civic and business leaders, public and private agencies, and residents and other local community institutions (Bureau of Justice Assistance, 1994). Decentralization, proactive officers, and building personal relations with communities are important in creating security in the community policing paradigm. However, implementing community policing has been difficult and often criticized for not truly changing the policing paradigm which is still based predominantly on principles of crime control (Manning, 1988; Zhao & Thurman, 2004). Community policing may be part of a bigger response to changes in society, particularly population increase and related advancements in technology. According to Foucault's (1979) panoptic analysis of dynamic power, as society increases in size, a set of complex functional hegemonic relationship will develop. The number of people being controlled can be exponentially increased using fewer, more efficient resources. As a result, more and more specialized resources are necessary to develop and exercise social control.

The demands of an increasingly complex and growing society require resources beyond the capacity of modern policing. Specifically, information and communications technologies in society coupled with fiscal pressures have placed a greater burden on police to perform more efficiently despite higher police-citizen ratios.[17] To control increased populations with disproportionally fewer resources, social control is accomplished by the ability to manage social dangers, conceptualized by levels of *risk*. Risks are adverse external conditions that exist in modern society created by both natural and technological means. Accordingly, "risk society" is shaped by the discourse between danger and security governance (Ericson & Haggerty, 1997).

Police, by their efforts to professionalize, have adapted to this risk environment to become *experts* in managing danger. Jerome Skolnick (1966) underscored this shift in his study of police officer culture, finding that rule of law objectives are often supplanted by arbitrary decisions for the purpose of managerial efficiency. Consequently, police departments have become organizations that function to calculate and manage risk. Police officers act as "knowledge workers" who are driven to collect and process information to obtain more and more perfect information for the purpose of managing risk in these "risk institutions" (ibid; Huey, 2002).

---

[17] Law Enforcement Management and Administrative Statistics, 2000: Data for Individual State and Local Agencies with 100 or More Officers. U.S. Bureau of Justice Statistic. *See* www.ojp.usdoj.gov /bjs/pub/pdf/lemas00.pdf.

The use of policing technologies has been instrumental in managing risk. Over the last century, police have adapted many technologies intended to increase crime control efficiency. Two technologies in particular were instrumental in reorienting police towards a model of professionalism and efficiency: (1) the widespread adoption of the patrol vehicle and (2) use of the Uniform Crime Reports (UCR) as a measure of success (Walker, 1984: 76). The integration of computer systems in patrol vehicles, for example, has given the officer an information platform to assess risk, which further solidified their role as professionals and experts in crime. From 1990 to 2000, the use of in-field computer systems in patrol vehicles increased from 14% to 59% in state agencies and from 19% to 68% for local agencies (Reaves & Hickman, 2004).

The convergence of information technologies with crime control and the reorientation of measures of success have served to ameliorate the image of the corrupt officer, but consequently removed community interaction (Walker, 1985). Dupont (1999) draws out three major eras in police adoption of technology in the twentieth century that are attributed to this disjuncture: (1) the mechanization of police work from foot patrol in the 1930s, (2) the refinement of communications technology such as the two-way radio and command centers up to the 1980s, and (3) the Information Age. Despite greater efficiencies using technology in a risk-management model, law enforcement efforts remain insufficient in overcoming the greater demands of the information society. This insufficiency has forced police to expand security functions to non-state entities.

DECENTRALIZED SECURITY AND SECURITY NODES

Security is no longer the exclusive duty of police (Bayley & Shearing, 2005; Dupont, 2006; Shearing, 2006: 26). Commercial and volunteer entities that participate in "pluralized" forms of policing and security have replaced the old "monopolistic" model of security, where State-sanctioned police handle crime unilaterally (Bayley & Shearing, 2005: 715). Non-State entities, ranging from private security companies to industries, often fill an important security role when state policing is insufficient. During transitional periods when the state alone cannot adequately provide security, for example, high crime often results which leads to anomic conditions and ultimately nation-state failures

(Genov, 2004; Bayley, 2006). Comprehensive policing plans that involve a large and active role for the public are often required for successful political transitions during these periods of "security gaps" (Bayley, 2006). The demand for security is also filled by the emergence and growing role of "hybrid" security entities that are neither completely State oriented nor private entities that perform professional security functions (Dupont, 2006). These commercial security institutions have served in greater security capacities in recent decades (Wood & Shearing, 2006). According to the U.S. Department of Labor, the *private security industry* is expected to grow by 17% by 2016 over growing concerns about crime, vandalism, and terrorism (Gamiz Jr., 2008). These private security firms consists of individuals privately employed with some security component such as guards, floor detectives, auditors, escorts, couriers, security consultants and other forms of hybrid actors (Shearing & Stenning, 1981:196).

Security in the information age is "governed" by a social network of security stakeholders, or *nodes*. This stands in contrast to the old model of security, which consisted of exclusive centralized coercive state power using crime control technologies. In the nodal security framework, "nodes" are defined as entities in a system with its own set of capital in the form of mentalities, technologies, resources, and institutions (Burris, Drahos, & Shearing, 2005; Wood & Shearing, 2007). Nodes can be public, private, or *hybrid* institutions, ranging from police departments to private companies. It is important to note that nodes must be situated in some form of organizational infrastructure with boundaries, and are not individuals (Burris 2004).

Benoît Dupont (2006), a leading expert in developing the *nodal governance* theoretical framework, classifies five interdependent forms of capital that nodes possess: (1) economic, (2) political, (3) cultural, (4) social, and (5) symbolic. First, *economic capital* is amount of monetary resources possessed by a node and the ability of the node to obtain funding. Private industries, for example, have historically possessed more economic capital than other nodes by operating under capitalist motivations of wealth accumulation.

Political capital is the power to mobilize and use government and political resources. Forms of government resources can include the ability to secure a percentage of a fiscal year budget. In addition, political capital also includes the ability to influence public discourse.

The federal government often possesses this form of capital to sway public opinion in supporting its agendas. For example, the war on drugs discourse was prevalent throughout the 1980s and 90s, which drew public attention and massive funding to drug enforcement.

Cultural capital is defined by Dupont (2006) as "actionable and explanatory knowledge." It represents the knowledge base possessed by a node that can be mobilized for security. For example, law enforcement's unique expertise gained through decades of investigative experience in forensics can be considered a form of cultural capital.

Social capital is the ability to institutionally "initiate and maintain social relations with other groups or individuals" (Dupont, 2006). This form of capital is often possessed by police agencies to maintain community relations required for effective community policing.

Finally, *symbolic capital* is the legitimacy gained from complimentary outcomes of the aforementioned forms of capital. Police can act as a nodal hub, or central point, in a security network through its exclusive form of legitimate state sanctioned power. These five forms of capital are used to determine position and influence in the overall security network of each node. Possessing greater amounts of each type of capital can give certain nodal sets or clusters greater social advantage and influence over security agendas and decisions. Regardless of a node's position within a network, security is derived from shared security capital.

At the heart of the nodal governance theoretical framework is the idea that security is co-produced through inter-nodal relationships. These alliances consist of "isometric" relationships amongst government and non-law enforcement stakeholders (Drahos, 2004). This means each actor can have multiple sets of relationships with other nodes, both state and non-state. In a traditional hierarchical model of security, a "locus of power" concentrates power to the state. In a nodal governance model, power is distributed to a "shifting network of alliances" (Johnston, 2006: 34). In this model, nodes are given agency to contribute to security by sharing resources and actively employing their expertise in areas of need. By forming multiple simultaneous relationships with other nodes (both government and private), security needs that were once insufficiently handled exclusively by police are addressed by the collective expertise of different nodes that form a "multilateral" dynamic network of alliances.

Police Reform and the Nodal Governance Theoretical Framework

The nodal governance theoretical model stresses a fundament shift in power from police "monopolization" of security responsibilities to nongovernmental bodies (Bayley & Shearing, 2001; Dupont, 2006; Wood & Shearing, 2007). Police were placed at the top of a security hierarchy to handle all crimes in the old model of security. The role of everyone else was to passively report crimes to the police, who have established themselves as "experts." However, in the network model of security, the police hierarchy is flattened. Law enforcement is considered simply one of many nodal clusters capable of producing some form of security within a given security network. Police are distinguished only as the state sanctioned body to apprehend and punish offenders. Law enforcement is not considered superior to other nodes, but simply contributes a different form of security capital to the network. This is not to imply, however, that power distribution is even across all nodal relationships.

Some nodes exert more influence than others. Nodes within a network often have conflicting interests and agendas. More powerful nodes generally wield greater authority in advancing their priorities. The nodal capacity to exert influence within a given network is determined by each node's access to capital or resources (Burris, Drahos, and Shearing, 2005:39). The degree of power or influence of a node or nodal cluster within a network is determined by the level of connectedness in the network and to other nodes. This is measured by a combination of the "density," or "ratio of existing to possible connections between organizations and stakeholders belonging to it," and "centrality," or the "number and pattern of connections" (Wasserman & Faust, 1994 in Dupont, 2006: 106). A powerful node, or one that exerts a high level of influence in a given network, has all possible relationships with others (density) and has relationships across multiple industries (centrality). Having these relationships means a node has access to and can mobilize a variety of resources from multiple sources which can be used to leverage security agendas.

The overall robustness and effectiveness of a security network is often influenced by the number and nature of relationships within a network. Networks with many nodal participants having sustained relationships can detect criminal activities and mobilize appropriate resources to address what the group identifies as a problem. Moreover, more shared security capital is available within a given network. Higher levels of collective action or efficacy often take place when nodes share similar desired outcomes or have a common purpose. These ideas can be found in neighborhood watch programs that are designed to "induce people to exercise some degree of social control in environments where they live" (Garafolo & McLeod, 1989: 327). Similarly, the way policing is being implemented on the Internet shares many community policing ideals of using community resources to control crime. The community policing paradigm incorporates non-police and community resources that were severed or abandoned during police professionalization. The development of community policing is a synthesis of earlier reforms. Police professionalization beginning in the 21st century was intended to eradicate corruption during political era of policing. Police stressed self-efficiency and exclusivity in handling crime. However, police became too insulated from the community, resulting in strained relations. The community policing era sought to reestablish community relations and reverse the insulated model of public cynicism and ineffective safety and order (Greene, 2004).

The use of non-governmental resources is perceived as desirable and legitimate in dealing with crime under the community policing ideology. Security is achieved through reciprocity and collective action between police and citizens (Kahan, 2002). For example, police have partnered with church organizations under the umbrella of community oriented policing.[18] Critics however, have questioned the community policing model's impact on crime. Community policing has often been criticized for being more rhetoric than producing real change (Klockers, 1988; Manning, 1988). This criticism, however, is not aimed at the effectiveness of the principles of community policing but the disjuncture between the model and actual praxis. Specifically, critics have questioned the degree to which community and police are integrated.

The strength of nodal security networks lies in the degree of integration and resource sharing between police and non-governmental nodes. Similar to community policing, the nodal model of security requires community institutions to be active participants in sharing their respective forms of security capital. In addition, sustained relationships allow for better two-way communication of security needs and available capital. For example, Skogan (2004) found a strong

---

[18] *See* www.ncpc.org/cms/cms-upload/ncpc/File/6_community.pdf.

correlation between residents' priority of addressing graffiti and abandoned cars and the allocation of police services addressing those needs in Chicago. These networks are not limited to one localized neighborhood and can be scaled for greater access to more security capital. Many sub-networks are situated or nested within other network layers. For example, local police departments can expand their security capacity by partnering with larger regional and state agencies.

A comparison of the anatomy of computer networks and the Internet with the structure of a nodal security framework can assist in understanding nodal governance. A computer network consists of interconnected nodes, or input/output computing devices controlled by end-users. A series of interconnected nodes forms a simple computer network. These autonomous small networks, or *subnets*, can be nested within larger networks. The largest global network (World Wide Web) is the Internet. Explained simply, the Internet is a "network of networks." The Internet[19] is not a single network, but a distributed system interconnecting multiple internets, or smaller autonomous computer networks, using the Internet Protocol (IP) (Tanenbaum, 2003). For example, a university campus will have a main network that is connected to the Internet, meaning it is connected globally to other institutions, but will also contain smaller departmental subnets. Multipurpose resource sharing is the main purpose of this interconnectivity.

Security in this distributed model of computing shares the same principles of the nodal governance model of security. There is not one entity that is exclusively handles all the security duties in cyberspace. Instead, online security is traditionally derived from a combination of technologies, private and public organizations, and online social communities that detect and respond to deviant or criminal activities. For instance, network security is a multi-level combination of cryptographic technologies, authentication tools, surveillance and monitoring technologies used by companies,

---

[19] Tanenbaum (2003) defines an internet is a system of autonomous separate interconnected computers using a single technology. The "Internet" (notice capitalization" denotes the distributed system known as the World Wide Web, or interconnected "network of networks" running the Internet Protocol (IP).

individual users, and even law enforcement (Kaufman, Perlman, and Speciner, 2002).

In computer security, deviant or unusual activity is detected by nodes in smaller networks using a distributed system of "trusted intermediaries" for authentication to each node. Any non-authorized activity is detected by these smaller networks, not an overarching police force; a virtual neighborhood watch. For example, online community groups often enforce group norms and behavior in a given domain (Preece, 2004). Nodal governance relies on this smaller "communal space" to enforce group behavior that contributes to the overall security network (Shearing & Wood, 2003; Bowles & Gintis, 2002). Small-scale surveillance and security resource sharing in cyber enclaves is a key to policing cyberspace. According to Dr. Larry Smarr, director of the California Institute for Telecommunications and Information Technology (CalIT^2) and a chief architect of the Internet infrastructure, the Internet represents a global "nervous system" that can sense and monitor activities (McCarthy, Rakotobe-Joel, & Frizelle, 2000).

Nodal security is the functional and dynamic channeling of capital to problem areas by a network of nodes (Burris, Drahos, & Shearing, 2005). Community members, non-governmental nodes, and nodal clusters sense and detect security breaches. These nodes take action or report these activities to the appropriate nodal security partners, such as police. Instead of being passive individuals, individuals and groups are encouraged to take ownership virtual spaces to form online communities and participate as active "denizens," akin to a virtual neighborhood watch program. *Denizens* are groups of active participants that belong to a "sphere of governance" in a domain that shares social capital in order to create public *communal spaces* (Shearing & Wood, 2003).

The Internet can be more effectively policed when it is broken down into smaller online spaces where community members can collectively detect and enforce crime. Cyberspace cannot be policed in a traditional sense in which state-sanctioned law enforcement agencies monitors the entire Internet. Instead, online enclaves can better detect abnormal activities and respond to them using collective efficacy or even report malefactors to the proper authorities. Emile Durkheim (1979) argued that collective responses to crime can serve to reinforce and strengthen group solidarity. For example, neighborhood watch programs often create a sense of community through the common purpose of crime prevention by residents at the block or neighborhood-level (Garofalo & McLeod, 1989). This does not imply that police have no role policing cyberspace. Police have historically adapted to changes in society and crime types. The rise of private policing in the United States can be attributed to the emergence of industrial cities and the need for policing services in urban environments (Forst & Manning, 1999). The new online policing model must consider a paradigm shift to adapt to a decentralized environment. The new nodal policing strategy which is based on distributed shared power with other non-police nodes is the ideal framework for the "borderless" cyberspace environment. Specifically, the model provides the flexibility to implement security in small and large scale crime areas across geographic borders. However, the overall policing effectiveness is dependent upon the capacity of the entire criminal justice system to handle crime.

Historically, there have been substantial systemic bottlenecks when dealing with complex crimes. White-collar crime, for example, has encountered many similar policing issues that plague cybercrime. Comparing white-collar crime and cybercrime, it is apparent that both crimes are often hidden, require expertise to enforce, and are often expansive in nature. Assessing the similarities between white-collar crime and cybercrime can elucidate policing and criminal justice issues in policing cyberspace.

WHITE-COLLAR CRIME AND SYSTEM CAPACITY

White-collar crime is a term coined by Sutherland (1939) to describe a "crime committed by a person of respectability and high social status in the course of his occupation." While this definition has been historically debated, a more contemporary definition is offered by the FBI, stated as "illegal acts which are characterized by deceit, concealment, or violation of trust and which are not dependent upon the application or threat of physical force or violence" (USDOJ, 1989: 3). Regardless of the definitional discord, the complex nature of white-collar crime and systemic response is the focus of his research. Similar to computer crimes, white-collar crimes requires additional resources and expertise in investigations, difficult to detect and enforce, and pose prosecutorial challenges (Jesilow, Pontell, & Geis, 1993).

Identifying and analyzing the points of inefficiencies in the criminal justice system is necessary to assess the overall capacity of enforcement and legal processing of cyber cases. According to Henry Pontell's (1982, 1984) System Capacity Theory, criminal deterrence is undermined by points of inefficiency within the criminal justice system. Ineffective policing and punishment of white-collar crime and cybercrime has resulted in little deterrence on criminals. Similarly, prosecutorial unwillingness to accept complex white-collar and cyber cases can also affect the overall capacity of the criminal justice system's ability to deter criminals (Nhan, 2009).

Prosecutorial reluctance to take on complex crimes stems from structural and pragmatic barriers. In cyber cases, digital evidence from multiple sources, ranging from computers to cellular phones, requires expertise and time to process for trial. In addition, national and international jurisdictional issues place additional bureaucratic and legal burdens on prosecutors. Consequently, prosecutors have a propensity to plea bargain cases and only pursue cases meeting minimum loss thresholds, resulting in "discounted justice" and "free zones," where criminals are free to operate without fear of apprehension and criminal prosecution (Nhan, 2009). Furthermore, prosecutors are given further disincentive to prioritize white-collar and computer crimes by the general public's demands for attention towards traditional street crimes.

The reluctance to prosecute white-collar and computer crimes is reflective of its marginalization by the general public, media, and legislators. Compared to more dramatic violent street crimes, white-collar crime is labeled as the "other" crime problem (Rosoff, Pontell, and Tillman, 2007). In other words, white-collar crimes have failed to illicit public fear and indignation despite causing widespread *real* harm. The savings and loans "implosion" during the late 1980s and 1990s, for example, caused thousands of households to lose their life savings and employee retirement accounts, costing taxpayers an estimated hundreds of billions to over one trillion dollars in the long run (ibid; Strader, 2006). University of California, Davis School of Law Professor John Poulos states in one interview that the harm created by the Enron/Arthur Andersen fallout was devastating. He states, "In a way, white collar crime, in terms of the number of its victims and the devastating impact on its victims, ranks right up there among even the most heinous violent street crimes imaginable" (Pleyte, 2003: 1). Nevertheless, the public remains disproportionately fixated on violent crimes. Poulos adds, "We live in culture that almost admires violent crime." Similar to white-collar crime, computer crimes also come at a high price. According to 2008 industry estimates, survey respondents reported an average annual loss of $350,000 to their company from computer crimes ranging from virus attacks to theft of information (Richardson, 2008). In addition, identity theft is considered by government estimates as the fastest growing crime in the U.S. (Foley, et al., 2005).

Identity theft in particular, can have a devastating impact on victims. According to a study published by the Identity Theft Resource Center (ITRC), in addition to the monetary costs, the average victim surveyed spent 116 hours over 12 months to repair the damage (Foley, Gordeon, et al., 2007). The same report finds 49% of respondents suffered from stressed family life, with common feelings of rage, betrayal, unprotected from the police, powerlessness, frustration, exhaustion, sleeping problems, mistrust, and despair. Many psychologists have recognized the symptoms of identity theft victimization as resembling those of Post Traumatic Stress Disorder (PTSD) (Carey, 2009). These findings were echoed by one California Office of Emergency Services (OES) coordinator interviewed, who states, "One ID theft can destroy a person's life!"

The public remains generally apathetic towards cybercrime despite a growing awareness in cases of identity theft. Similarities can be drawn with public perceptions towards white-collar crime, which took several major scandals before public attitudes began to accept the phenomenon is a real crime. During the 1960s and 70s, white-collar offenders were perceived as respected community members. Negative perceptions of white-collar criminals as being "bad guys" began to take place only after more recent high-profile scandals such as Enron and WorldCom revealed the level of callousness and greed of white-collar offenders (Cullen, Hartman, & Jonson, 2008). Without a major cybercrime incident with widespread victimization, however, public attitudes remain marginalized, or worse, supportive of certain types of online criminal activity.

In cases of media and computer software piracy, enforcement and legal actions against offenders often incite strong public backlash and increased criminal activity (Nhan, 2008). This Robin Hood-effective and general apathy translates into little pressure to generate legislative action, continuing a cycle of under-funding and light penalties. The combination of weak social and legal controls means companies and individual victims are left mainly to fend for themselves. Moreover, offenders are largely undeterred against future criminal activities without adequate enforcement or meaningful negative stigma.

Another similarity between white-collar and computer crimes are cover-ups and anti-forensics activities deployed by offenders which make investigations and prosecutions very difficult. For example, the General Accounting Office (GAO) discovered that 42 out of 179 alleged criminal violations for 26 failed thrifts were for obstruction of justice through manipulating accounting and recordkeeping during its savings and loans investigations (Pontell & Calavita, 1993). The end result has been reluctance by law enforcement agencies and prosecutors to accept and process cases, reducing overall criminal justice capacity. Likewise, cyber malefactors employ a variety of sophisticated anti-forensics technologies that make enforcement and prosecution very time consuming and costly.

Sophisticated technologies, such as data encryption, Internet Protocol (IP)[20] masking and spoofing[21] technologies, and botnets, are often used by cyber criminals. Botnets in particular are extremely harmful and difficult to enforce. A botnet is a network of infected "zombie" computers that are remotely controlled to perform malicious functions such as overwhelm a website or server with frivolous data requests. Botnets also farm for credit card information. One film studio Internet security expert explains, "When you have 100,000 computers at your disposal, that's power." He adds, "You pay me $50,000 or I take down your online gambling site for three days; that's

---

[20] Internet Protocol (IP) is the single standardized software protocol that runs the Internet. Large chunks of information, such as files, are broken up into smaller datagrams, or packets, that is transmitted through the transportation and network layers and reassembled at the destination computer (Tanenbaum, 2003). Each computer has an IP address, similar to a phone number that identifies a computer's physical location. Data that is transmitted contain source and destination information. IP masking uses software that conceals these addresses.
[21] IP spoofing is when data packets are transmitted with a forged IP source address, making it appear to come from a different location.

real money." These botnets make investigations difficult by serving as the "middle man" and masking the source of illegal activity (Nhan, 2008). While law enforcement and industry have formed social networks to aid in enforcement, so too have criminals to counter these efforts. Countering "bright" security networks are "dark" criminal networks in both white-collar and computer crimes (Wood, 2006b). Complex financial crimes often take a concerted effort between many functional actors. One Senate Banking Committee investigator who was investigating the thrift industry during the savings and loans scandals exposed a "mafia-like" system of "fraudulent mutual support" (Rosoff, Pontell, & Tillman, 2007). For example, in one scam, lenders evaded loan restrictions by performing "reciprocal lending" where insiders made loans to corroborators in a "daisy chain" resulting in a taxpayer loss of $26 million.

Similarly, illegal file-sharers have created highly structured, sophisticated, and lucrative social and computer networks to distribute copyrighted digital content. These networks not only allow for the sharing of technical capital, but insulate top members from prosecution. These criminal networks are highly-organized and arranged in a hierarchy of individuals and organizations, collectively known as "Darknet," or simply, "The Scene" (Biddle, England, Peinado, & Willman, 2002; Howe, 2005; Lasica, 2005; Nhan, 2008). These dark networks shield illegal activities from elite members by employing low-level tech-savvy youths and disgruntled individuals to perform risky activities, such as obtaining unreleased and original copies of software and digital media (Nhan, 2008).

Similar to the flexibility and scalability of security nodal networks, criminal networks are also dynamic to allow for quick responses to major disasters, albeit those of a different nature. Decentralized file-sharing networks that distribute copyrighted content often operate overseas in countries with lax laws and enforcement. However, when law enforcement activities disrupt their operations by raiding or taking down a site, these networks are able to quickly reroute activities to other locations. For example, popular Internet Peer-to-Peer (P2P)[22] file-sharing portal, The Pirate Bay, was briefly shut down by

---

[22] In a traditional client-server computer network, information is routed from a source server, which contains a database of information that can

Swedish authorities only to resurface week later in the Netherlands fully operational with higher levels of traffic (Harrison, 2006; Sandoval, 2007). More recently, in November, 2009, The Pirate Bay announced the permanent shutting down of its tracker. However, Hollywood has suspected that it has merely changed names to OpenBitTorrent, which was established by one of the founders of The Pirate Bay (Kravets, 2009). The "cat-and-mouse" skirmishes between piracy groups and law enforcement still continue at the time of this writing with no end in sight.

Summarizing this chapter, the comparison of cybercrime with white-collar crime framed around nodal governance and system capacity theory has given a good framework for analysis. While white-collar and computer crimes are not mutually exclusive, their comparison for the purpose of this research shows the historical context to criminal justice and legal response to complex crimes. This will highlight any pre-existing structural inefficiencies while distinguishing those attributable exclusively to computer and Internet technology. We will find that many security actors involved with financial crimes are the same ones involved with cyber-crimes using similar tactics, particularly, the use of task forces to deal with the problem. However, there are some added difficulties with distributed digital information associated with cyberspace that makes sustained security extremely difficult to be explored in subsequent chapters. We now turn our attention to the methods of inquiry before examining the formation of the California cyber security network.

---

be downloaded to individual nodes or client computer systems. In a peer-to-peer network, data stored from one or more computers is directly transferred to another computer without a central server to store information. Without a central server storing all the information, this decentralized network makes dismantling the network and removing information extremely difficult. The Pirate Bay serves as a directory portal that connects these separate nodes but does not store files for downloading.

CHAPTER THREE:
Methods of Inquiry

The purpose of this study is to assess the policing of cybercrime and overall cyber security scene in California. This is accomplished by first identifying key actors, their respective assets and roles in cyber security and enforcement. Next, an assessment of how each actor operates will help identify important variables that influence the nature of participation in cyber security. In addition, an analysis of how each actor interfaces with other actors will draw out structural, cultural, political, and economic variables that enable or inhibit cooperation. These variables will be important to understanding not just how cyber security operates in California, but also the underlying cultural and structural mechanisms that influence organizational behavior.

California was selected for convenience as well as its unique situation in cyber security. California is a considered a high-tech hub with major technology industries located throughout the state. The American Electronics Association (AeA) ranks California as the overall top "cybercity" in the United States, with Silicon Valley being the nexus for high tech with Southern California employing nearly as many tech workers.[23]

California is also headquarters to the entertainment industry in the United States. This includes every major motion picture studio as well as their trade association, the Motion Picture Association (MPA) world headquarters and its American division, the Motion Picture Association of America (MPAA). One of the primary duties of this organization is to protect intellectual properties, which includes the

---

[23] AeA *Cyberstates* 2007: A Complete State-by-State Overview of the High-Technology Industry. Data was derived from the U.S. Bureau of Labor Statistics. *See* www.aeanet.org/publications/idjj_cyberstates2007_overview.asp.

deployment of anti-piracy technologies as well as developing partnerships with law enforcement.[24]

California, considered a central gateway to Asia, has historically had the greatest concentration of media and software piracy activity (Fisher, 1998). California's relatively close proximity to East Asian countries allows it to serve as a distribution gateway from and to the U.S. for both digital (soft goods) and physical (hard goods) piracy. Between 2001 and 2007, Microsoft and its law enforcement partners busted counterfeit software operations in Los Angeles, seizing an estimated $900 million worth of illegal goods (Mintz, 2008).

Having chosen California as the target population, it was first necessary to start with a literature review of cybercrime enforcement in general. The purpose of the literature review is to gain a better understanding of how cyberspace is currently policed and to identify important actors. The current literature has generally categorized cyber security actors into two groups: public policing and private industry. For example, two prominent cyber researchers, Susan Brenner (2007) and David Wall (2007) have explored tensions between public police and private industry. However, *private industry* was often used as an aggregate without identifying specific industries. It was felt that this was too broad and needed to be further defined. In addition, these studies were based on little empirical evidence and none were specific to California. To identify specific cyber security actors in California, direct initial inquiries were made with law enforcement officers and computer security practitioners.

Supplementing a review of the literature to identify key stakeholders and determine the proper research design in California were pilot phone and face-to-face interviews and queries with law enforcement throughout California and the high-tech industry. Initial interviews with law enforcement officers led to identifying the network high-tech crimes task force network in California. Pilot interviews were conducted at a large national computer security conference to identify the appropriate private industry security actors. Informal interviews and discussions with attendees led to identifying the appropriate research subjects. Based on these interviews and

---

[24] *See* www.mpaa.org/piracy.asp.

discussions with law enforcement and industry security professionals, appropriate subjects and methods were chosen.

QUALITATIVE METHODOLOGY

Qualitative methodologies were deemed the most appropriate method of inquiry. In depth-interviews would provide the appropriate depth of answers to extract important variables deemed appropriate by each security actor directly. The *grounded theory* approach, while subject to researcher biases, would allow for more depth and substantive answers not possible by quantitative surveys (Strauss & Corbin, 1990; Lofland & Lofland, 1995). A combination of convenience and snowball sample was used. Consequently, it was anticipated that random sampling and the distribution of surveys would yield extremely low returns.

The exploratory nature of this research makes qualitative methods more appropriate because of the unique population. There is simply not enough known about the high-tech crimes policing scene in California to quantitatively test variables for statistical significance. The elite population examined is relatively small with access given by a limited number of high-level gatekeepers. This was extremely important given the sensitive nature of information discussed, such as weaknesses and inadequacies in areas of cyber security.

Privacy concerns did not permit inquiries that involved specific cases and financial information, which was considered potentially harmful to the organization. Tech sector company representatives explained that computer security breaches and losses were highly guarded information that is considered potentially harmful to the company reputation.[25] This is consistent with industry surveys which cited potential harm to company reputation was a major reason for not reporting crimes to police (Richardson, 2008). This meant that collecting quantitative data for analysis was not appropriate. For example, it was common for public companies to simply refuse to disclose specific numbers of computer security incidents, citing potential insecurity can trigger a loss in consumer confidence which can result in negative shareholder reactions.

---

[25] Several public company representatives cited potential impact on stock prices and possible legal ramifications of disclosing specific losses from security incidents.

Pilot interviews also indicated that the true scope financial losses from unauthorized intrusions and piracy were not generally known to the subjects interviewed. Instead, these individuals often dealt with problems of a technical nature with little knowledge of business and financial information and decisions. Business and financial information was usually handled by a separate department or entity within the company. This made obtaining descriptive statistics from surveys, such as using a localized version of the CSI Computer Crime and Security Survey (Richardson, 2008), not possible. However, some internally published reports and surveys were obtained with some restrictions on their uses.

Law enforcement also gave certain restrictions on data used. Members from some government and law enforcement agencies interviewed were not permitted to discuss specific strategies and cases related to terrorism and cyber-terrorism, citing national security. In addition, information on active cases was not disclosed. Qualitative methods would be most given the sensitive nature of the research data.

SECURITY STAKEHOLDERS

Data were derived from four main sources: interviews, observations, published works, and documents provided by participants. Direct interviews, discussed in detail later in this chapter, provided both descriptive and substantive insight into each stakeholder's cyber security role and the nature of relations with other nodes. Supplementing interviews were observations made in several steering committee meetings between public policing and private industry groups. Observations at these meetings served to confirm the dynamics and frictions between actors. Furthermore, attendance to these meetings served to identify and gain access to more subjects. A review of the literature and initial pilot interviews with law enforcement and the technology sector initially helped identify stakeholders and served as a guide for developing appropriate interview questions. Finally, some documents (published and unpublished) were provided by interview subjects to supplement the interview data.

Four specific groups were determined to be important security stakeholders: law enforcement, government, private industry, and the general public. The identified security actors are similar to those found by other cybercrime researchers. Wall (2007), for example, has defined cyber security as a synthesis of public police, private industry (Internet

Methods of Inquiry

Service Providers), government (European Union), and private organizations (Internet Watch Foundation). A snowball sample was collected from subject referrals which led to relevant groups and individuals. Access to data will be discussed before discussing each group in further detail.

ACCESS TO DATA

Subjects were asked permission to conduct interviews after introductions were facilitated by colleague referrals and snowball sampling from known references. Industry subjects were initially referred to by individuals from pilot interviews and initial inquiries from attendees of a computer network security conference and previously known contacts in the law enforcement community in California. Subjects were then directly contacted via telephone or email to arrange for face-to-face interviews. Further snowball sampling from interviewed subjects allowed for additional subjects in law enforcement and each industry.

Initial access to the law enforcement nodal cluster was granted by one high-ranking task force supervisor. This supervisor was initially referred to by a known contact in law enforcement that was an acquaintance of the supervisor. This supervisor was initially contacted via email, followed by a telephone conversation. Finally, a face-to-face meeting was arranged, where the details of the research project was discussed. Verbal consent was given by the supervisor, who acted as a gatekeeper for access to all members of his task force, regardless of agency association.

Access to the five California regional task forces was facilitated by snowball sampling originating from one task force. The task force supervisor that initially granted permission for interviews facilitated contact to other regional task force supervisors. This was done via telephone call or email which briefly explained the study. This resulted in very receptive and cooperative task force supervisors. Task force supervisors were then contacted directly by the researcher either by phone or email, who also gave verbal consent or consent via email to arrange for interviews with their respective team. Members of all five task forces gave permission to conduct interviews.

Task force referrals led to access to the state of California governing body of the five regional task forces, the Office of Emergency Services (OES). This node works under the auspices of the state of California Governor's Office, which directly represents state government. The OES sets policy and submits annual budget proposals to the state fiscal year budget. It was identified as a key stakeholder in cyber security in California. One task force supervisor gave the name and contact information of an OES employee, who was contacted via email by the researcher. Consent was given via email and arrangements were made to conduct interviews at the OES offices in Sacramento, California.

Permission was explicitly granted directly by each subject after an explanation of the research was discussed and certain conditions were met. The nature and purpose of the research were discussed before asking permission for an interview.[26] The intent for publication along with privacy issues were also discussed in detail. A single page, IRB-approved letter of research intent was given to each subject via email before each interview. This letter outlines the researcher's responsibilities for confidentiality in accordance with the University of California, Irvine guidelines. This letter also specifies that all identifiers will be masked along with the names of specific organizations whenever possible.[27] The letter also contains all contact information of the researcher and research committee.

After approval was granted, face-to-face interviews were conducted at each subjects' locations during business hours. All subjects interviewed were working professionals. Some interviews were conducted inside restricted buildings and required authorization to

---

[26] Most subjects were contacted previously by the referring colleague before the initial phone or email exchange, which increased the likelihood of gaining permission. Subjects that were not contacted by referring colleagues were informed of this referral, which also allowed for easier access.

[27] Some public institutions could not be masked, such as the California Office of Emergency Services (OES), because it can easily be identified at a descriptive level. Permission was granted to identify these organizations by name, with the condition that individuals be masked.

enter the facilities. Subjects were given a physical copy of the letter of research intent and confidentiality policy before each interview.

INTERVIEWS

In person (n=47) and phone (n=5) interviews were conducted from 2005 to 2007. Interviews were conducted at the subjects' work locations in California, Arizona and Washington. Interviews generally lasted between one to two hours. On several occasions, two subjects from the same agency or company were interviewed simultaneously, including one phone interview. Some subjects were interviewed multiple times for clarification and to ensure validity of answers.

Subjects were asked semi-structured and open-ended questions to allow for discovery. Questions were asked within subject areas relevant to their respective industry. Prepared questions served as a subject guide rather than a strict linear inquiry to allow for flexibility. In addition, questions were also constantly adjusted during and in subsequent interviews as important issues surfaced, allowing for more in-depth and rich answers (Lofland & Lofland, 1995). For example, tech sector companies were asked specifically about unauthorized network intrusions in addition to general questions regarding the nature of relationships with law enforcement and government. Similarly, the movie industry practitioners were asked questions on Internet piracy and the impact of peer-to-peer (P2P) file-sharing technologies.

Interviews began with prepared thematic questions but subjects were allowed to expand on details and dictate the flow of questioning. The open-ended and dynamic questioning format allowed issues not anticipated by the researcher but relevant to each subject to be brought forth by subjects throughout the course of the interview. For example, multiple subjects from the technology industry repeatedly brought up the impact of the Sarbanes-Oxley Act [28] (Sarbox) on their roles and their respective companies. As a result, questions specifically

---

[28] The Sarbanes Oxley Act of 2002 (Public Company Accounting Reform and Investor Protection Act of 2002) informally referred to as "Sarbox" or "Sox" was enacted to ensure accounting integrity in public companies in the wake of major financial scandals of the early 2000s. *See* http://frwebgate.access.gpo.gov/cgi-bin/getdoc.cgi?dbname=107 _cong_bills&docid=f:h3763enr.tst.pdf.

referring to Sarbox were incorporated into questions for subsequent subjects. Subjects were also given the opportunity to define "cybercrime" according to relevance to their specific industries with the only requirement being an Internet component. This inductive approach produced very rich answers that gave a good sense into what each subject perceived as being important, including enforcement activities as well as relationship dynamics between nodal clusters. Furthermore, an analysis of how each subject defined cybercrime gave an in-depth insight into organizational cultures and how they situate themselves in the security network. While these interview data can be quantified and analyzed, it was felt that sample sizes for each group individually were inadequate to develop any meaningful inferences.

Questions were semi-structured and arranged to cover important cultural, structural, and inter-nodal factors from each actor's point of view. Examples of general guide questions included:

SAMPLE GUIDE QUESTIONS FROM TECH SECTOR

What is "cybercrime" to your organization? What is the biggest threat?

Do you work with law enforcement and what is the nature of your relationship?

Why do you choose to report or not report incidents to law enforcement?

What happens when there is a computer incident?

How has the Internet impacted your business in terms of crime?

Does your organization take legal action against attackers? When do you take them and why?

Do you feel the current laws are adequate to deal with the situation? Why or why not?

Specifically, what types of laws do you use?

Methods of Inquiry 41

What forms of technologies are you employing to curtail this problem? What are the difficulties? What types of individuals are you hiring?

What value does law enforcement bring to you in terms of cyber security?

What is your relationship with the general public in terms of security?

SAMPLE GUIDE QUESTIONS FROM MOVIE INDUSTRY

What is "cybercrime" to your organization? What is the biggest threat?

Do you work with law enforcement and what is the nature of your relationship?

How has the Internet impacted your business?

Do you take legal action against attackers? When do you take them and why?

Do you feel the current laws are adequate to deal with the situation? Why or why not?

Specifically, what types of laws do you use?

What has been the impact of these lawsuits? How has the impact of music lawsuits affected your business?

Being a steering committee member, what is the nature of your relationship to state government? Please explain what areas of need are met or unmet?

What technologies are you employing to curtail this problem?

What types of individuals do you hire?

SAMPLE GUIDE QUESTIONS FROM LAW ENFORCEMENT

What is "cyber-crime" to law enforcement? What is the biggest threat and being reported the most?

Do you work with industry and other law enforcement agencies? What is the nature of your relationship?

Which industries do you work most closely with and which do you not? Why?

Please explain how law enforcement get involved with policing cybercrime and the formation of the task force.

How do cases get brought to your attention?

What determines which cases you choose to pursue? Why?

Why are your investigations not outsourced to private investigations companies that specialize in computer forensics?

Why are computer science graduates and other individuals with technical backgrounds not hired as task force investigators?

How has limited state budgets and staffing affected your ability to handle cyber cases?

Have private companies been offering you employment? Why haven't you left your position at the task force for more lucrative opportunities in the private sector?

How do individuals report cybercrime and what procedures and steps are taken?

Have you asked for donations from companies in terms of training and equipment? What has been the response and why?

[SAMPLE GUIDE QUESTIONS POSED TO TASK FORCE PROSECUTORS]

What types of crimes are you seeing the most?

Methods of Inquiry

How has being in the task force affected your relationship with law enforcement and private industry?

What factors determine if you are going to pursue a case? Why?

What laws do you typically use to prosecute a case? Are current laws adequate for cyber cases or are a new set of 'cyber' laws necessary? Why or why not?

What is your success rate?

How are cases reported and handled once they are reported?

What sorts of defenses are you seeing in cyber cases?

Why are plea bargaining used so prevalently?

Is special training required to prosecute cyber cases?

What is the workload of cyber cases compared with non-cyber cases?

SAMPLE GUIDE QUESTIONS FOR STATE GOVERNMENT

What is the state's role in cybercrime? Why?

What is the nature of the state's relationship with private industry and law enforcement?

Why hasn't cybercrime been given more attention and larger budgets compared with traditional street crimes?

What is the biggest problem facing the state in terms of cybercrime?

What are the sources of strain between your organization and the federal government, law enforcement, industry and the general public? Are these needs met and how so?

Why were the task forces created and why was this model used for cybercrime?

What are the state's priorities in terms of cybercrime in general and types of cybercrime?

What types of legislation and policies currently govern cyber security in California?

These examples of semi-structured and open-ended questions allowed for detail-rich answers.

Interview data combined with observations of steering committee meetings and documents gave a fairly accurate view of cyber security in California as a whole. It is felt that questions were appropriate in capturing the multiplicity and complexity of issues related to policing cybercrime. It is also felt that sample sizes were appropriate relative to the small population of high-tech investigators and computer network security personnel in the private sector nodal clusters.

Patterns of similarities in answers emerged across interviewees within nodal clusters. Consistencies in answers between different clusters allowed for identifying structural and cultural frictions between actors, suggesting appropriate questions were asked enough times. For example, both law enforcement and tech sector interviewees confirmed conflicts between what should be policing priorities but gave differing perspectives to why they exist. As a whole, it is felt analysis of this data provided a fairly accurate depiction of cyber security in California as well as cultural and structural conflicts between security actors. Furthermore, while generalizable inferences cannot be made beyond California, many interviewers have collaborated with different law enforcement and private organizations in different states. This suggests the possibility that future research should confirm these structural and cultural difficulties.

Interview Table 1*

Participant Category	n
Police Personnel	22
Private Industry	
Film	10
Tech	18
State Representatives (OES)	2
Total	52

* Excludes pilot interviews

     Interviews with members of each of the four primary security actors gave a holistic view of cyber secuirty in California. First, the law enforcement nodal cluster was chosen for its growing role in cybercrime. Law enforcement has been playing a growing role in protecting cyberspace and was formally recognized as part of an overall strategy to protect national critical infrastructures ("The National Strategy to Secure Cyberspace," 2003). This important role reiterated recently by the Obama administration's desire to appoint a national cyber security czar.[29]

     Second, the film industry and technology sectors, representing the *private industry* security nodal cluster, were chosen based on their contrasting relationships with law enforcement. It will be discussed in the following chapters that the film industry has similar desirable security outcomes with law enforcement, creating a strong partnership. In contrast, the tech sector has historically avoided or has had relatively little utility for law enforcement assistance. Despite these differences, these two industries have been victims to cybercrime and have been at the forefront of policing cyberspace.

     Third, the state government cluster was selected for its role in coordinating resources and communications between law enforcement, private industry, and the general public. There has been growing demand for a stronger leadership position by the government. One

---

[29] As of the time of this writing, the cyber security advisor is vacant since the resignation of Melissa Hathaway, President Obama's original appointee, in August, 2009.

industry group, The Cyber Security Industry Alliance, criticized the federal government for lack of leadership and accountability (Krebs, 2005). Finally, the general public is considered a key security stakeholder. Unfortunately, members from this cluster were not interviewed given the limited scope and constraints of this research. However, the general public's role will be discussed from the point of the view the security actors interviewed as well as assessed using published literature.

LAW ENFORCEMENT NODAL SET

The law enforcement sample consisted of members from five regional high-tech crimes task forces throughout California. These task forces were coordinated by the Office of Emergency Services (OES) under the auspices of the California Governor's Office. The California High-Tech Task Force Committee designates each task force to consist of city, county, and state law enforcement agencies, prosecutors, and federal agencies ("Combating High Tech Crime in California", 1997). Each regional task force is supplemented by a steering committee consisting of high-tech businesses, trade and professional organizations, and insurers.

The task force members are comprised of investigators from federal, state, county, and local agencies. Task force members, regardless of their home agency, are under the direct supervision of the task force supervisor. The task force supervisor is often a high-ranking peace officer or a district attorney. Each supervisor coordinates and distributes cases to each investigator and handles budgets. Task force members are comprised of detective-level officers from state, county, and local agencies. Several federal law enforcement agencies have task force members. In addition, specialized prosecutors are embedded within each task force to ensure compliance to evidentiary guidelines and to streamline the prosecutorial pipeline.

Task force members are often transient in nature. The task force training is often used by a growing number of police agencies developing in-house computer forensic and cybercrime capabilities. Many officers dedicate several years of membership to the task force in exchange for knowledge, training, and experience in cyber investigations. Upon completing their task force assignment, these investigators can take back the skills learned to their home agency or department. During times of fiscal constraint, however, many departments often "take back" their investigator and reassign him or her to local duties before their task force commitments are completed.

PRIVATE INDUSTRY NODAL SET (TECH SECTOR AND FILM INDUSTRY)

Representatives from the private industry nodal cluster were interviewed. The private industry aggregate was too broad to be considered for a single unit of analysis. "Private industry" can depict numerous companies in different fields throughout California. Instead, two specific industries were selected for the nature of their relationships with law enforcement: the technology sector and film industry. The technology sector encompasses companies involved in the research, development, and distribution of technology-based goods and services[30] such as computer hardware, software and information technology companies. The tech sector was chosen for several reasons: (1) Its history of underreporting crimes to law enforcement (Richardson, 2008), (2) its historic role in developing and deploying technologies to monitor and police the Internet, and (3) its expertise concerning the Internet infrastructure (Government Accountability Office Report, 2007).

A sample of network security specialists and practitioners from computer hardware and software companies were interviewed. These individuals also referred colleagues with similar positions in other companies. It must be noted that software engineers and other security experts have a fraternal network with equivalent associates across the entire industry. These experts regularly shared security information with colleagues even in competing companies. Only individuals working directly in cyber security were interviewed to maintain consistency and reliability.

Interviews were conducted with tech sector subjects from Washington and Arizona in addition to California despite the California cyber security network being the focus of the research. While many tech sector companies are based in California, some companies have computer security individuals and teams working remotely that handle security functions in California. This is not uncommon in computer

---

[30] *See* www.investopedia.com/terms/t/technology_sector.asp.

security, where security personnel are often not required to be physically located in the area of business. In all, eighteen subjects (n=18) were interviewed from the technology sector from California, Washington and Arizona.

The film industry was chosen for the nature of its relationship with the law enforcement. The film industry has historically worked closely with law enforcement on investigations to bust groups and individuals illegally distributing *hard goods* ranging from VHS tapes to DVDs. This industry has also taken legal action to enforce piracy and copyright infringement. This group continues to work closely with law enforcement on investigations and the criminal prosecution of Internet piracy (*soft goods*). The MPAA in particular, actively monitors Internet copyright infringement activity on Internet forums and P2P file-sharing networks.

Ten subjects (n=10) were interviewed from the film industry. Interview subjects consisted of security professionals from the MPAA and its international counterpart, the MPA. The MPAA is considered a subdivision of the MPA but shares the same facilities and functions, differing only on its focus on the U.S. This paper will refer to both MPA and MPAA as a single entity, the MPAA. The MPAA represents every major motion picture studio and plays an important role in protecting intellectual property. Interviews were also conducted with security practitioners from several studios. Many studios also have in-house security teams that perform similar copyright enforcement functions to supplement security provided by the MPAA. It must be noted that this group has a much smaller population than the tech industry, reflected by the smaller sample size.

Only MPAA and studio Internet security specialists and practitioners were interviewed. This was the case in order to remain consistent with the research focus on Internet crime. The goal was to match employees with similar functions in the technology sector. The exclusion of individuals not directly involved with security, such as lawyers and public relations representatives, allowed for a more accurate depiction of Internet crime directly from individuals working in cyber security. Moreover, the Internet security practitioners interviewed routinely conduct investigations and work directly with task force investigators.

Both the tech sector and film industry (including the MPAA) are members of California's high-tech crimes steering committee. Members of the steering committee represented a large number of companies throughout that state, totaling hundreds of high-tech firms. These companies range from major hardware and software manufacturers to banks and other industries concerned with cyber security. While nearly all companies have some form of cyber security team, the steering committee represents the only state-coordinated body that bridges industry and law enforcement in dealing with high-tech crimes. The state plays an important role in developing and maintaining industry-police relations.

NODAL CLUSTER INTERVIEWED: STATE GOVERNMENT

State government is a key stakeholder in California's cyber security social network. Two Office of Emergency Services (OES) representatives directly in charge of the high-tech crimes task forces were interviewed. State OES representatives oversee legal, budgetary and policy matters regarding cyber security. The subjects interviewed coordinated steering committee meetings and administered budgets and policies that govern the high-tech crimes task forces. While not involved with daily Internet security operations, OES members served as law enforcement-industry liaisons and communicated general concerns and priorities between nodes. The OES also heads a high-tech crimes steering committee, which also includes members from several high-tech industries.

One high-ranking task force supervisor facilitated access to the OES. The OES is headed by the California Governor's Office. The two representatives (n=2) were interviewed from this node. The OES, which is today known as the California Emergency Management Agency (CalEMA), handles a broad range of state emergency services, ranging from natural disasters to homeland security. The small sample size of this node is reflective of a very small population at the OES that deals with cyber and high-tech crimes. Access to the OES was extremely important to gaining insight into the financial and political aspects of policing cybercrime in California.

The OES allowed access to high-tech private industries. Snowball sampling was possible from OES referrals to high-tech steering committee members. Furthermore, direct contact with industry representatives was made possible from attendance in public quarterly steering committee meetings. Technology sector and film industry representatives were introduced to and encouraged to participate in the study by OES and task force members familiar with the research project. This resulted in very receptive industry representatives and positive attitudes towards the research. Arrangements were later made with industry subjects for face-to-face interviews via email or telephone.

HIGH-TECH CRIMES STEERING COMMITTEE

The OES, law enforcement, and private industries interfaced quarterly during state-sponsored steering committee meetings. A total of three meetings were observed. The OES-led steering committee consists of all five task forces and representatives from major high-technology industries throughout California. Committee members include a variety of industries ranging from movie and music, as well as the technology industries such as computer software to banking. The common thread shared amongst industry committee members is the desire for collaboration with industry and law enforcement. These meetings served as open forums to share information, bring forth and discuss issues, settle disputes, and network. Observations of these meetings provided insight into interactions and dynamics between law enforcement, private industries, and state government.

While steering committee meetings are considered public, it is not advertised to the general public and no members of the general public were observed to be in attendance. This was not surprising considering each meeting took place in secure buildings at the state OES headquarters or regional task force offices. Non-members in attendance were mainly made aware of the meetings through colleague referrals. These guests were mainly representatives from industries interested in committee membership. For example, a member from the telephone and telecommunications industry was in attendance during one observed meeting. Most industry representatives in attendance were interested in learning about the security assets offered by the task forces and sharing their specific industry needs.

Non-member industries were allowed to voice their input on issues presented but did not have voting privileges. Many individuals in attendance inquired about obtaining committee membership and desired to make connections with law enforcement. Non-steering committee industry representatives were approached for interviews, which led to further snowball sampling.

GENERAL PUBLIC

Members of the general public were not interviewed for this research. This does not discount the general public as a key stakeholder in cyber security. However, several factors contributed to their exclusion. First, interviews with members of the general public were beyond the scope and resources of this research. It was decided by the researcher that the primary goal of the research is to bring to light policing efforts in cyberspace. Next, it presented methodological problems. Establishing a representative sample from a large population would require a substantial sample size and random sampling. With a larger sample, quantitative methods may be more appropriate to gauge public attitudes. Mixing interview data with three nodal sets (law enforcement, the state, and private industry) with a quantitative nodal set (general public) may be inappropriate. Instead, the general public perspective was measured using secondary data and indirectly with interviewed nodes.

Public attitudes were gauged indirectly using a variety of methods. Subjects from state government, law enforcement, and private industries were asked about the nature of their relationship with the general public. While these interviews gave only a one-sided representation of the nature of relationships with the general public, direct attitudes and activities of the public were gauged using published secondary data. It was felt that a fair assessment can be derived from combining published public perception studies with interview data.

Public perceptions of cybercrime have been considerably researched. For example, many studies have focused on piracy amongst college students by sociologists, economists, and other social science researchers (Sims, Cheng, & Teegen, 1996; Higgins, Fell, & Wilson, 2007; Aiken, Vanjani, Ray, & Martin, 2003). Cross cultural comparative studies of the public reveal cultural influences that explain piracy activity (Husted, 2000; Condry, 2004). In addition, many researchers have examined Internet and hacker culture (Levy, 2001; Kleinrock, 2004; Holt, 2005) and the public's attitudes towards cybercrime (Wall, 2008) and in general. The Pew Internet and American Life Project, for example, has surveyed and tracked trends amongst thousands of Internet users since 2000.[31] While these studies

---

[31] See www.pewinternet.org.

did not draw samples exclusively from California, they collectively allow for a better understanding of public mentalities and behaviors towards social control and policing in the Internet.

QUALITATIVE METHODS

In-depth interviews and observations were determined to by the most appropriate level of inquiry in this research design. The purpose of this is to not only describe the cyber security scene in California and identify key participants, but also to assess the nature of inter-nodal relationships. A grounded-theory qualitative approach, where theory is derived from empirical data, provides the necessary empirical depth for the complexities of policing cybercrime. A primary goal of the research is to contextualize cybercrime from a criminological perspective that takes into account cultural, economic, structural, and political forces. A discussion of qualitative methodology will expand upon why in-depth interviews and observations were chosen for this research.

Deriving theory from empirical data is the basis for grounded theory research (Glaser and Strauss, 1967). Through a process of systematic discovery, categorization of testable variables can emerge using a best-fit theory. In sociological theory development, the purpose of theory is: (1) produce predictive and explanatory power, (2) be useful the theoretical advancement of sociology, (3) be useful in practical applications, (4) provide a prospective on behavior, and (5) serve as a research style guide (ibid: 3). In this sense, the nodal governance framework is a tool for understanding behavior for further development of predictive behavior in cyberspace.

Using an inductive approach with the actor's point of view is an important element of social science discovery (Becker, 1996). This is consistent with the exploratory nature of qualitative studies with an "open-ended and emergent process" (Lofland & Lofland 1995: 5). Interviews produced empirical depth allowing for a holistic understanding of cybercrime, identifying variables for future testing. Using interview data, general patterns of activities were identified, taking into account the complexity of perspectives.

There are drawbacks to using grounded theory methodology. Known problems include the subjectivity of data collection, the lack of equivalent comparison groups makes causal inferences difficult, relatively small sample sizes, lack of generalizability, and dependency

Methods of Inquiry

on interviewer skills (Bryman, 1999). They have also been criticized for being incoherent and unscientific (Morse, 1994). However, some argue there are some misconceptions about this methodology, including the lack of generalizability, hypothesis testing and theory building, and bias (Flyvbjerg, 2006). These critiques of grounded theory are reflective of broader criticisms of qualitative research design. Kvale (1994) points out ten stereotypes of qualitative research stereotypes in the social sciences, stating qualitative research interviews are: (1) not scientific but based on common sense, (2) subjective and not objective, (3) untrustworthy and biased, (4) not reliable with leading questions, (5) not intersubjective and open to differing interpretations, (6) not quantitative, (7) not generalizable with too few subjects, (8) exploratory with no scientific hypothesis testing, (9) not formalized but dependant on researcher skills and (10) not valid but rests on subjective impressions.

This study does not suggest that qualitative designs are inferior. It is felt that the research design should be selected on the basis of being the best fit to the research objectives. Hammersley (1996) argues that a strict dichotomy between quantitative and qualitative paradigms in research methods is not realistic, citing that much of social sciences data does not fall neatly into these two categories and suggests practitioner choices are often attributed to paradigm loyalty and dogma.

In this particular study, qualitative methods are the most appropriate. Small sample sizes of an elite population makes meaningful survey design invalid. In addition, there is very little known about the cyber-policing scene in California. The exploratory nature of the research seeks to identify the variables that can allow for future quantifiable hypothesis testing. Moreover, in-depth interviews allowed for the nuances and patterns to emerge in determining what was important to each security actor.

Semi-structured and open-ended interview questions allow subjects to freely express opinions on what is important to the subject without imposing researcher judgments on what is important. Furthermore, it allows subjects to bring forth ideas and topics about policing cybercrime not initially known to the researcher and highlight those expressed as worthy of attention. Having subjects dictate the relevancy of issues prevents an influence or bias of topics deemed important by the researcher. Closed-ended survey questionnaires can omit important variables and possibly overestimate the importance of other variables. Eliciting sensitive information is one primary advantage of a qualitative approach using open-ended interview questions (Edwards, Rosenfeld, Thomas, & Booth-Kewley, 1996: 26). Straub and Welke (1998: 447) consider information security "an extremely sensitive subject for all organizations." To examine managerial responses to security situations, they used minimally intrusive open-ended questions during intensive interviews to encourage thorough and candid participation.

Subjects greater likelihood to explain answers in detail and reliably is one particular advantage of qualitative research design. Some subjects were interviewed multiple times for clarification to ensure consistency and greater validity. Consistent answers in repeated interviews of the same subject indicated reliability and minimal interviewer bias effects. In addition, consistency across multiple interviews subjects minimized the possibility of subjects answering what are "expected" of them. None of the interview subjects interviewed two or more times in this study were not found to give contradictory or conflicting answers to previous interviews.

The qualitative analysis of empirical data in this research is intended to be compliment future quantitative and mixed designs. The depth of answers and richness of information can be readily used for further analysis and as guides for future research designs. Closed-ended survey designs often capture less additional information than intended, which limits secondary analysis.

EMPIRICAL MAPPING

Qualitative design is implemented in this research using empirical mapping. Empirical mapping is a method of inquiry used in the nodal governance theoretical model designed to (1) specify each security actor's functions and assets, and (2) situate each actor in the security network in relation to others. This information is derived primarily from interview data. The nature of their security assets and relationships will be useful in assessing overall cyber security in California.

Methods of Inquiry

This research builds upon this nodal governance theoretical framework using Wood's (2006) exploratory guidelines to empirically map out the California cyber and high-tech security network. This functional mapping is used to identify and examine main actors in the security field and their respective assets (capital) contributing to security in order to extract structural and political variables that affect levels of participation and security outcomes. More importantly, mapping allows for the analysis of inter-nodal synaptic gaps, where points of cooperation and conflict occur. Inter-nodal frictions can reveal structural, cultural, political, and economic incompatibilities. For example, desired outcome misalignments and divergence can result in weak or non-existent partnerships, while sustained collaborations can be formed when inter-nodal security goals are similar. Collectively, examining these relations within a network can determine the overall strength of cyber security.

To begin an exploratory and *explanatory* empirical analysis of a security network such as attempted in this research, nodes must be identified through a "mapping exercise" (Dupont, 2006; Wood, 2006). Key security stakeholders, their capital or attributes, and their relationship to other security stakeholders are identified. Wood (2006: 230) proposes a mapping framework methodology as follows:

(1) A comprehensive empirical "mapping" of existing governance nodes and networks within specific sites.

(2) An assessment of gaps, limitations and ethical problems with the operation of existing nodes and networks.

(3) Designing and tailoring of an innovation, involving the participation of actors with different forms of tacit and expert knowledge, aimed at transforming, or even inventing, new mentalities, institutions and practices of governance that serve to enhance the effectiveness and/or democratic character of security provision. The adaptation and translation of the innovation within a specific site should consist of a continuous, flexible and iterative process of evaluation and reflection that adjusts to forms of resistance and contestation on the part of local actors.

Wood (2006) also proposes a general set of questions as a guideline for explanatory mapping:

- Who are the actors (both formally organized and informal) who participate in the promotion of safety and security?

- What forms of knowledge, and what capabilities and resources, does each of these actors bring to bear in promoting security outcomes?

- What does this set of knowledge, capabilities and resources reveal about the word-view of such actors?

- What are their state outcomes and how do they measure success?

- What are the ways in which these different actors relate to one another in the security field?

- Depending on the nature of each nodal relationship, how often does each node/actor 'interface' with another and in what situations?

In addition, questions are posed to identify the nature of nodes, such as the modes of production of commodities, variables that make certain nodes the target of crime, and structural factors that make some nodes insecure.

In one mapping example, Manning (2006a) maps an *ad hoc* security network to identify security strengths and weaknesses. During the 2002 Winter Olympic Games in Salt Lake City, Utah, police forces from several local, state, federal organizations, and the National Guard (nodes), were mobilized for quick response to potential terrorist incidents and to provide security. This security network was further enhanced by access to several crime databases, including two national databases from the Immigration and Naturalization Services (INS) and Federal Emergency Management Agency (FEMA). Despite a major coordination and access to shared information, Manning found inter-nodal friction between federal agencies and municipal police forces. He identified communication breakdowns attributed to an imbalance of power, different communication technologies and protocols, and differing appearances as factors that weaken overall security. He concludes that structural variables led to "inter-agency conflicts, inefficient technology, lack of intelligence and analytical capacity," making security procedures "ritualistic and symbolic rather than instrumental and preventative" (Manning, 2006a: 65).

DATA COLLECTION

One critical issue of this study was the problem of mapping and analyzing California's cyber security network using interview data collected outside of California. To overcome this problem, limitations and boundaries on the study were theoretically and functionally defined using an actor's relation to California. While traditional studies have stressed study limitations contained to subjects in a specified area, this did not violate the nodal governance theoretical framework.

Wood's (2006) mapping exercise stressed identifying and analyzing security networks functionally in relation to other security actors. This underlying framework was essential and specifically chosen in analyzing security in the Internet's non-geography oriented boundaries. It would simply be inappropriate to superimpose geographically and politically defined borders and notions of territory on the Internet geography. Huey (2002) discusses the dichotomy between terra-bound entities of social control (police) with an "abstract", relatively borderless Internet space. In other words, a study of the Internet using strictly geographic limits as in traditional social science research is not an ideal methodology. In this sense, it does not violate research methodology to examine California's cyber security network using data collected from sources outside of California that have functional relationship to the state.

It is felt that the methods used in this exploratory study accomplish the goal of describing the cyber security network in California and understanding underlying mechanisms that shape each security actor's role in cyber security. Furthermore, this study helps in developing future research with quantitative or mixed methodologies. While it is acknowledged that qualitative data can be codified and analyzed quantitatively, it was felt that larger sample sizes are needed for more accurate findings. This should be possible in future studies for a more complete understanding of policing cybercrime in general. Mixed methods of inquiry have been shown to give more robust understandings of complex social problems (Jick, 1979; Johnson and Onwuegbuzie, 2004).

Having discussed the methods of inquiry, we now turn our attention to the formation of nodal networks and the development of cyber security in California.

CHAPTER FOUR:
The Formation, Expansion, and Function of Nodal Networks

This chapter will apply the nodal governance theoretical framework to examine the development of California's high-tech crimes task force network. First, the conditions that led up to the development of a high-tech crimes task force network will be examined. Next, the Internet geography and some of the difficulties policing this space will be considered. Specifically, applying traditional geographic territory-oriented police to a virtual geography will be explored. Finally, two cases in particular, online auction fraud and homicide, will be deconstructed to show how cyber investigations are currently conducted. Implications of the proliferation of computer technology in all crimes will be discussed.

THE NEED FOR SPECIALIZED POLICING

The exponential growth and integration of computer and Internet technology into everyday life has facilitated an unprecedented increase in crime using the new medium. The dynamic environment has been the subject of much debate to whether it is a new crime type or merely manifestations of old forms of crime (Grabosky, 2001; Brenner, 2001; Wall, 2004). Regardless of this debate, one uncontested assertion is that Internet technology facilitates crime with greater speed and ubiquity than previously possible. Moreover, Internet crime has been extremely lucrative, spawning a multi-million dollar "shadow economy" (Espiner, 2007). For example, the digitization of personal information coupled with the ease and anonymity of Internet technology has resulted in a dramatic increase in identity theft and other criminal acts (Pontell, 2002). In some instances, automated processes for identity theft and credit card fraud have resulted in large-scale financial losses and victimization (McCarty, 2003).

Despite increased industry investments in computer security, cybercrimes such as network intrusions (Richardson, 2008) and media piracy (Siwek, 2007) continued to rise dramatically. The growing security deficit prompted industry groups to solicit state government and law enforcement for assistance. One OES coordinator explains, "[Industries] came to the [California state] legislature saying we have a problem; this is a growing trend." She adds, historically, "Law enforcement wants to lock 'em up, throw away the keys. They weren't addressing business' needs." Increased victimization both by individuals and corporations has created a growing need for specialized police services. With industry lobbying and an increasing number of individual and corporate victims, law enforcement was thrust into taking a significant role in policing cybercrime.

THE TASK FORCE MODEL

Law enforcement responded to industries' inability to adequately self-police by forming of a high-tech crimes task force network in California. A task force is a temporary *ad hoc* assembly of separate security entities for a specified purpose. The task force model is often used by law enforcement to offset insufficient knowledge and expertise in dealing with complex crimes. The model has many advantages, such as broaden expertise, share resources, minimize costs, and overcome inefficiencies and legal complications associated with overlapping jurisdictions. In the context of the nodal governance model of security, collaborations are used to mobilize collective resources and knowledge to manage risk.

Today, nearly every state has adopted the task force model to deal with electronic and cybercrime in the United States. These task forces are coordinated either by state or federal government. They range from very developed state-wide and federal collaborations to more localized cyber units. For example, the New York Electronic Crimes Task Force (NYECTF)[32] headed by the U.S. Secret Service consists of 50 law enforcement agencies, 200 corporations, and 12 universities. In Illinois, the office of attorney general coordinates the High Tech Crimes Network,[33] which includes the Illinois Computer

---

[32] *See* www.secretservice.gov/ectf.shtml.
[33] *See* www.hightechcrimes.net.

Crimes Institute, Illinois Computer Forensics Lab, the Regional Computer Crime Enforcement Group, and other government agencies. Federal or state government plays a central role in cyber security, functioning to connect all regional nodes and nodal clusters.

Security partnerships have been effectively utilized to share expertise in complex white-collar and organized crime cases. The 2001 Enron/Arthur Andersen scandal, for example, required the resources and expertise of a large investigative team consisting of federal agents, accountants, Internal Revenue Service, lawyers, and other specialists ("Report of the Investigation of Enron," 2003). The collection of specialists uncovered illegal financial activities that were purposely obscured by company insiders. In another case, complex medical fraud required an assembly of expert investigators from multiple agencies and organizations to be familiar with esoteric medical terminology and differentiate between legitimate and unlawful activities as well as decipher accounting misconduct (Jesilow, Pontell, & Geis, 1993). Similarly, the New York State Organized Crime Task Force was used to investigate the construction industry in New York City in the 1980s (Goldstock, Marcus, Thacher II, & Jacobs, 1990).

Security alliances allow for pooling financial resources. White-collar crime cases are often expensive and time consuming, requiring greater amounts of resources and specialized knowledge than traditional street crimes (Williams, 1997). For instance, the FBI alone had over 4,300 open fraud investigations during the peak of the savings and loans scandals of the late 1980s and early 1990s (Calavita & Pontell, 1994). Resource-intensive cyber investigations can also be very expensive, giving incentive for some industries to form alliances with law enforcement.

An industry's desire partner with law enforcement is dependent upon their level of utility for law enforcement's security capital. For some industries, law enforcement's expertise in digital forensics can be a valuable and cost-saving security asset. One network security explains, "Forensics is *very* expensive...to do a full forensic work for eventual litigation can cost [our company] $50,000 to $100,000." Another computer network security engineer described the importance of law enforcement's investigative capability as "the biggest area of need," adding, "Law enforcement will become more critical because information is becoming more digitized." In addition to cost reduction by sharing resources, the task force model serves to streamline jurisdictional issues in the cyber environment. The Internet is often considered a "borderless" environment from its lack of strict confinement to geographic territory. One particular advantage of the task force policing model is its flexibility to handle multiple jurisdictions. Specialized prosecutors embedded within these task forces are given enough flexibility to overcome territorial issues associated with overlapping legal turfs to ensure the integrity of evidentiary processing. According to the National Institute of Justice (NIJ), one of the biggest challenges facing police in cyberspace is eliminating prosecutorial impediments such as out-of-state warrants, subpoenas, and court orders (Ritter, 2006). The NIJ emphasizes using a strategy consistent with the nodal governance framework by recommending a "multidisciplinary team of professionals." The network of task forces in California was designed to eliminate many of the legal and structural issues underscored by the NIJ.

Cyber and high-tech security in California consists of a network of five task forces guided by high-tech oriented directives. Successful industry lobbying resulted in the passage of California Penal Code §13848-13848,[34] which covers the following acts:

1. White-collar crime, automatic teller machine and credit card fraud committed electronically or using a computer.

2. Unlawful access and destruction of private, corporate, and government computer networks which includes any disclosure or manipulation of data.

3. Money laundering or banking transfers using computer networks.

4. Telephone and cable television theft using electronic devices.

5. Intellectual property piracy.

6. Theft and resale of computer equipment and technology.

---

[34] *See* lawyers.wizards.pro/california/codes/pen/13848-13848.8.php.

7. Counterfeiting computer hardware and software.
8. Theft of trade secrets.

Furthermore, California law is supplemented by The Digital Millennium Copyright Act[35] (DMCA), a federal law which specified computer security circumvention and added more severe criminal penalties along with civil liability. These laws are used in conjunction with non-cyber specific laws applicable to cyber cases to give law enforcement the necessary legal tools to enforce high-tech and computer crimes. CPC §13848.6 also mandates the formation of the High-Technology Crimes Advisory Committee (HTCAC) and funding for the high-tech crime task forces.[36]

The establishment of the HTCAC mandates extending membership to private industry representatives throughout California. Industry representative members consist of a variety of industries, such as computer software, banking, film, and music. Police services are not limited to committee members, but extend to all companies with operations in California. Non-member industry and company representatives are invited to attend quarterly steering committee meetings. These industry representatives can observe and give input during the public proceedings and request to join the committee. Prospective members often attended these meetings to present what security capital they can offer to the task forces and learn of the benefits. New memberships can expand the security network, increase the security capital, and expand the overall security capacity. However, an abundance of security capital in a large network does not guarantee effective or better cybercrime enforcement.

Task forces can be ineffective without clear guidance and leadership from a central node. Geller and Morris' (1992) informal study of Washington, D.C.'s International Narcoterrorism Unit underscores the important role the state plays in managing a task force. They explain, "Poor husbanding of resources and deficient coordination

---

[35] H.R. 2281 The Digital Millennium Copyright Act of 1988 signed in to law October 28, 1988 as Public Law 105-304 amended Title 17 U.S.C.

[36] CPC §13820 under the High Technology Theft Apprehension Program.

of anticrime and order maintenance assets may make for weak strategic and tactical planning and ineffectual operations." Furthermore, problems "simply fall between the institutional stools as federal, state, and local law enforcement agencies, unaware of one another's priorities, assume that someone else is taking care of the problem" (Geller & Morris, 1992: 232). California has divided its task forces by geographic region to minimize bureaucratic inefficiency.

REGIONAL SUB-NETWORKS

Law enforcement-industry nodal relations are often formed regionally in smaller regional security sub-networks. The makeup and functions of each regional network differs, reflecting clientele demographics and security goals. The Southern California regional task force, for example, has many more piracy cases having nodal alliances with the film and recording industries from being close to Hollywood. In contrast, the Sacramento Valley regional task force has a much heavier load of computer intrusion and hacking having close proximity to high-tech Silicon Valley companies. Each task force has a set of private industry representatives from a variety of companies within their jurisdiction. All five task forces and industry representative members are officially governed by the OES via steering committee membership.

THE FORMATION OF *AD HOC* SECURITY ALLIANCES

There are several ways in which new security partnerships are formed. First, industry-law enforcement alliances can develop from private industry and company representatives joining the high-tech crimes steering committee. Second, nodal partnerships are often formed through informal personal referrals rather than structured arrangements. Industry representatives often have a single task force investigator who is contacted directly when problems arise. This is not a pre-arranged protocol but result of positive rapport and mutual trust gained through previous investigations. These relations are expanded when through colleague referrals by industry practitioners. One new task force investigator who replaced a former detective explains, "They'll just get all my information and before you know it, another company will call asking for me, being referred by so and so. They come looking for me."

The expansion of the nodal network is not limited to the creation of industry-law enforcement relationships. Nodal alliances can also be expanded within the law enforcement community. Each regional task force consists of a variety of investigators from local and federal agencies. Relatively few local law enforcement agencies have investigators assigned to a task-force. Low participation amongst local agencies is due to two main factors: First, smaller departments with fewer personnel resources cannot afford to "donate" an investigator to investigate cases outside their home jurisdiction. Second, many local agencies are simply unaware of the existence and purpose of the task force. Task forces face a constant problem of retaining and gaining new law enforcement members. Task force supervisors are often actively recruiting new members through all opportunities.

The expansion of task force membership and partnerships with law enforcement agencies is often done informally, in *ad hoc* fashion, and fortuitously. Routine police activities can lead to interactions with the task force. This serendipitous interaction can result in greater exposure to the task force and potentially expand nodal network connections with other law enforcement agencies. One task force supervisor gives an example:

One time there was a police chase that ended right outside our office in the parking lot. So the cops were wrestling the guy and finally take him into custody. We were just watching them from inside over there. The building's not marked so when they were all done we went out there and I handed him a card and told [the arresting officers] about us.

The goal of expanding the task force is twofold: (1) by increasing the number of personnel hired and (2) expanding alliances with other law enforcement organizations.

It is important to recognize task force capital expansion is oriented around human capital with a much smaller emphasis on increasing technological capacity. One goal long-term ambition of the task forces is the creation of a unified database system to facilitate information sharing. Ideally, such a database can serve as a central information hub to allow law enforcement instant access to information and an active directory to facilitate members of the law enforcement community to communicate with each other without prearranged introductions. In practice, however, a central database has yet to come to fruition mainly due to investigator apathy and reservations with its usefulness. One task force prosecutor explains:

> The way it works in law enforcement, you work with people, you know them; I may not know the guy in Boston but I worked with a guy in New Hampshire who knows the guy in Boston who hooks me up with the guy in Boston. The old time personal communication vouching for somebody is what cops works on. Having an official network where you can go online and talk to somebody is not necessarily going to foster that.

The expansion of the task force and security capital is through increasing the number of nodal connections and by hiring more investigators.

BUILDING LAW ENFORCEMENT CAPITAL

Building capital also requires expanding the security network to other law enforcement agencies as well as increasing knowledge capital of all law enforcement. One task force supervisor from a large urban agency underscored the general lack of security capital by law enforcement by stating that less than 1% of the department is trained to handle high tech crimes. He emphasized two important elements within law enforcement to expand security capacity, stating, "One, the [task force] unit is important and needs to be expanded and two, there needs to be some training curriculum and base knowledge."

One goal of the task forces is to expand their knowledge capital. Police have generally avoided complex high-tech and computer crimes due to a general unfamiliarity with the technical requirements in handling cybercrime cases. Task force investigators often select cases that expand the knowledge capital for use in future scenarios with similar circumstances to expand their base knowledge and experience. According to one task force prosecutor interviewed, task force investigators have very large case loads which require minimum victim and loss thresholds in order to be pursued. However, his task force will pursue cases that do not meet this threshold if they present unique learning opportunities. He explains his criteria by asking, "If we do respond to this [case], will it facilitate a growth of an appropriate response in the law enforcement community for this type of situation?" However, this open attitude is not representative of the law enforcement community as a whole, which remains largely apathetic to cybercrime. It is necessary to examine the nature of cyberspace to understand why cybercrime is largely marginalized amongst police departments. What makes policing this space difficult extends beyond the general lack of technical knowledge, but extends into social-structural arrangements of policing itself.

THE INTERNET GEOGRAPHY

Cyber-geography is an emerging field that seeks to expand the study of cartography to cyberspace. This field uses visualization techniques by converging geographic information systems (GIS) with networking. Johannson (2000: 67) points to the increasing applicability of GIS systems in computer networks, which categorically flows from 1) traditional geographical space, to 2) computer media, to 3) cyberspace, and to 4) traditional geographical space of physical reality as organized by cyberspace.

Some cartographers attempt to superimpose physical mapping methods and spatial boundaries on to an abstract space. Dodge and Kitchin (2001) categorize three ways to map the Internet space: (1) Maps of the Internet infrastructure (a purely functional map such as routers, "pipes", connectivity etc.), (2) maps of Internet traffic, and (3) temporal maps of information communications technologies (ICTs). However, some problems arise with mapping the Internet. For instance, connectivity mapping often suffer from *ecological fallacy,* where aggregate characteristics are wrongly attributed at the individual level (Dodge & Kitchin, 2001: 83).

Wilson and Corey (2000) classify the Internet into three distinct geographies: (1) the *physical infrastructure*, or location of hardware assets such as servers and routers, (2) *virtual disparities*, or separation between the "haves" and the "have-nots," and (3) spaces defined by demarcation and interaction of places, or online communities. They argue that space remains important component of the Internet in connecting places and markets despite the overly simplistic declaration of "the death of distance" (Wilson & Corey, 2000: 2). The inability to use traditional mapping techniques based purely on physical geographic location is the common thread amongst Internet cartographers.

The Internet is not governed geographically using legally and politically-defined notions of territory. Instead, it functions as an "abstract" medium (Huey, 2002) commonly described as "borderless." This is not to suggest that the Internet is entirely disconnected to the physical world, but that it is governed functionally using gateways to data. Conceptual boundaries and territory can be defined functionally by setting differential limits to information (Marx, 1997).

The social movement towards an online society is one of social integration and embedded technologies used to enhance human interaction. It is not a dichotomous disconnect between an online and offline world. Calhoun (1992) argues that face-to-face interactions do not disappear with computer-mediated communications but become more specialized with a different social significance (Lyon, 1997). Furthermore, Doheny-Farina (1996: 13) argues that cyberspace can serve "to help reintegrate people within their placed communities."

Social behavior on the Internet often reflects social interactions in non-virtual spaces, including criminal behavior. Casey (2004: 17-18) brings forth three reasons why the Internet should not be considered disconnected from physical space. First, Internet crimes mirror crimes in the physical world. Second, criminals are observable and vulnerable on cyberspace despite misconceptions of anonymity. Third, the ubiquitous use of the Internet makes digital evidence an extension of most crime scenes today. Police, therefore, have a significant role in cyberspace.

Police function to connect virtual space to geospatial territory. Police capacity in cyberspace mirrors their traditional functions in the physical space: to apprehend criminals, reestablish geographically-defined territorial bounds, and gather evidence to fit with legal evidentiary guidelines. In essence, cyber investigations entail "following a cybertrail" in order to find and apprehend a physical perpetrator that has committed a crime using a virtual space (Casey, 2004). One predominant role of police in cyberspace is regulatory in nature; to intervene only to reestablish institutional fairness when self-regulation breaks down (Lenk, 1997). To explore this bridging role, it is necessary to understand the operations of the Internet environment and infrastructure.

THE INTERNET INFRASTRUCTURE

The Internet is a decentralized "network of networks" that distributes information by breaking down large pieces of data into smaller *packets* that are sent through the various routers and networks to arrive and reassembled at its final destination (Tanenbaum, 2003). The Internet as a whole is often described as a "cloud" of complex interconnected networks. All packets traveling across this cloud leaves behind a digital trail or footprint that is associated with physical location. Transmitted data contains information of the path the data has travelled as well as destination information. Understanding how this data travels and how its relationship to the physical world is the necessary key to conducting all cyber forensic investigations.

The universal protocol that governs cyberspace is the Internet Protocol (IP) address, a unique numeric identifier that gives the domain, the network, the sub or local area network, and physical location of the computing device. Each packet contains a *header* with a source IP address and destination IP address used to navigate the various *routers*. Routers use software tables that direct these packets to their destination in the most efficient way. Data hops across various routers until reaching the final destination IP address, where the packets of information are reassembled. Each IP address is unique, liken to a telephone number.[37] The physical location of a computer system can be located by using IP addresses.

LAW ENFORCEMENT INVESTIGATIONS

Connecting the physical with the Internet space is the primary function of law enforcement investigations and is the basis for computer forensics. There is a twofold process of cybercrime investigations: *digital investigation* and *digital forensics*. A digital investigation involves finding the location of the computer used in the crime from the victim's computer. Once found, the investigator needs to perform digital forensics, or "the process of using scientific knowledge for collecting, analyzing, and presenting evidence to the courts"[38] on

---

[37] *See* www.3com.com/other/pdfs/infra/corpinfo/en_US/501302.pdf
[38] *Computer Forensics*. US-CERT (Computer Emergency Response Team) report. *See* www.us-cert.gov/reading_room/forensics.pdf.

computer systems. First, investigators must work backwards to decipher the IP history recorded in logs as information passes each point. The IP history tells the investigator the path that the data has traveled. These points, or "hops", correspond to a geographic location. For instance, one email can travel across different IP locations before reaching its final destination. Logs only contain numeric values that correspond with physical locations with no end user information.

The actual physical address of the suspect computer can be obtained from an Internet Service Provider (ISP) or phone company using these logs. A warrant often required to be presented to the ISP to release the end user, or customer information. The computer can then be seized by trained investigators at the location of the end user to conduct a digital forensics investigation. The investigator must be wary of the ephemeral and changing nature of digital information. Seized data can be easily and inadvertently altered, which jeopardizes the integrity of the evidence. The examination of a cybercrime case will illustrate the complexities and ubiquity of crime and cybercrime.

According to the FBI's Internet Crime Complaint Center (IC3)[39], online auction fraud is the second most prevalent form of reported crime on the Internet (NW3C/BJA Internet Crime Report, 2008). The typical case involves a scenario where a customer of the popular Internet auction site EBay makes a payment and does not receive the advertised item or receives an item that is different from the agreement (commonly known as "rocks in a box").

A typical investigation begins by working backwards from a victim's computer. The EBay subscriber information of the seller is checked and is often found to be fraudulent. Next, using the victim's last received email from the seller, a *traceroute*, or computer command that shows the network data path between two computers systems, is performed to obtain IP addresses (Branigan, Burch, Cheswick, & Wojcik, 2001). Email systems often log the path and time of data transmission. Next, investigators use IP address information to check under which ISP a particular domain is registered to. These service providers possess registered subscriber information such as home addresses and telephone numbers. Telephone companies can also provide physical addresses. One investigator interviewed explains the process:

---

[39] *See* http://ic3.gov.

The Formation, Expansion, and Function of Nodal Networks

The first thing is we go to EBay and get the subscriber info which is usually bogus. We then run a trace backwards from the victim's computer. We check the logs via email and *whois*[40] the [Internet service provider] for the IP address. We then get the subscriber info and phone number. We can then do a subscriber search using the phone number to find the exact address of the person and issue and get a search warrant.

Warrants are often required to obtain end-user or customer information from ISPs and phone companies. Once the physical address information is obtained from an ISP, another warrant is required to enter and search the physical address and contents of the suspect computer system.

One task force supervisor explains the four criteria for obtaining a search warrant. He explains that warrants are only sought if: (1) the crime is a felony, which is $400 or more in losses in California; (2) the person or place is connected to the crime; (3) the person expected to search is in control of the space or instrument of crime, and (4) there is evidence to support or exonerate the person at the location of the search.

Investigators cannot presume the registered ISP account holder is the person who actually committed the crime. Various scenarios can occur that absolves the account holder from the actual crime. In more devious cases, the account holder may be a victim of unauthorized Internet access by a neighbor or computer system of close proximity through an insecure wireless network or by hacking. In one recent trend, *wardriving* is the act of driving around in search of insecure wireless signals for the purpose of obtaining data from the network. In a more serious situation, perpetrators can use the wireless connection to commit a cybercrime easily flee the scene, making it nearly impossible to identify the suspect.

Shared computers in a household are a typical scenario encountered by task force investigators. According to one prosecutor, "While it is possible to trace IP addresses back to the origin, it is difficult to prove who was actually on the keyboard at the time of the incident." This phase of the investigation often requires more

---

[40] *Whois* is a search command that queries a database for a domain registry for registration information.

traditional detective skills and experience over technical expertise. One investigator asserts it takes "shrewd investigator skills" to determine "whose fingers were at the keys." According to the task force investigator, it becomes a process of elimination and making circumstantial connections. To understand this function, an examination of the line of questioning illuminates the police point of view. The investigator explains the algorithmic flow of questioning and reasoning during investigations once a location is identified and a computer is seized:

> Who was logged on to the computer? They use a user name and password. We also demonstrate activities immediately before or after the time of the crime, such as sending emails and other business that's specific to that person. Who else has access? Where were you? We use timecards to eliminate the person if they were at work.

Investigators are able to reconstruct the timeline of the crime and more importantly, identify the suspect using this circumstantial evidence. For example, if a suspect was accused of soliciting sexual activities from a minor, investigators can check for computer use activities immediately before and after the incident. If the suspect performed certain activities that require a login, such as checking emails and online banking, immediately before or after the crime, it is very likely that the person in question in the perpetrator.

    Extra precautions must be taken when searching digital evidence such as emails to ensure the integrity of evidence. The task force clones and timestamps all digital evidence seized in a secure area inside the department to prevent defense lawyers from claiming evidence tampering or contamination. In addition, task force members conduct their own warrant searches and seizures of computer systems rather than rely on untrained police officers. Many factors can compromise digital evidence during seizures, including inadvertent damage during hardware collection and itemization, as well as hostile individuals destroying evidence immediately prior to the raid (Sommer, 1998). These precautions are especially important with the growing convergence of cybercrime with traditional street crimes.

A CASE OF HOMICIDE

Street crimes increasingly have a cyber component. Crime scenes with computers present are becoming commonplace as more computers and computing devices become ubiquitous in society. This ubiquity erodes the distinction between "street crime" and "cybercrime." One particular case illustrates the growing convergence of computer technology with street crime. Moreover, it highlights importance of computer and cyber forensics in detective work. A task force investigator gives the following scenario:

> We had a case where a girl was rushed off to the hospital with an infection. The hospital determines that it's a uterine infection from giving birth. The mom finds a plastic bag with a fetus and notifies the police. The police coroner determines that the baby was alive before death, which makes the case a homicide. The hospital says that the girl's infection was post-childbirth but the girl says, "I didn't know I was pregnant." She denies it's human or its growth. Is this a slam dunk case? Is there a possibility the jury might say a 17 year old never gave birth? Is it plausible? Do we go back and interview?

While this case does not appear to have any computer or Internet component to it, the suspect's home computer can contained valuable information. The investigator explains the investigative thought processes after seizing her computer:

> What do you need? What evidence? Did she visit any sites on home birth? Did she search for safe havens? Childcare? Parenting? We search emails. Everything we do is to strengthen the case and eradicate decent defenses.

The task investigators were able to establish a motive using evidence found on the computer to ultimately convict the suspect. This example investigation highlights the growing importance of electronic evidence in street crime cases (Coren, 2005).

Building a solid case is a critical element for task force investigators. All investigations must function to this end in order to ensure a successful conviction. Currently, task force investigators and prosecutors are confident they have established and adhered to very strict evidentiary procedures which have resulted in strong cases. However, digital forensics is a relatively new field and has not established universal guidelines for collection and analysis (Gausnell & Stoll, 2007). Their early success may be attributed to the infancy of digital evidence and a learning gap between defense attorneys who have not yet been able to successfully call digital data collection procedures into question. In comparison, DNA evidence in the courtroom has experienced a history of procedural challenges from defense attorneys who have cited contamination, interpretation ambiguity, and improper laboratory conditions (Thompson, 1995; Thompson, Ford, Doom, Raymer, & Krane, 2003).

CHAPTER SUMMARY

It was shown that growing demands for police services have thrust police into a new and oftentimes uncomfortable role as "cybercops" in an unfamiliar virtual environment that is not governed by traditional boundaries. Investigations of such complexity in an unfamiliar environment require the collaboration and cooperation of many security actors. Law enforcement has responded by using a model that has worked well in the past in dealing with complex crimes, task forces. California's network of five task forces significantly expands the capacity of law enforcement and security resources available to fight cybercrime in the state. However, law enforcement's culture often prevents truly integrated and sustained partnerships with non-police entities. Moreover, each actor has differing security agendas and brings different assets to the table. These incompatibilities and frictions can be better identified by examining the nature of relationships between actors.

In the next chapter, we investigate the function and culture of each security stakeholder using Wood's (2006) exploratory guidelines for empirical mapping.

CHAPTER FIVE:
Theoretical Mapping of Key Security Stakeholders

In the previous chapter, we discussed the formation of California's high tech crimes task force network. In this chapter, we use Wood's (2006) nodal governance exploratory mapping to analyze each security actor in greater detail. This functional "mapping exercise" includes identifying each stakeholder's security capital, definitions of successful security outcomes, and organizational culture. Four key security stakeholders in California will be mapped using this framework: law enforcement, state government, private industry, and the general public. This will allow for in-depth analysis of the points of cooperation and conflict in the subsequent chapters.

To recall, Wood (2006) outlined several guidelines for empirical mapping. First, governance nodes and networks must be identified. Second, an assessment of the relationships between nodes ("gaps") can reveal limitations and problems within networks. Finally, new and innovative models of policing can be considered using the knowledge gained from mapping and gap analysis. Some important factors to be identified include forms of knowledge or security capital each stakeholder possesses, stated outcomes and measures of success, the nature of nodal relationships, and frequency and nature of interactions. Structural, cultural, economic, and political mechanisms can be extracted performing these empirical mapping steps that can be used to better understand inter-nodal systemic frictions and inefficiencies. We begin by mapping the law enforcement nodal set.

LAW ENFORCEMENT NODAL CLUSTER

The law enforcement cluster consists of local, county, state, and federal law enforcement agencies, as well as specialized county and state prosecutors. These law enforcement bodies are assembled in high-tech crimes task forces in five regions of California. This network of task forces is the backbone of policing cyber and high-tech crimes in California, serving under the auspices of the California State Governor's Office of Emergency Services (OES). Collectively, the five task force nodes make up the law enforcement nodal cluster in California's cyber-security network. Task force investigators are specially trained in computer forensics to meet the policing needs of private industry as well as law enforcement agencies seeking technical assistance.

The task forces are mandated to enforce laws under California Penal Code §13848,[41] providing law enforcement and district attorneys "with the tools necessary to successfully interdict the promulgation of high technology crime." California law specifies the enforcement of

---

[41] CPC§13848 specifies: (1) White-collar crime, such as check, automated teller machine, and credit card fraud, committed by means of electronic or computer-related media.
(2) Unlawful access, destruction of or unauthorized entry into and use of private, corporate, or government computers and networks, including wireless and wireline communications networks and law enforcement dispatch systems, and the theft, interception, manipulation, destruction, or unauthorized disclosure of data stored within those computers and networks.
(3) Money laundering accomplished with the aid of computer networks or electronic banking transfers.
(4) Theft and resale of telephone calling codes, theft of telecommunications service, theft of wireless communication service, and theft of cable television services by manipulation of the equipment used to receive those services.
(5) Software piracy and other unlawful duplication of information.
(6) Theft and resale of computer components and other high technology products produced by the high technology industry.
(7) Remarking and counterfeiting of computer hardware and software.
(8) Theft of trade secrets.
(c) This program is also intended to provide support to law enforcement agencies by providing technical assistance to those agencies with respect to the seizure and analysis of computer systems used to commit high technology crimes or store evidence relating to those crimes.

high-tech and computer crimes targeting businesses, such as unlawful access to computer systems, unauthorized duplication of digital information, and theft of trade secrets. It also contains a section for technical assistance to other law enforcement agencies. Law enforcement's forms of capital are derived its inherent power and situation within criminal justice and legal systems. Law enforcement serves as the gatekeepers into the criminal justice system. This front-end position of the criminal justice system gives law enforcement two important functions: apprehension and investigation. Law enforcement possesses the exclusive state-mandated legitimate power to apprehend and arrest perpetrators (Manning, 2006b). In addition, they possess the power to investigate crimes and collect evidence for legal processing. Evidence collection, by nature, requires police to conduct forensic investigations in preparation for the prosecutor. With cyber and high-tech crimes, investigators' roles ranges from seizing computer equipment to perform computer forensics to finding the physical location of a cyber suspect for apprehension. Law enforcement's primary desired security outcome is the apprehension of suspects for prosecution.

Law enforcement's security capital is desirable or necessary for individuals or organizations seeking retribution, criminal restitution, or visible deterrence, as desired security outcomes. Task force members are comprised entirely of sworn law enforcement officers, agents, and specialized prosecutors.

JOINING THE TASK FORCE

Prospective task force members are selected from a pool of detective-level applicants from various federal, state, county, and local agencies. These experienced detectives, with no required technical background, are provided training and equipment by the task force. Task force membership is considered a specialized detective division for detectives from non-federal law enforcement agencies. The minimum requirements for joining a task force are: (1) completion of mandatory Peace Officers Standards and Training (POST) certification, (2) police academy training, (3), patrol duty (plus two years of jail operations for sheriff's deputies), and (4) two years of general detective experience, totaling approximately 15 years of police experience.

New recruits are not considered for task-force membership. One investigator explains, "We don't hire investigators in the very beginning. We want someone very mature, methodical, and experienced." Membership to the task force is considered a prestigious detective assignment, with additional financial compensation. However, rank promotions can remove task force detectives from cyber to traditional street duties.

One structural impediment of the task forces is the acquisition and retention of investigators. Recruiting detectives from other law enforcement agencies to join a task force is a difficult task despite the increased pay and prestige of membership. Many departments often perceive assigning a detective to the task force as removing one investigator from dealing with more important street crimes. Instead, task force duty is recognized by departments as policing lower priority corporate crimes. This viewpoint is especially prevalent amongst smaller departments with fewer resources, who oftentimes have only a small number of full-time detectives.

Competing demands for police services that are not typically crime control-oriented in a traditional sense, such as corporate and cyber crime, are not prioritized by law enforcement. Law enforcement generally value street crime and crime control aspects of police work (Wilson, 1968; Manning, 2006b; many others). One task force supervisor is puzzled by the reluctance of departments to commit detectives to his task force considering the benefits of membership, stating:

> [The contributing departments] are not losing an officer, but gaining a fully staffed high-tech crime lab. Part of the attractiveness of the package is, for a one year commitment, the task force will train and provide equipment to the officer or agent. This is worth over $250,000. At the end of the one year term, if the department feels they are in need of the detective to return, the fully trained officer or detective can keep all the forensic equipment to basically open up a lab at their department. This would not have been possible with the small department's budget.

Structural disincentives often prevent task forces from obtaining new members. Participating departments facing staff shortages and budget shortfalls have reassigned task force investigators back to street crime duties. These departments may have little incentive to keep investigators in the task forces knowing that high-tech services are still available to them. One investigator explains the situation in one task force:

> [Two large and several smaller] agencies have pulled their members out of the task force to use in other duties. The task force tries to sell their membership as gaining a task force, not losing a man. However, these agencies that pull their members out continue to ask the task force for help in high-tech investigations.

The difficulties of staffing the task forces reflect cultural and bureaucratic factors associated with policing.

THE INFLUENCE OF POLICE CULTURE

The police organizational subculture is attributable to viewpoint that prioritizes violent-street crime. Law enforcement professional development has produced a strong collective identity, commonly referred to as an "us (police) versus them (civilian)" mentality. This cynical worldview stems from the professional developments of the quasi-military command structure, academy training, and the real and perceived dangers of the profession, that have produced a strong group introversion (Bittner, 1995; Skolnick & Fyfe, 1993; Wilson, 1968; Kappeler, Sluder, & Alpert, 2006). This research has been substantiated by the Knapp Commission Report in 1972 (Knapp, Monserrat, Sprizzo, Thomas, & Vance, 1972) and the 1991 Christopher Commission Report.

The Christopher Commission Report found that the LAPD bureaucratic command structure and organizational subculture was responsible for a number of problematic areas in need of reform. The commission attributed the strong subculture to the regular use of excessive force by a number of officers, strained relations between the public and police, an unwritten code of silence amongst officers, and structural barriers within the department that make external oversight and reporting officer misconduct difficult (Report of the Independent Commission on the Los Angeles Police Department, 1991; Bobb, Epstein, Miller, & Abascal, 1996).

Police reform since the Christopher commission in many large urban departments have centered on eradicating this strong subculture by hiring more women and minority officers. Despite these efforts, cultural and structural conditions systematically "weed out" many women recruits. Traditional crime control litmus tests, such as physical agility, results in the women who successfully pass to be perceived as "token" officers, which reinforces existing organizational norms (Lonsway, Moore, Harrington, Smeal & Spillar, 2003). Rigid recruitment requirements and mandatory patrol duties emphasizing crime control agendas, makes hiring technically-oriented recruits difficult.

HIRING *GEEKS*

August Vollmer's police professionalization movement centered on college educated recruits as its archetype (Vollmer & Schneider, 1917). Vollmer's recruits would be proficient in academic topics ranging from criminology to the hard sciences, such as physics, biology, and chemistry. This specialized educational background would help officers become skilled and efficient crime fighters. However, structural and cultural impediments have undermined Vollmer's lofty vision. For example, the Plano, Texas, Police Department lowered its four-year college degree requirement to two years of college or three years of military experience to meet recruitment goals (Johnson, 2006). Nationally, less than five percent of local departments with over one hundred officers require a four-year degree (ibid). Recruitment of college graduates having computer degrees is especially difficult, considering the high opportunity of joining a police department.

Several structural disincentives deter computer experts and university educated candidates with computing degrees to join police departments. First, recruits are hired based on historically crime-control oriented requirements and performance measures, such as physical fitness. Second, police recruits are required to undergo formal academy training. Academy training often serves to filter out weaker recruits and those who do not mesh or successfully socialize with the existing police culture (Walker & Katz, 2002). College education was not found to be a significant indicator of academy performance (White, 2008). Third, potential computer science recruits must undergo mandatory patrol requirements and general detective experience before being considered for promotion to cyber and high tech divisions in policing. In Goodyear, Arizona, police detective applicants are required to have a minimum of three years patrol experience before considered for promotion. This entire process can take over a decade before the computer expert can be considered for a cybercrime assignment.

The large pay differential between policing and private industry careers often prevents highly skilled computer practitioners from joining the ranks of law enforcement. According to one computer network security specialist from a software company, a comparatively lower salaries and negative reputation of working in law enforcement makes joining law enforcement unappealing. He explains:

> There are some decent crime labs for data recovery and analysis on the federal side, but with our skill set, who would want to work in law enforcement? The salary differential is very large. Even with higher steps [in a government job], it's still $10,000 below market. [People in the industry] might consider careers to go in to government much later in their careers, but not work up through an agency. At the local and state level, gee, I can be a sheriff with computer investigations but I'll get zero respect from colleagues and make $30,000 less than the private sector counterpart.

Significantly higher industry salaries also create a potential for a "brain drain" effect on law enforcement, where skilled investigators with experience are lured away from police work. One task force investigator explains, "[Computer forensics software companies] hire guys with six-figure incomes away from the [department]." One film industry Internet security supervisor explains that investigatory skills and experience is highly desirable to their industry. The MPAA tries to hire task force members and other experienced investigators with digital forensics skills on a regular basis. He states, "The type of people we're looking for is more in-line with law enforcement's." However, most task force members are not lured away by the better pay, citing loyalty as the primary reason.

The police subculture creates a strong sense of loyalty to policing. One former task force supervisor explains that a strong sense of loyalty causes most investigators to turn down more lucrative career opportunities in the private sector. She states, "Even when [task force investigators] do leave, they never join the *other side*." "Other side" refers to companies or organizations that might employ former investigators to use insider knowledge to develop software or strategies to circumvent security measures or avoid detection. Instead, these former investigators often work for companies that perform parallel work, such as private computer forensics or security. Cultural factors make hiring skilled practitioners and outsourcing cyber investigations to non-police entities virtually impossible. The law enforcement culture values traditional detective experience over purely technical skill. Consequently, the task forces opt for expensive and lengthy technical training for existing officers over hiring technically competent individuals without a law enforcement background. It takes approximately four years to fully train a task force detective with no computer background. When asked why not simply hire recent college graduates with computer science or equivalent degrees as investigators, one task force supervisor replied, "We need detectives, not *geeks*. We will train you to be a geek." He reasoned, invaluable investigative skills cannot be taught, but can only be gained through years of patrol and investigations experience. He further explains:

> Geeks and cops aren't a compatible skill set. The ideal candidate for the task force is someone with a lot of patrol experience, a little computer base knowledge, and investigative experience. The proper way is from detective to the computer. Not the other way around. What makes a good police investigator is the ability to *think like a crook*. The ability to develop skills and learn resources available are only available to cops. It takes approximately three years as a police officer or detective to learn this.

The importance of police experience was echoed by task force prosecutors. One county district attorney assigned to a task force explains, "Since the paperwork generated for each case is immense, it is necessary for the officer to have a good understanding of evidence collection." He adds, "This is more important than [possessing] only computer skills."

Investigative experience serves as a highly desirable capital for prosecutors. Experienced investigators are able to identify evidence more quickly than inexperienced technical individuals. One state prosecutor explains:

It is better to train officers and detectives to be cyber investigators than computer science students because they are actually *faster*. The huge amounts of data can more effectively be searched by a seasoned investigator who knows what he's looking for than a college grad with no clue.

This opinion was resonated amongst several investigators, who stressed that investigative police experience is becoming more valuable as the amount of digital information found at crime scenes continues to grow at a rapid rate.

Some industry practitioners disagree on the value of experience as a security capital. One director of fraud and security at a telecommunications company disagreed strongly, exclaiming, "*We* know *more* investigative techniques!" She adds, "We've done the case and there are a few items that [law enforcement] need and you don't need a degree for it!" This inter-nodal friction can often undermine strong and sustained relations between police and private industry. However, there is one form of security capital that private industries desire from law enforcement: leadership.

Businesses and individual victims highly desire is the ability to serve as a single point of contact during emergencies. Law enforcement's central nodal position in the security network makes this possible. Cyber and high tech investigations begin when the victim contacts the local police station and files a report. The station can then refer the case to their regional task force. Some businesses, particularly steering committee members, can contact the task force directly and can establish personal relations with investigators. At the federal level, victims can report crimes to the FBI and National White Collar Crime Center's (NW3C) Internet Crime Complaint Center (IC3) via an online website.[42] These reports, if meeting minimum thresholds, are forwarded to the regional task forces.

HIERARCHY AND AUTONOMY

Task forces have relatively less bureaucratic limitations than traditional police organizations. The hierarchical command structure of a task force is significantly flatter. The task force supervisor, often a high

---

[42] *See* www.ic3.gov.

ranking officer or senior-level district attorney, serves as an office manager who assigns cases to investigators. The investigators are veteran officers and agents, which includes detectives, sergeants and federal agents. Rank within task force members was is considered very important since each investigator works independently on cases, allowing for relatively more autonomy and flexibility needed for effective investigations.

The task forces have higher levels of autonomy than more traditional police departments and are generally insulated from the outside world. First, task force offices are physically separate and independent from their home agencies. Task force offices are remotely located and physically dissimilar to typical police departments. Task force offices have little to no law enforcement insignia. These buildings are often located in remote industrial areas. Second, task forces do not directly interact with the public. Cyber and high tech crimes are reported to local stations before being referred to the task forces. Third, Investigators "like to stay low-key," including their dress and demeanor. The police uniform signifies and legitimizes group membership, organizational goals, status, and a framework for group control (Joseph and Alex 1972; Crank and Langworthy 1992). However, this and other symbols of authority, power, rank, and legitimacy, such as a firearm and badge, are shed in favor of more casual office attire. When one new federal agent joined the task force wearing a uniform, one task force supervisor remarked, "He learned real quick that's not how we dress around here." One task supervisor jokingly said it has been years since he can fit his uniform. Uniforms and suits are also not ideal when working on computers.

Work autonomy is a primary reason why task force members desire to remain in law enforcement and on the task forces. First, many task force members of the task forces who have turned down more lucrative career opportunities in the private sector cite autonomy of the task force as a reason for staying. When asked why he forgone several job offers in the private sector, one investigator explained, "[Law enforcement] is governed not by company policy, but by law; that's why I don't leave. There's great autonomy." Second, most task investigators forgo promotional ranks to remain on the task force. Oftentimes a promotion from detective to sergeant will require reassignment to non-cyber duties. These more traditional supervisor assignments, such as sergeant, will mean less autonomy, more direct supervision, and rigid and undesirable work shifts. Task forces normally operate during normal business hours and are closed during the weekends. There are negative ramifications to the decreased supervision associated with increased flexibility from the flattened hierarchical structure of the task forces. Task force supervisors often find it difficult to keep track of investigators who are jointly supervised by their home department of agency and by the task force supervisor. Cyber investigations often require investigators leave the office frequently for field work. This absence creates a situation for task force supervisors, who are generally unaware of the whereabouts of any given investigator at any given moment, which can potentially lead to abuse. One supervisor explains:

> One problem we have is that I don't know where all the guys are at any given moment. A lot of times it's based on trust. Some officers can take advantage of the system. These are guys who aren't in [my department], who are 'loaned' from other departments. [My department] and other departments don't coordinate to keep track of the officer. Some people do this.

The supervision issue appears to be a relatively minor issue to the overall performance of the task forces. There does not appear to be widespread abuse of autonomy by investigators, who are often overburdened by large and lengthy caseloads.

The task force model is successful when sufficiently staffed, funded, and equipped. In theory, this network of officers and federal agents integrated into a single unit provides the resources and communications needed for cyber cases while overcoming many bureaucratic and jurisdictional obstacles of a single police department. This is further streamlined by embedded prosecutors that specialize in high-tech cases, providing fast and direct feedback on evidence admissibility. However, praxis is hindered by issues of insufficient staffing stemming from inter-agency conflicts.

INTER-NODAL CONFLICT AND COOPERATION

Inter-agency friction can sometimes cause staffing shortages and affect internal power dynamics. Task forces are comprised of a collection of individuals from different agencies. Task forces are continuously recruiting officers and detectives from local police agencies. These recruits are not required to have technical backgrounds. However, staffing is sometimes affected by differing inter-departmental priorities and inter-agency cultural strains. One task force supervisor explains:

> Each department or organization has a sense of pride and feels superior. For example, [my agency] will feel like their reputation and leading role in the task force makes them the "big dogs". However, every agency within the task force must be made to feel equal. This is my job to ensure that each department or agency's needs are met.

Supervisors must minimize any indications of favoritism or bias towards investigators for any particular agency. In this instance, the supervisor's home agency is the leading agency within the task force with the most number of investigators. Any real or perceived bias can create strain within a task force which can ultimately compound problems of member attrition and recruitment of prospective investigators from local agencies.

The lack of guaranteed returns on investment to the task force is a major structural barrier to local departments desiring to assign a detective or agent to the task force. Many agencies often fail to see the benefits of "lending" or "donating" a detective to the task force and do not anticipate any returns for this human capital investment. This situation creates two problems for task force supervisors. First, supervisors must persuade prospective agencies of the *value-added* of task force membership. Second, once the agency has agreed to assign a detective to the task force, the supervisor must balance allocating task force resources to assist the home organization of the detective. Local agency task force needs often compete with higher priority cases. One supervisor gives an example:

> [City A] Police Department might provide a person to the task force. This officer or detective's constituents are in [his respective city]. The task force handles cases from all jurisdictions in the [entire] area. [City A] provides this detective not for "free", since they would be down one member. Instead, they want to allow that officer to take cases using the task force resources to solve cases in [City A]

jurisdiction. My job is to make sure the officer's needs are met while appropriately prioritizing the roles of the task force as a whole. This balancing act means that [City A's] case will be looked at maybe in a week or two, after higher priority cases. Sometimes this is too long of a timeframe, which causes a lot of conflict.

Inter-nodal relationships amongst regional task forces are generally good. Collaborations are usually formed between task forces on *ad hoc* case-by-case basis. Task forces may request assistance for a variety of reasons. For example, some cases that span over a large area within California may require expanding the task force jurisdiction by collaborating to another regional task force. In other instances, collaborations may be formed for cases that require another regional task force's expertise for particular types of crime. Typically, each regional task force caters to different clients with different needs. For example, some task forces prioritize child pornography, while others focus on corporate intrusions, depending on its location.

Inter nodal relations amongst task forces and with the federal government are limited. Task forces are set up to handle in-state cybercrime and do not generally handle national matters. One task force investigator explains that the task forces are considered a "regional law enforcement agency." Adding, "Information is not shared in a collaborative database and the capacity of the task force is not in-line with national security." This was echoed by another investigator, stating, "At the local and state level, collaboration is generally good," however, "there is no centralized way to disseminate information." It may be the responsibility of the state to take on this role.

THE GOVERNMENT NODAL CLUSTER

The state government is a central stakeholder in the security network. The state is the legitimate body that sets policy, controls budgets, legislate laws, and addresses public needs. Naturally, the state by default has taken on a central role in governing cyber security issues for its constituents, the general public. The state's priorities often reflect public opinion and sets public policy and allocating budgets accordingly. The public generally supports cyber and high tech crimes and the state's leading position in the security network. An analysis of the government nodal shows important security capital to cyber security in California, which includes setting policies that govern cyber security, budget allocation to high-tech and computer crimes, and drafting laws that govern cyber and high-tech crime.

The government or state node in this study is represented by the California Office of Emergency Services (OES), which governs the five regional high-tech crimes task forces. The state node sets policy and controls finances for each regional task force. Each quarter the OES organizes a steering committee meeting to discuss current issues brought forth by each task force, private industry representatives, and the general public. The steering committee consists of law enforcement members from each task force, private industry representatives operating within the state, and members of the OES. This steering committee is the recommending body to the OES, which has authority over policy and monetary decisions. While the OES distributes funding, it is situated within the California State Office of the Governor, which is the ultimate authority for budget allocation.

Structural barriers limit funding for cybercrime. Computer and high-tech crimes were originally conceived as having low importance to the state. Consequently, the low importance of cybercrime is reflected by how it is situated within the state budget. High-tech crimes funding is a line-item, meaning, each fiscal year, it must be added as an item in the state budget. In comparison, some state programs automatically recur in the state budget and are adjusted for inflation. However, line-items do not have an automatic mechanism and are in risk of not being approved by the governor. One OES high ranking supervisor explains this structural difficulty:

> In the end, [the OES only has] budget authority to disperse. Every year the cost of business goes up and there are no automatic mechanisms that increase funds. Cumulatively it adds up. That's a difficulty for task forces; every year unless there's an action by the governor or legislature, the dollar amount is the same.

In a recent steering committee meeting, one committee member from law enforcement highlighted the budget frustration of operating at the "1999 budget" level. This requires individual task forces, which draw funds from participating members' organizations, to compensate for the difference. For example, one county agency, which is the lead agency for a particular task force, invests more departmental funds to supplement the task forces than the state contribution. Task forces are not funded entirely by the state and do not receive any federal assistance. Task force funding from the state comes from the California state budget and is matched by at least 25% by each task force. According to one task force supervisor, this matching figure is much higher due to the expensive equipment that needs constant upgrades, training, and rising personnel salaries.[43] Despite growing demands for services by private industries, local law enforcement agencies, and the general public, collective sentiments still marginalize cybercrime that does not warrant funding levels that match those of street crimes.

The marginalization of cybercrime is apparent when comparing cyber and high-tech crimes to traditional street crimes. For example, drug enforcement receives much higher public attention and funding. One OES supervisor explains:

> [The task forces receive a] total of $13 million from state general fund. This year there's $30 million in state funds going to methamphetamines enforcement. This year the federal government is allocating to California $34 million to drug enforcement. In terms of need and amount of money, we can easily double that amount and the task force can catch up the work they have now, let alone expanding.

Without wide range public and political support, the task forces do not have sustained growth and annual budget adjustments. Each year, the OES receives reports from the five regional task forces. These reports are used to generate a final report from the OES to the governor's office. The governor has approve this funding before submitting the line item to the legislature for adjustments, which then goes back to the governor for his signature for final approval. The OES report merely requests that task force funding be included with the annual budget but

---

[43] Personnel salaries are compensated for the specialized skills. For example, a detective assigned to the task force can earn income as high as a sergeant.

does not ensure additional funding to meet rising costs. As a result, the budget has remained stagnant.

Ramifications of this stagnant budget have truncated expansion plans, resulting in the large sections of California without task force services. According to the 2006 High-tech Crime Annual Report, [44] seven task forces required for full coverage for throughout state. Currently, there are only five task forces. One OES supervisor describes these non-service areas as "big holes...in the Central Valley and Central Coast." Another OES coordinator describes these areas as "blank spots" that are in serious need of digital forensics and investigative police services. These areas remain without sufficient high-tech policing services without additional funding. Sufficient increases in funding would require federal assistance.

Structural and bureaucratic obstructions prevent additional funding for the task forces. State employees cannot petition for additional funds from the California legislature. Therefore, the OES cannot submit direct requests for funding. An OES coordinator explains, "We as civil servants from the state are prohibited from lobbying the legislature." Instead, the OES submits annual descriptive reports to the California governor's office that contain the performance statistics of each task force. The OES coordinator proclaims, "We can [only] provide information."

The OES must rely on law enforcement officers, private companies, or the general public to lobby for additional funds. There is little or no lobbying effort by task force members or industry representatives in spite of pleads by the state for steering committee members to lobby for federal funding. One OES coordinator voices her frustration at the general apathy amidst the growing cybercrime problem, stating:

> We just need someone to bang on Washington's door and say we need funding. It's getting worse, it's not getting better. You have funds for victims against women and they get funding, but based on ID theft, that's devastating [also]. But

---

[44] *High Technology Crime in California: Annual Report to the Governor and Legislature for 2006.* Submitted by the High Technology Crime Advisory Committee High Technology Theft Apprehension and Prosecution Program.

since it's not violent, it doesn't qualify. You talk to any law enforcement agency; we just don't have enough funds. We're on a shoestring budget.

Finding the appropriate person for lobbying is a difficult task. The same OES coordinator explains:

> We only need one authentic voice who has been in [a task force member's] shoes. I don't see money being thrown our way from [the state of California]. We need to lobby Washington to sell [the importance of cyber and high-tech crimes].

Federal funding may be one form of financial assistance, but private industry is potentially a bigger source of revenue. However, private industry does not generally contribute direct funds to enforcement efforts.

Cultural differences have contributed to inadequate task force funding. The task forces were originally conceived from business' needs to secure intellectual property. During the 1990s, "[Industry] came to the legislature saying 'we have a problem, [computer crime] is a growing trend'," states one OES coordinator. She adds, during that time the mentality of law enforcement was "to lock 'em up throw away the keys. They weren't addressing business' needs." As a result of industry lobbying, the state formed the high-tech crimes task forces.

Business contributions to the task forces are minimal despite spearheading the creation of the task forces and being the primary beneficiaries of this specialized enforcement. The same OES coordinator expresses her frustration at the lack of industry donated funds, stating:

> One million dollars to [a large company] is nothing. Task forces have not been getting donations. We received [a onetime] $50,000 [donation] from [a large software company]. It's like a penny for them.

The $50,000 donation was in light of a major bust that prevented millions of dollars in company losses. She explains that when companies pay fines for misconduct, high-tech task forces do not receive compensation from fines, stating:

> High-tech should be getting more of that [money from fines]. But if it's [a large computer hardware company] that's paying a fifty million dollar fine, a piece of that should be supporting programs.

One task force supervisor echoes this frustration from the lack of donations from industry. There is a trust fund that accepts direct industry donations. However, the long delay in setting up the trust fund and lack of donations is very revealing about the nature of the task forces, which is seen by businesses as a free *public good*. He states, "It took us around five years to set up that trust fund, but to my knowledge no one has ever deposited money into it."

The lack of law enforcement's lobbying efforts and minimal industry contribution, despite the growing need for services, may have less to do with unwillingness to help or the inability of companies to afford donations, but may be indicative of larger structural issues. A task force supervisor explains:

> The law allows a trust fund to be established for the purpose [of company donations], but what we found out is that it's the state's responsibility to set up the trust fund. The state doesn't have a mechanism to distribute funds. By legislation, any money left in the fund when the state does the next budget goes back to general funds. There's really not a mechanism for the state to establish trust funds, trust boards, rules, how it's distributed, *et cetera*. No one wants to put money in that because it goes to the general fund. The law says the state has to do that. Some steering committee members wanted a lawsuit against the state to force them to do that. But who's going to file the lawsuit? The state attorney general is part of the task force, he would have to file the case and receive the case. That's impossible.

Despite these structural issues, the trust fund was ultimately established. However, there has yet to be any industry contributions. In addition to budgetary issues, inter-nodal conflicts deter more agencies from participating in the task force.

Inter-departmental politics and power dynamics cause some agencies to turn down participation in the task force. The refusal to join the task force is often in the face of monetary incentives. An OES coordinator stresses, "If [County B] (a smaller county) wanted to participate, there would be additional funding for them, but so far, they have not chosen to do so." She questions, "Why is [County B] not playing? There's two million dollars there." The lack of interest by some nodes to participate as security stakeholders can be explained by inter-nodal conflict. All investigators in each task force, regardless of home agency, must take assignments from the command of the task force supervisor. Some agencies have turned down monetary incentives due to wariness of allocating resources and personnel to address the needs of other jurisdictions at the cost addressing home jurisdictional needs. One OES coordinator explains the situation:

> There's a whole thing about control. I know counties don't like other counties messing with their business, but it's a growing problem. It's just getting worse and worse.

This inter-nodal conflict between law enforcement agencies underscores perhaps the most important function of the government nodal cluster: a *communications hub* and *resource broker*.

THE STATE AS A *COMMUNICATIONS HUB* AND *RESOURCE BROKER*

While the government nodal cluster is theoretically situated in a non-hierarchical, decentralized nodal governance security network (Johnston, 2006), it has a more significant role compared to other nodes. Herbert (2006) stresses a normative framework for effective community security as being anchored by a public institution. The state nodal cluster serves in a position of centrality which acts as a communications hub and distribution center for security resources to other clusters. In computer networking terms, the state cluster serves as a router, an important device allowing connections between computers, networking devices, and other networks (Tanenbaum, 2003). The state's legitimate powers to control funds and draft policies that govern policing make it the *de facto* router for information, communications, and resources. One OES supervisor describes the state's role as a "resource broker", stating, "Part of our job is to share with other parts."

This is consistent with the nodal governance theoretical framework that is based on the concept of resource sharing between nodes. He explains:

> One of the services we provide is being a bridge linking task forces, state agencies, Office of Privacy Protection, consumer affairs, et cetera. All state agencies make a concerted effort to work with each other.

Specifically, the state's and managerial role includes distribution of grant funds, ensuring efficient use of funds by regional task forces, and according to the OES supervisor, "getting everyone on the state's perspective."

Political factors can affect the state's central nodal function to form new relationships between nodes, increase communications throughput ("bandwidth") between existing nodes, and mediate inter-nodal conflicts. One OES coordinator explains the difficulty facing the OES, stating:

> We as the state have a responsibility. We really do; to bring people together. Senator Poochigian had some great ideas and [is] very much a friend of high-tech and ID theft. Are we doing the best we can do on a statewide process? We used to be [The Office of Criminal Justice Planning (OCJP)][45]. It's politics. They threw us in with OES. Is this the best fit? I don't think so. Are we getting the most out of the money? Are we lobbying enough in Washington? Are we doing enough? I would say not.

This inter-nodal competition within the state cluster to secure funding for computer and high-tech security is, perhaps, the most challenging role for the OES. The OES is a state government organization and must compete with other state organizations for the same general funds. Competing for a larger portion of the law enforcement budget is extremely difficult. Funding priorities typically go towards more visible street crimes instead of computer and white-collar crimes with

---

[45] The Office of Criminal Justice Planning implements the California state governor's public safety plan.

corporate victims (Penalties for White-Collar Crime, 2002; Rosoff, Pontell, & Tillman, 2007). Nevertheless, the state nodal cluster plays a central role in California's cyber security, particularly coordinating the different stakeholders and distributing vital resources.

THE PRIVATE INDUSTRY NODAL CLUSTER

Private industry is an important stakeholder in the cyber security network and has been at the forefront of policing cyberspace long before law enforcement and state government participation. Examining the scale of victimization, it is clear to see why. Online malefactors have targeted company networks and databases that store valuable information from trade secrets to employee and customer records. A University of Maryland study found that computer systems are attacked every 39 seconds by hackers, averaging 2,244 times a day (Ramsbrock, Berthier, & Cukier, 2007). According to a CSI/FBI computer security survey, the annual average cost of computer crime has more doubled from 2006 to 2008, from $168,000 to $350,000, citing increasingly targeted sophisticated stealth attacks (Richardson, 2008). Protecting these assets has meant deploying *ad hoc* security technologies, such as encryption and authentication software, along with information technology (IT) and network security staffs. An examination of this technological capital and business culture will reveal why this cluster often opts for technological solutions over criminal apprehension. This analysis will illustrate the types of security capital and overall security capacity of the private industry nodal cluster.

Private industry owns, operates, and develops the vast majority of the Internet infrastructure despite being developed by the U.S. government [46] (United States Government Accountability Office,

---

[46] The U.S. Defense Advanced Research Projects Agency (DARPA) began research for interlinking computer networks for information packet distribution in 1973. The result was a universal protocol suite known as Internet Protocol (IP), a simple yet robust network when combined with Transmission Control Protocol (TCP), a type of border gateway protocol. This was further developed in the 1980s by academic researchers using grant funds from the National Science Foundation (NSF) before ultimate release to the public. (Source: "A

2006). Conceived as an academic research network, the Internet was developed without security in mind, making it inherently vulnerable to exploitations and attacks (Dekker, 1997). Attacks on software vulnerabilities are often confronted by anti-virus software, intrusion detection systems, and the deployment and installation of security software patches (updated code that fixes the problem) (Castañeda, Sezer, & Xu, 2004). However, even these security patches are reverse engineered and exploited by highly skilled groups and individuals. According to one security engineer at a software security company, "The window of time for attacks is shrinking. We're seeing a quicker exploit, such as *zero-day attacks*." He adds, "The goal now is intrusion prevention: *zero day protection*." Zero day attacks refer to exploits that are executed the day of any software release.

Nearly every security measure has been trumped by attackers, leading to an endless cycle of security patches and exploitations. To the film industry, these exploitations have led to widespread piracy and distribution of intellectual property through ubiquitous peer-to-peer (p2p) networks,[47] costing billions of dollars in potential revenues.[48] As a result, lucrative and highly organized criminal networks, likened to organized crime groups, have profited and driven illegal activities (Biddle, England, Peinado, & Willman, 2002; Nhan, 2008). It was clear that this model of security was inadequate to protect business interests.

Security in businesses in the tech sector has undergone a paradigm shift which reflects the changing nature of business and

---

Brief History of the Internet and Related Networks," The Internet Society. *See* www.isoc.org/internet/history/cerf.shtml)

[47] A Peer-to-Peer (p2p) network is a decentralized computer network for the purpose of sharing resources and files. In a 72 hour period, a single file, such as a movie, can be copied and distributed to over 4 million computers worldwide. The Motion Picture Association of America (MPAA) describes this as an "avalanche" effect. *See* www.mpaa.org/avalancheofpiracy.htm.

[48] According to the MPAA, illegal motion picture and television piracy costs the industry an estimated $18.2 billion in 2005 from potential revenues. In the same year, the MPA's Asia-Pacific region investigated more than 34,000 cases of piracy. Source: Anti-Piracy Fact Sheet: Asia-Pacific Region. *See* mpaa.org/AsiaPacificPiracyFactSheet.pdf.

attackers. One network security expert at a large software company explains the cybercrime trend:

> In the 1990s, you had a single paranoid expert who provided *ad hoc* opinion. This was not good. It was a "domain of exception." There was a need for a structure engineer who would map out everything related to security. These were the early days of security and few experts were around.

This security, which was the responsibility of a single expert with little transparency, was similar to a form of security described as "security through obscurity," a principle term used in cryptography to describe fallible methods of security through code secrecy instead of an open and transparent system based on mathematical difficulty (Anderson, R., 2001; Mercuri & Neumann, 2003). Faith in this fallible system gave companies a false sense of security.

The security paradigm has shifted to prevention and risk management with increased sophistication by attackers. One security expert interviewed explains the overwhelming task of securing a network:

> There are basically two parties involved. There is the attacker and the defender. The defender, in this case legitimate businesses, has the daunting task of securing their networks in addition to [performing] daily functions. For this function, businesses must secure all ports of entry and be vigilant in monitoring activity and safeguarding. The attacker, on the other hand, simply needs only know one thing and know it extremely well.

The security model has fundamentally changed from the responsibility of a person or small group to the entire organization and collaborations with other organizations. He further describes the nature of hacking has been overblown and is considered somewhat of a "red herring" in terms of the real threat to network security. He criticizes a lot of network security consultants who lack a realistic perspective on security by not recognizing security as more of a human and social engineering issue. He explains the new model of security:

Today, organizations that really understand [security use] the engineered approach that consists of *threat models*. These threat models are about building bridges between all business functions that give an optimal cost/benefit with limited resources; basically, focusing on the important issues.

To private industry, this has meant expanding their security network and sharing resources to include law enforcement. Consequently, the high tech crimes task force was conceived by private industries' request for assistance.

The high-tech task force network in California's existence is a direct result of lobbying efforts by overwhelmed private industries. However, each industry has different security needs and desirable security outcomes. This differential can affect the level of need and utility for law enforcement assistance.

INDUSTRY COMPARISON: TECH SECTOR VERSUS FILM INDUSTRY

The usefulness each industry finds law enforcement's security capital depends on the desired security outcomes for each industry. For example, industries dealing to piracy find law enforcement's security capital of criminal apprehension and digital forensics is compatible with their security agenda. Moreover, these criminal and legal actions can serve as a deterrent for future criminality. For other industries, such as a large segment of the tech sector, security means a discreet proactive prevention model based on uninterrupted business functions.

The tech industry generally uses a *private model* of security. Underreporting remains high amongst tech sector nodes due to security and commercial ramifications. The risks of a negative commercial impact associated with potential bad publicity and intrusive evidence confiscation of vital computing systems outweighs the benefits of utilizing law enforcement (Wall, 2005). In this model, deterrence is based on prevention through strong security. One network engineer explains, "Our interest is in making money, not upholding the law." Instead of deterrence, the aggressive pursuit of criminals and publicizing strong security can antagonize attackers and escalate attacks. He states, "It's a challenge; calling the attackers."

The film industry, in contrast, utilizes an incapacitation and retribution model of security. Their primary goal is to protect against the illegal distribution of their intellectual property in the form of "hard goods" (optical discs) and "soft goods" (digital content). The security goals of this industry are twofold: (1) increase public education and (2) dismantling criminal distribution networks, or "darknets". One film industry security expert describes the organized distribution of hard goods and soft goods as the "next generation of white-collar crime." He explains that similar to the sale of illegal drugs, revenue generated from the sale and distribution of copyrighted material is often used to fund other illegal activities. Another studio security expert describes the situation as "a battle between us and the peer-to-peer networks."

Studio enforcement branches must also compete with funding from other entertainment divisions. This situation is similar to the task forces, who must compete with general law enforcement funds. A studio security expert explains the cultural and financial strains within his company:

> We're seen as a cost center to the studio. It's difficult to get money dedicated to us. We're a proactive studio, but some studios don't have an in-house security team, so we collaborate a lot.

The biggest hurdle the film industry must overcome is general apathy and perceived diminished importance of cybercrime within their organization. Organizational attitudes are reflective of what is perhaps the biggest challenge facing the film industry: overcoming an antagonistic relationship with public and get them to share the same security perspective.

The general public is a large part of the film industry's overall security strategy. According to both the tech sector and film industry, long term security is dependent upon good relationships with the public. The current strategy is less partnership and more educational. The MPAA holds workshops, speak in academic institutions, and publishes online material to educate the public of the harms of piracy. One film industry security expert frames public relations as an issue of legitimacy, stating the industry's main goal is "winning the hearts and minds" of the public. Getting the public to buy in as security stakeholders is a difficult, but necessary task for long-term security.

Currently, there are three active participants in California's cyber security network: The state, law enforcement, and industry. A more robust nodal governance security infrastructure cannot be sustained without the fourth branch, the general public.

THE GENERAL PUBLIC NODAL CLUSTER

The largest security gap in the security network is the general public. The public is the largest potential source of security capital. Specifically, the general public can participate as security stakeholders in three ways. First, the public can development social capital in the form of communities within cyberspace. These communities can develop a social fabric that can be a source of self-efficacy and resistance to crime. Second, community members can form active partnerships with government, police, and industry nodes that allow for greater surveillance, knowledge capital, and defensible spaces online.

Social capital has been developing online. Online communities and digital enclaves, such as social networking websites, Usenet newsgroups, and message boards, have emerged where community members actively participate and shape a social experience of common interests, while maintaining the integrity of the medium through self efficacy. For example, user-driven interactions and relationships in online health communities spawn from patients and professionals sharing information and mutually supporting in patient recovery (Preece, 2000). Moreover, member-maintained and moderated online communities were found to be more robust and valuable due to regulation of harmful member behavior (Cosley, Frankowski, Kiesler, Terveen, & Riedle, 2005).

Community members of these cyber-social spaces are similar to those in non-cyber nodal governance "communal spaces." The term "Netizen" is used to describe Internet users who actively engage the medium and challenge the top-down power distribution model by interjecting a variety of intellectual discourse using communication through "an interactive creative process" (Hauben & Hauben, 1997; Licklider & Taylor, 1968). Shearing and Wood (2003) describe this participation in non-virtual spaces as "Denizenship," where "Denizens" (active participants) share "social capital" across multiple domains. More active participation in these domains results in greater collective capital, transforming public spaces into more secure communal spaces (ibid).

The transformation from public to communal spaces has not yet occurred despite the widespread adoption of the Internet in the U.S. According to a 2005 Pew Internet and American Life Project survey, over 70 million adults go online in a typical day, up from 52 million in 2000 (Rainie et al, 2005). The Pew Research Center claims that Internet adoption in the U.S. has reached nearly 80% in 2009 (Pew Internet & American Life Project, 2009). Another Pew survey found that 55% of youths ages 12-17 use an online social networking site, representing tens of millions of individuals (Lenhart & Madden, 2007). This social capital has not been transformed into security capital. Instead, the reverse has occurred, where the vast majority of Internet users have utilized the Internet to illegally download and share intellectual property. Moreover, many of these Internet users exhibit negative attitudes towards policing efforts, ranging from apathetic to hostile.

A HOSTILE PARTNERSHIP

The public has developed a dichotomous relationship with companies and police instead of participating as active security stakeholders and partners. The film industry, in particular, has suffered from a longstanding antagonistic relationship with the public. Enforcement efforts have triggered public backlashes. In a 2005 Pew survey, 27% of Internet users polled (approximately 36 million Americans) say they illegally download music and video files (Madden & Rainie, 2005). The same poll showed that 42% of respondents felt the government can do little or nothing about it (ibid). This has developed into contentious and hostile relationships between the public and any organization enforcing illegal file distribution. Moreover, many Internet users perceive enforcement or external regulation of the Internet as an attack on the Internet itself, a medium that represents innovation, openness, expression, democracy, and end to inequality (Lessig, 2005; McLeod, 2005).

Negative attitudes towards social control on the Internet are substantiated by film industry security professionals, who have become vilified by the public. One film industry security expert questions, "Why are we the bad guys again?" Another studio security expert articulates the antagonistic relationship using public reaction towards security efforts. He states, circumventing security by the public is summarized by the following sentiment: "It's a challenge. I can beat 'The Man.' It's fun to beat The Man. At the end of the day I feel I have the right to do this." Industry security professionals have the daunting task of overcoming these negative attitudes and sense of entitlement held by the general public when it comes to piracy.

Film industry professionals feel file sharers use the democratic ideals of the Internet as rhetoric and neutralizations for unlawful behavior. For example, when asked about the possibility of piracy functioning as a form of competition that drives away bad products, one industry Internet security expert exclaimed "bullshit!" He questions, "What's [a studio's] incentive [for making big budget movies or releasing optical discs] if they have to compete with *free*?" He also sees piracy as "devaluing" work which ultimately hurts smaller companies. Ironically, Internet culture values the products of small companies as being more authentic than large corporate conglomerates (Lasica, 2005). He questions, "Why buy $30 software when the bootleg high-end stuff is for free?" In essence, software packages produced by smaller companies must now compete with pirated versions of more expensive, full-featured software that is free to download illegally. In the long run, these smaller companies cannot absorb these losses and are ultimately put out of business.

These public attitudes often marginalize cybercrime and white-collar crime as victimless crimes. However, white-collar crime, which is often masked and justified as routine business, is very costly and "exacts a gigantic social toll" on all citizens (Rosoff, Pontell, & Tillman, 1998: 219). Similarly, the public has not personified or refused to acknowledge illegal Internet activity as being committed by actual criminals. These illegal acts are often perceived as being a righteous defense of Internet freedom and not associated with criminal networks seeking gain.

The lack of a clear public perception of who are the villains and victims is one of the difficulties in establishing the public as a security partner in cybercrime. According to the MPAA, the public have ironically reversed the villains (illegal distribution sites administrators) and the victims (movie studios). According to one MPAA Internet security expert, file sharers often perceive illegal file sharing network administrators as modern-day *Robin Hoods* that challenge corporate greed. Corporate victims and law enforcement have difficulties convincing the public that there are, as one MPAA security expert puts it, "real bad guys".

The contentious situation is aggravated by aggressive legal actions by the recording industry, which further strains public relations and justifies public refusal to participate as security stakeholders. The Recording Industry of America (RIAA), the enforcement branch of the music industry representing numerous record labels, sues end-users as a primary security strategy (Nhan, 2009). Consequently, aggressive civil litigation has created a very adverse relationship between the RIAA and the public.[49] In a 2007 Consumerist poll, the RIAA beat out Halliburton as the "worst company in America".[50] Transforming the adversarial relationship between industry and the public to one of collaboration is an extremely difficult task that requires changing the predominant public discourse of piracy from "freedom" to "criminal".

TWO MEANINGS OF THE WORD "FREE"

The majority of public Internet users are resistant to social control on the Internet and lack incentive to participate as security stakeholders. Public opposition is especially strong in cases of software and media piracy. According to one film industry Internet security expert, the public perceives the Internet as open democratic environment associated with liberty and autonomy. It is simply "free" in a postmodern sense that it is owned by no one person or group and is an unbiased medium for open expression of ideas and truth. For example, restrictive copyright laws have been blamed for stifling not only artistic creativity in audio and visual media, but exploiting artists as well (Lasica, 2005). However, industry insiders from both the tech sector and film industry perceive this mentality as a cover up to the *real* meaning of the word "free," defined as *without cost*. According to the same expert explains, "It's not about free speech, it's about free movies." He elaborates, "When someone obtains a perfect version of something, would they go out and buy it after that? They're stupid if they do! In fact, I wouldn't either." He explains in detail:

---

[49] RIAA lawsuits have sparked numerous anti-RIAA sites on the Internet, such as fucktheriaa.org.
[50] *See* http://consumerist.com/consumer/top/riaa-wins-worst-company-in-america-2007-245235.php.

These pirates are after profit, not freedom. There is always a motive of gain behind the actions of pirates. The gains are not only for money, direct or indirect. To say that [top site[51] administrators] are providing free services is not true. Bandwidth and equipment costs aren't free. For file sharers, their gain is the music they obtained. For some, it may be the notoriety or fame associated with the activity. For others, maybe the service is free, but the ad space sold is not. So in some way, there is always personal or group benefit at the cost of someone else.

This opinion was supported by controversial file sharing index, The Pirate Bay, which made millions in advertising revenue in 2006 according to Swedish authorities.[52] The security expert summarizes his frustration with a catchphrase, "You can't compete with free!"

Criminal organizations use public sentiments to their advantage. File sharers generally maintain that Internet regulation and legal action equates to harming the Internet's "free" principles and file-sharing is not considered a serious criminal offense. According to industry experts, organized piracy groups use this mentality to their advantage by exploiting young individuals who willingly perform criminal acts, ranging from recording movies in theaters to hacking. One studio security practitioner explains:

> There is no complete tie in with movies, but there is an organized crime element. It's supplying organized crime with the masters and leveraging talent. They're servicing organized crime; talking about the Robin Hood-types who are being exploited by organized crime groups. Organized crime pulls the strings and all the minions follow.

---

[51] Top sites are high-speed file servers that store illegal software ("warez") and pirated media such as movies, television shows, and music. These "sites" are the source of pirated material that gets distributed to millions of file sharers. Access to top sites is limited to "elite" trusted members of the community (Nhan, 2008).

[52] "*TPB Raking in Millions.*" See rixstep.com/1/20060708,00.shtml

Despite this apparent exploitation of the skilled labor that buffers top groups and members from apprehension, the majority of the public does not perceive the harm and criminal element involved in piracy. Instead, individuals involved in piracy can get paid a significant amount of money and are often given access to large libraries of illegal content. Moreover, copyright security measures deployed by studios are seen as an affront and direct challenge to tech-savvy individuals who are often paid by organized groups to circumvent these technologies.

The general public's reluctance to accept responsibility for computer crimes and securing cyberspace is reflective of broader theoretical issues on perceptions of victimless crimes. Pontell and Rosoff (2009) suggest these ambivalent attitudes of white-collar and computer delinquency by the public is attributed to Lemert's (2000) explanation of tacit acceptance derived from: (1) the lack of understanding of complex crime and (2) many persons maybe have been engaged in such illegal activities themselves.

CHAPTER SUMMARY

It is clear that each security stakeholder has different agendas and understanding of security. Having mapped each actor, it was shown that the state, in addition to setting policy and task force budgets, functions to bridge security nodes and serve as a resource broker and communications hub. This is especially important for matters of national security and critical infrastructure emergencies, where a central point of contact and mobilization of security resources must be efficient and timely. The police, considered an extension of the state, carry out these agendas accordingly with what they function for and know best, apprehending criminals and preparing cases for prosecutorial processing. In cybercrime, this has translated into digital forensics, a security capital that is more useful to some industries than others. This was specifically why a comparison between the film industry and technology sector is significant in this research.

The film industry and tech sector were ideal models for comparison under the umbrella of "private industry". The film industry and tech sector have divergent desirable security outcomes. The film industry's successful outcome centers on incapacitation while the tech sector prioritizes prevention. The utility of inter-nodal security capital sharing depends on the degree to which each node is compatible to one another. Nevertheless, both nodal clusters consider security a top priority and have relations with both law enforcement and the California state government.

One untapped potential security partner, the general public, also factors into the overall security network. At this point, the general public do not consider themselves security stakeholders, but instead maintains an antagonistic relationship with any form of authority, especially law enforcement and companies exercising social control on the "free" Internet. The focus on the subsequent chapters will explore these conflicts in greater depth. Chapter six will examine inter-nodal structural and cultural friction that take place in the nodal "gaps" and how these variables can affect security outcomes as well as the overall criminal justice system capacity.

CHAPTER SIX:
Compatibility of Desirable Outcomes

The overall strength of a security network is derived from the number of participants and resources shared in the given network. Each security stakeholder has different sets of behaviors, definitions of success, and cultures. The degree to which each actor finds the security assets offered by other security stakeholders useful depends on the compatibility of desirable security outcomes. As explained in the previous chapter, the film industry finds police security assets of criminal apprehension and digital forensics very useful compared to the tech sector, which prefers a low profile approach to security. The level of capital sharing and outcome compatibility affects the strength of nodal connections and overall security. Many variables affect inter-nodal collaborations despite a common desire amongst government and private industry stakeholders to maintain a secure and stable Internet environment.

This chapter explores the compatibility of security outcome variables beginning with the nature of victimization. Next, a comparison between law enforcement's relationship with the film industry will be juxtaposed with its relationship with the tech sector to elucidate cultural and structural points of collaboration and conflict affecting security. Finally, the law enforcement subculture will be explored in greater detail in the context of the criminal justice system and Pontell's (1982; 1984) System Capacity Theory. Specifically, the influences of prosecutorial decision-making processes on enforcement activities are assessed.

THE NATURE OF VICTIMIZATION

The utility of nodal security capital and strength of network connections is influenced by the compatibility of security outcomes amongst nodes. The degree of success of co-produced security outcomes depends on the extent to which end goals of each industry can align with law enforcement's end goals. Similar measures of success will result in more utility for law enforcement security capital (apprehension, digital forensics etc.) while divergent goals often result in less use of this form of capital, resulting in weaker inter-nodal relations.

Security is most effective when there are sustained inter-nodal relationships. The sustainability of relationships is derived from high levels of compatibility of security goals and capital sharing (Nhan & Huey, 2008). The strength and nature of inter-nodal relationships are often influenced by the nature and self-perception of victimization. For instance, corporations who perceive their victimization as being part of the normal cost of doing business instead of a crime *per se*, will tend to opt for business-oriented solutions over law enforcement. Businesses typically absorb the costs and pass them along to consumers and generally prefer to implement preventative security patches. As a result, their utility of law enforcement security capital (oriented around incapacitation) is limited, resulting in weaker and less sustained relations.

Corporations who perceive their victimization as being similar individual victims often more compatible with law enforcement's crime control security goals. Higher levels of collaboration results in more sustained security alliances. The strength and nature of security industry-law enforcement partnerships are influenced by the level usefulness of security measures. For instance, actors who value incapacitation and retribution find a greater degree of utility for law enforcement's crime control oriented capital. While attitudes and measures of success for each security actor can change in the long run, it will be assumed for the purposes of this research that they are fairly static in the short term. Therefore, the degree of compatibility of desired security outcomes are based on current security outlooks by each actor.

Law enforcement's cyber security capital is oriented around crime control agendas. This is derived from a strong emphasis on crime detection and criminal apprehension that largely ignores the reality of reactionary service-based roles (Webster, 1973; Skolnick, 1994). Measures of success are crime control oriented and meet public expectations to "catch the bad guys". Attempts to realign measures of success with more preventative strategies for cyberspace have failed due to longstanding intrinsic police informal *normative orders* (values) that dictate behavior (Herbert, 1998). Moreover, police recruits tend to reflect values in the community in which they are drawn from (Walker, 1983) and police officers are indefinitely defined by a process of socialization that reinforces group norms (Van Maanen, 1975). Any attempts to redefine the roles and expectations of law enforcement are often met with strong structural and cultural resistance. Therefore, industries looking to utilize law enforcement capital must be align themselves with crime control security goals and cannot expect law enforcement to change in order to fit their security needs.

THE FILM INDUSTRY AND LAW ENFORCEMENT

The film industry's high degree of compatible security outcomes with law enforcement allows for a more robust and sustained security partnership. A primary security goal of this industry is to stop the spread of piracy at the source: elite release groups that illegally obtain and distribute copyrighted content. This strategy considers that once a file is shared in the massive Peer-to-Peer (P2P) distribution pipeline,[53] it is virtually impossible to stop its spread.

The source of piracy is not identified by the film industry as an abstract computing device, but actual criminals. One film studio Internet security expert explains that stopping the source of Internet piracy begins with apprehending individuals before digital content even reaches cyberspace. He asserts:

> Two sources of the crime plague the industry: insiders and camcorders. With the growing technology, it becomes cheaper and the quality is better. Pirates are very organized and can influence insiders as well as teenagers to film something. The rewards are high; a clean camcorder copy can pay $10,000 or more. A pristine copy from a company insider can cost even more. They will even pay off projection technicians. When these teens get caught, they're still juveniles so the risk is extremely low.

---

[53] It is estimated that P2P file sharing accounts for tens of millions of downloads. *See* mpaa.org/pyramid_of_piracy.pdf.

The film industry's ability to connect the physical with the abstract Internet space makes it compatible with law enforcement's geographic and crime control oriented capabilities in forensics and apprehension. The perception of whether the Internet is a new crime type or merely a new means for traditional crime often influences security strategies.

The film industry does not perceive piracy as cybercrime *per se*. Instead, it views the Internet as a new medium for traditional crime. One film industry Internet security expert states, "Piracy is a traditional crime moving online," further explaining, "The principles of the crime are the same, including motives and methods; manufacturing, distribution, and sales." Since Internet piracy is perceived as being no different than street crimes by the film industry, it is treated in a similar fashion to street crime. This agenda finds great utility in law enforcement's security capital of apprehension and legal processing. Fighting crime online, however, may not be as simple as applying the same street crime enforcement strategies despite this perception.

Diminished time and space makes enforcement difficult for both industry and law enforcement. One film industry security expert explains, "The Internet has affected crime by the sheer speed and volume of piracy." There is a misconception that large movie files deter downloaders, making the effort of the crime outweigh the benefits. However, technological advancements have diminished this barrier. The same expert states, "A growing problem with broadband and faster connections is moving this along quickly." Moreover, once digital files are uploaded on to P2P networks, it gains momentum and allows for exponentially faster transfers. He explains, "The Internet is *viral* and allows for millions in distribution from just one copy." This was evident in 2009, when an unfinished copy of the movie *X-Men Origins: Wolverine* was leaked on to the Internet, resulting in over one million downloads (Ernesto, 2009). The film industry still must convince law enforcement to serve their policing needs as a corporate victim despite having significant losses and compatible security outcomes with law enforcement.

The film industry has attempted to change the discourse of piracy as an Internet and high tech crime to piracy as a form of street crime to garner more law enforcement and public support. Innocuous terms such as "digital files" and "movie files" are replaced with a more terms that denote street crime, such as "stolen goods." "File sharer" and "downloader" are replaced by more provocative labels such as "dealer," and "thief." The concerted effort to identify piracy with street crime is reflected by the language used by the MPAA. According to an MPAA security supervisor, "Piracy is theft and pirates are thieves, plain and simple. Downloading a movie off of the Internet is the same as taking a DVD off a store shelf without paying for it." Changing the discourse, however, does not guarantee law enforcement attention.

The film industry still finds it difficult to compete with traditional crimes for law enforcement resources despite application of street crime labels to Internet crimes and offenders. One studio Internet security expert reasons, "This is because [law enforcement does not] see the *real bad guy* with this and how this can relate to physical harm. They focus more on immediate safety." The much stronger association of piracy with a "bad guy," which often illicit a stronger and immediate police response, has not yet manifested into the law enforcement mindset. However, the difficulties of this strategy do not diminish the importance of law enforcement to the film industry.

Successful security outcomes by the film industry are highly publicized, often serving as a form of deterrence. To entice law enforcement support, successful investigations that result in big busts are framed as giving law enforcement positive reputation. For example, the largest Australian movie piracy bust resulted in the seizure of over 400,000 pirated DVDs and copying equipment in 2008. An agent from the Australian Federation against Copyright Theft (AFACT), stated, "The enforcement action of the Victorian and Federal Police sends a very clear message to those involved in movie piracy - that it is a crime, it will not be tolerated and it has consequences" (Hendry, 2008). High profile arrests send a deterrent message to potential Internet criminals. In contrast, the technology sector prefers a more discreet approach to security.

THE TECHNOLOGY SECTOR

The relationship between the tech sector and the task forces is often much weaker, stemming from divergent measures of success and desirable security outcomes. The film industry defines criminal apprehension as the principal security outcome. In comparison, the tech sector prioritizes prevention and uninterrupted business activities without apprehending offenders. Recall that the primary state-mandated function of police is criminal apprehensions and investigations (Manning, 2006b). There are variances in the degree to which tech sector nodes find utility in law enforcement security capital despite divergent security functions between law enforcement and the tech sector. There are two dichotomous considerations that determine the likelihood and degree to which the tech sector uses law enforcement capital: the level of perceived value-added versus the level of perceived consequences of using that capital.

Some tech sector companies only incorporate law enforcement during emergency incidents as a small part of a comprehensive security framework (Schultz & Shumway, 2001). The first priority for this nodal cluster in an event of a security breach, such as a compromised host or widespread malicious code, is to immediately contact their incident response team (close the vulnerability in order to minimize damages (West-Brown et al., 2003) instead of law enforcement. Moreover, the decision to engage law enforcement is complex and often involves corporate and legal consultation during the decision making process in cases where it is not required by law to disclose security breaches[54] (Schurr, 2006).

Certain types of tech sector companies find law enforcement security capital very useful. Nodes such as computer software companies share many desirable security outcomes with the film industry. Software companies, who face similar intellectual property protection concerns as the film industry, often seek incapacitation and retribution as forms of deterrence. Computer software, similar to movies, is pirated in the form of hard goods (duplicate optical discs) and soft goods (downloadable software or "warez"). Similar to the film industry's copyright enforcement division, the MPAA, this industry also employs a collective copyright enforcement trade group, the Business Software Alliance (BSA).[55]

---

[54] SB 1386 (2002) under California Civil Code Section 1798.29 requires businesses operating in California to "disclose in specified ways, any breach of the security of the data, as defined, to any resident of California whose unencrypted personal information was, or is reasonably believed to have been, acquired by an unauthorized person." See info.sen.ca.gov/pub/01-02/bill/sen/sb_1351-1400/sb_1386_bill_20020926_chaptered.html.
[55] See www.bsa.org/country/BSA%20and%20Members.aspx.

Compatibility of Desirable Outcomes 113

Many software companies with crime control-oriented goals often seek to develop security alliances with law enforcement. In the 2001, for example, collaborative efforts between Microsoft and several law enforcement agencies resulted in the largest seizure of counterfeit software in U.S history. This bust resulted in over $10 million of counterfeit software seized and more importantly, it disrupted a highly organized supply chain (Stenger, 2001). Similar to cases with the MPAA, law enforcement was able to publicize their success and garnering positive reputation. As a result, sustained security relations exist between Microsoft and the law enforcement community. Internationally, the working relationship between Microsoft and law enforcement has resulted in arrests in 22 countries and the recovery of over $900 million in pirated goods (Broache, 2008). In a similar bust, "Operation Cyberstorm" brought a lot of positive media attention to federal and local authorities in 2002 when the high-tech crimes task force in Silicon Valley arrested 27 people in an international software trafficking ring (Singer, 2002). However, the value of law enforcement security capital is not as clear when the nature of victimization involves computer systems.

Computer network intrusions, a form of *hacking*, often involve theft or destruction of information.[56] Estimating the value of private information stored in a database is much more difficult than intellectual property in the form of computer software and movie files. The value of law enforcement involvement and the decision to pursue criminal apprehension is often based on the evaluation of potential benefits and harm. Oftentimes the harms outweigh the benefits. Companies prioritizing network intrusions favor defensive and prevention strategies over incapacitation and retribution.

Several computer security experts explained the philosophical differences between law enforcement and companies primarily concerned with network intrusions. One states, "Corporations enforce their laws as standards and policy. This is only a means to an ends. For law enforcement, the enforcement is the ends." Another

---

[56] There are two main classifications of hackers: "black hat" hackers, who illegally gain access to computer systems for personal gain and "white hat" hackers who ethically motivated to discover weaknesses in computer systems for the purpose of rectifying and improving security (Bratus, 2007).

professional echoes this opinion, succinctly stating, "We minimize damage and move on." One network security professional explains the divergent philosophies in detail:

> Corporations are in business to make money. Law enforcement is in business to enforce law. [Security] is a function of making money as long as it's not greater than it in terms of investment. Corporations typically don't share their audit findings; don't want to share about weaknesses. Law enforcement wants to broadcast it by nature.

The sensitive nature of computer security further divides successful outcomes between law enforcement and the tech sector. Businesses have historically avoided reporting crimes such as network attacks and intrusions to avoid negative publicity that may undermine customer confidence in the safekeeping of their personal information (Richardson, 2008; Wall, 2007).

Aggressive stances on security are often perceived as affronts to the hacker community which can provoke further attacks (Townsend, Riz and Schaffer, 2004:27). One network security engineer explains the risk of advertising strong security and engaging law enforcement, stating, "Initially it's a challenge; calling the attackers. After you bust them quickly, then it might become a deterrent." This was consistent with a 2006 security survey, which found that employing more security technologies actually *increases* attacker activity. The study cites, "It is likely that organizations that are attractive targets are also mostly likely to experience attack attempts and to employ more aggressive computer security measures."[57] Apprehending an attacker remains a low priority in the overall emergency response strategy.

Corporate responses to network intrusions are often guided by set policies and procedures exercised by network administrators and computer security staff. Emergency response procedures often prioritize stopping immediate threats and restoring computing services before considering contacting law enforcement. The process of restoring network functionality can destroy potential evidence and

---

[57] It was requested that the title of the document was not provided due to the sensitive nature of the agency involved and research participants.

compromise any subsequent legal actions (Kornblum, 2002; Faulk et al., 2004). One network security supervisor explains the process in an event of a network intrusion emergency:

> We first have to consider the confidentiality chain of command. Legal and IT action is taken. Then investigators are deployed, even using outside contracting if necessary. A contingency fee is retained. Then we focus on damage control, VISA, MasterCard, the Attorney General is contacted. We devote time to internal processes. We're not even worried about the bad guys at this point. We keep outsourced things to keep an eye out on the bad guys. We're proactive on the perimeter.

Despite the same perception with the film industry in recognizing there is a "bad guy," digital information that is "stolen" or destroyed is more abstract.

Digital information is problematic for police, who focus more on tangible goods and quantifiable losses. First, legal complications can arise with estimates of potential losses. For example, the cost of a downed website for three hours or stolen social security numbers is difficult to quantify. Second, these virtual losses make law enforcement's desire to publicize "big busts" very difficult. Unlike thwarting a bank robbery or large drug busts, it is difficult for police to convey to the public that millions of dollars were saved by stopping a hacker attack without physical displays of success.

Public displays of strong security, which is a strategy often used by law enforcement agencies as a form of deterrence, can provoke malefactors to execute further and more aggressive attacks on tech sector companies. One network security engineer explains the conundrum:

> Law enforcement celebrate. For [our company] it's making money, not upholding the law. It's a delicate balance. [Law enforcement] needs to publicize to make progress. Is it a deterrent? No, it's the opposite. If [law enforcement] never come forward, they lose credibility. The question is how can they come forward? Do they have to say the name [of the

company]? Do we inform the press during the break in? Is it a deterrent?

In addition to structural incompatibilities, inter-nodal cultural similarities and differences can explain the nature of relationships between law enforcement and private industry.

CULTURAL ANALYSIS: LAW ENFORCEMENT AND THE FILM INDUSTRY

The film industry fits very well with the law enforcement culture. Law enforcement qualities are highly desirable for employment to the film industry due to the nature of investigations-based security outcomes. One of the main prerequisites of prospective security job candidates for the MPAA is investigative skills, which explains the significant number of MPAA employees with law enforcement backgrounds. An ideal MPAA job candidate is an individual who possesses both technical skills and law enforcement investigations experience. MPAA security employees having law enforcement backgrounds have several advantages. First, they are better able to communicate with law enforcement. Second, these individuals can establish and instant level of trust. Recall that law enforcement has developed a cynical subculture (Van Maanen, 1975; Skolnick & Fyfe, 1993; many others). Third, MPAA security professionals with policing backgrounds have a familiarity with legal evidentiary guidelines. One MPAA job posting for an Internet security position listed the following requirements:

- Conduct complete investigations, which will include conducting interviews, conducting physical surveillance, reviewing public records, and conducting all related follow-up.

- Refer investigations to federal, state and local law enforcement entities.

- Identify and track repeat offenders.

- Assist law enforcement agencies with investigations and prosecutions.

- Develop and maintain interdepartmental relationships to allow for free flow of information within the organization.
- *Strong knowledge of investigative techniques - required*
- *Ability to recognize developing patterns - required*
- *Knowledge of law enforcement structures and methods - required*
- *Knowledge of criminal justice system - required*
- Law enforcement experience, or equivalent experience conducting investigations in the private sector
- Experience in conducting and directing investigations of Internet activities, including intrusions, web hosting and programming, IRC (DCC and XDCC) transmissions, Usenet postings, FTP site operation, peer-to-peer systems, and e-mail.
- Extensive understanding of TCP/IP, DNS, WHOIS, NAT, and basic Internet protocols.
- Extensive understanding of Windows OS and applications; familiarity with Linux, UNIX, or other operating systems preferred
- Functional understanding of U.S. federal computer crime statutes, Title III (Wiretap Act), and the Electronic Communications Privacy Act (ECPA)
- Familiarity with copyright law and the Digital Millennium Copyright Act (DMCA) preferred
- Experience in evaluating and implementing LAN and WAN security

The only four required areas are not technical in nature, but they relate to law enforcement. This emphasis on investigative skills over technical ability is revealing to the culture and security outlook of this industry, suggesting high levels of compatibility with law enforcement and a high value for law enforcement security capital.

Having compatible cultures does not guarantee access to law enforcement capital. The film industry must still compete with street crimes for law enforcement resources and time. The film industry often offers free training to officers to entice law enforcement to take on cases. In addition, one MPAA supervisor with a policing background explains that the MPAA only presents "cases that are worthwhile, meaning that there is a substantial bust with enough for a successful outcome," to the task force. Moreover, these individuals are cognizant of law enforcement priorities and caseloads. The understanding of law enforcement culture and priorities allows the MPAA to operate relatively smoothly with the task forces.

The MPAA presents cases to law enforcement with convenience for police investigators in mind. The MPAA conducts investigations to a certain extent before handing it off to law enforcement investigators to complete. One MPAA security expert explains:

> State law allows for the MPA to do complete investigations all the way up to the arrest. They can even obtain search warrants. However, we don't do this; we share the responsibility with police. The role of police therefore is to one, identify the suspect, and two, obtain probably cause and continue.

It is still frustrating for film industry investigators to develop a level of trust with law enforcement despite having a highly compatible culture and functional relationship with law enforcement.

Structural and cultural obstructions in law enforcement prevent greater nodal bandwidth between film industry and law enforcement nodal clusters. First, law enforcement culture places low priority on corporate victims. Second, its closed nature prevents disclosure of investigative information, essentially creating an information abyss. Once information is passed to law enforcement, the investigative process is closed to outsiders. One film industry security expert describes his experience working with law enforcement in an investigation as "frustrating." He states:

> When [our studio] works with them, honestly it's mostly positive, but you're dealing with a government bureaucracy. You have those issues; doesn't keep you in the loop. It never

goes anywhere. It's all of the right reasons for them, but it can be very frustrating. I'm a strong supporter [of law enforcement]. It's the nature of the beast.

This is consistent with the closed police culture and strong group introversion. This cynicism, however, is not exclusive to law enforcement. The relationship between the tech sector and law enforcement reveals reciprocated distrust towards law enforcement.

THE TECH SECTOR AND LAW ENFORCEMENT GAP: THE EFFECTS OF CORPORATE CULTURE

The tech sector has a culture that is closed to outsiders. This is not without practical reason; corporate espionage and protecting proprietary information are daily realities of security departments. Unlike the film industry, tech companies are often unable or unwilling to properly prepare evidence for investigations when utilizing law enforcement. Many companies with more technology-oriented security staffs are not trained or fully aware of evidentiary requirements for digital forensics. One network security expert who has worked on several investigations with law enforcement highlights the cultural impediments on both sides. He explains, "[Law enforcement] depend on corporations to bring them everything in a neat and tidy bundle." However, the sensitive nature of information and resource constraints of companies often results in "frustration [for law enforcement] in that the corporation doesn't want to put out the package." Decisions to not disclose information to law enforcement is often reflective of the organizational culture that closely guards trade secrets and protects the company image.

Security incidents are often regarded as highly negative and should only be publicly disclosed if legally mandated to do so. One network security engineer describes the situation as "keeping your dirty laundry in-house." Another network security professional explains the closed-nature of businesses will perpetuate "because companies just don't want to admit they have a problem." He questions, "Is it more of a threat to not tell versus the embarrassment or is it companies are getting better? Hard to say."

Legal liability may also be responsible for general attitudes towards the non-disclosure of intrusions. One network security engineer expresses, "[Public relations] people don't like them because it's increasingly litigious." Adding, "You have to pick your battles very carefully and provide value to stockholders." This is consistent with industry surveys that cite negative publicity as a reason for underreporting cybercrime (Richardson, 2008). A network security consultant explains the risks while handling a security breach:

> The company will contact the software company who developed and sold the software to develop a patch. They will not announce the guy has been in the system for five years. It erodes confidence of the customer; runs the risk of litigation. If information of customers were potentially at risk, that customer can sue. It's the custodial responsibility of the company.

The security priority to restore business functions and revenue intake is greater than pursuing criminal incarceration. One network security supervisor explains this conflict, stating, "It might be too late if the system is already up and running - the job is done." The culturally closed nature of the tech sector further discourages reporting to police.

Tech companies' closed culture stems from pragmatic purposes. Allowing non-company outsiders access to sensitive information can potentially compromise proprietary information and jeopardize future earnings and stock prices. Many companies invest millions annually on research and development. Protecting these assets equates to protecting the livelihood of the company. In 2005, corporations spent an estimated $95 billion in protection of assets against corporate or industrial espionage, such as surveillance and physical security (Pisani, 2006). One Internet security supervisor at a hardware company interviewed was extremely distrustful of government agencies, likening them to an Orwellian "Big Brother." He states, "We don't need government guys coming in looking over our shoulder."

Government can be regarded as security competitors instead of security partners to some tech sector nodes. Many security companies consider law enforcement as a competitive entity that performs a similar security service at no cost. Information sharing with law enforcement may mean giving away expensive proprietary security technologies considered trade secrets. One network security engineer from a security company explains, "We're not going to pass info to them that we use to make a dollar." Another security professional shares a similar opinion, stating, "I don't want to become their laboratory." In addition, many companies simply do not know the security capabilities of law enforcement without having worked with law enforcement.

Nodal relations between industry and government/law enforcement is often constructed through past experiences. Positive experiences can foster stronger alliances while negative experiences of lead to criticism and little value-added for companies considering law enforcement for assistance or sustained partnerships. One particular network security supervisor with over 20 years experience in information technology expresses her negative opinion of government participation in cyber security:

> I'm not convinced government has their house in order. Government is always suspect. They might be useful if they can get their own act together. To them, everyone's brilliant but they're failing their own internal exams. There are things that government does that help like [Computer Emergency Response Team (CERT)][58] and Infragard.[59] Their advisories are helpful.

The decision to pursue partnerships with government and law enforcement nodes is often gauged by their practical value. The government node serving as a nodal information router is helpful, but in certain security instances, it may not be timely enough. A network security engineer shares his experience with security notices, stating, "CERT sends out bulletins, but when they say something, it's two days behind when it's already spread over the Internet." The same security expert explains, "The window for time for attacks is shrinking; we're seeing a quicker exploit, zero day attacks." Hackers are exploiting software vulnerabilities the day of discovery, often reverse engineering a software patch the very same day it is deployed (Arora, Telang, &

---

[58] *See* www.cert.org.
[59] *See* www.infragard.net.

Xu, 2003; Ward, 2004). For government to be valuable, it must be extremely capable and prompt. Government and law enforcement security assets are often affected by high caseloads. One security expert explains, "[Government security agencies] have a lot of competent very technically skilled people [but] they're overwhelmed." Corporate nodes often acknowledge the important role of government and law enforcement. A large software company network security expert expresses, "They will come in and help you, but you take what you can get. They are cooperative but they're just as busy." For maximum utility, corporate nodes must facilitate law enforcement evidentiary needs as best they can. He adds, "Corporations just need to do as much of the background work as they can." For some companies, government and law enforcement's slower pace has meant a greater reliance on internal teams. Another security professional explains, "Only the extreme cases [are law enforcement] involved. The company has an internal investigation team that deals with incidents."

Corporate nodes acknowledge that government and law enforcement serve a greater function than merely providing technical and investigatory capital. Law enforcement can serve as a legitimate external entity that ensures the integrity of investigations. One network security professional having a law enforcement background explains, "Corporations can*not* self-police. Look at the case of Enron," referring to the corporate scandals from energy industry deregulation. A former task force supervisor underscores this roll by law enforcement, explaining that the company insiders such as network administrators are often perpetrators or accomplices to the crime. Despite the perceived limited abilities of law enforcement security capital, tech nodes acknowledge that the ubiquitous growth of cybercrime requires the involvement of law enforcement may be legally necessary to protect against civil litigation.

The tech nodal cluster's incomplete information and under-utilization of law enforcement as a security partner can be attributed to the closed nature of policing.

LAW ENFORCEMENT AND THE TECH SECTOR: POLICE CULTURE

Police reclusiveness often hinders full collaborative efforts with the tech sector. Security partners participate passively during the police investigative processes. Corporate victims often hand over information requested by investigators and await an outcome in a non-transparent method. Any security capital offered by corporate nodes is not utilized unless requested in an *ad hoc* manner for a particular purpose. For instance, investigators may not request assistance tracking a suspect or investigating a digital trail by employees familiar with the system. Instead, the investigators may simply want the login information. This is problematic for businesses desiring to be active participants during the investigative process and establish long term nodal partnerships.

The imbalance in investigative power is a disincentive to engage with law enforcement during investigations. One security professional expresses, "If they get involved, they may or may not tell you what they found. They may classify it as counterintelligence." Furthermore, information that is shared with government or law enforcement nodes is filtered by law enforcement and government before dissemination. One security engineer describes the process of inter-nodal communications as "throwing information into a black hole." Another security professional expresses his frustration with law enforcement by stating, "It's never an open channel; they don't trust us. We tell them something then we want to be there too!" The flow of information is dependent upon inter-personal contact. He adds, "Sometimes they're responsive and engaged. It varies and depends on the agent." However, relationships between industry professionals and investigators are sometimes structurally capricious.

Organizational and political variables associated with law enforcement making sustained partnerships are difficult to establish and can undermine existing relations. One network security professional explains the difficulty of businesses to trust working closely with government due to the susceptibility of political and bureaucratic changes. He explains that administrative changes in federal and state government could mean agency priorities may also change, stating, "No matter what assurances they can give, they can be swept out the next election." In addition, bureaucratic rigidity within departments and agencies can also undermine long-term collaborative efforts.

The law enforcement paramilitary command structure for state and local investigators means highly trained personnel are often promoted away from cyber positions. One cyber security professional explains, "[Law enforcement] train people and lose people." Instead, he recommends using a more distributed model of security consisting of a "volunteer reserve corps" from a consortium of companies that actively conduct investigations. This reserve corps would pool their collective expertise in order to "get private industry to work with the government and law enforcement that wouldn't cost them money." In essence, the proposed model of security is a decentralized nodal model of distributed power where experts can contribute with their respective areas of expertise. However, the lack of full mutual trust and communication of nodal capital and abilities prevent more robust collaborations between law enforcement and tech sector nodes.

Both law enforcement and private industry underestimate the value of each other's security capital and often overestimate their own abilities. Law enforcement places a higher value on investigative acumen, while the tech sector stresses the importance of technical expertise. The major source of conflict stems from each side's belief that the skills they possess are mutually exclusive and often superior. One type of security capital that is stressed by police as being exclusive and superior is developed through years of traditional police experience. Law enforcement feel the ability to "think like the bad guys" is an invaluable security asset developed only through experience. This opinion was stated by both task force investigators and prosecutors. One task force investigator stressed:

> It is better to train officers and detectives to be cyber investigators than computer science students because they are actually *faster*. The huge amounts of data can more effectively be searched by a seasoned investigator who knows what he's looking for than a college grad with no clue. This can only be obtained via experience from street patrol and detective work. The biggest issue is people, training, and commitment.

Moreover, even outsourcing investigations are not possible, highlighting the closed police culture. One task force prosecutor explained simply, "The stakes are too high for that." When asked if non-police technical individuals can be trained to conduct investigations, one taskforce supervisor did not believe that was possible. He echoed the opinions of other investigators and prosecutors, underscoring "the ability to think like a crook" as an invaluable skill that cannot be taught.

Task force members also emphasize the practical advantages police have during investigations. Law enforcement is generally connected to government agencies and resources. Task force members have an awareness and familiarity with these resources and can more quickly access these resources. For example, an investigator, being in a node situated as a state entity can apply legal and political influence, access government resources, *et cetera*. A task force supervisor explains "the ability to develop skills and learn resource available only to cops" is an extremely important and exclusive form of security capital. Tech industry nodes, however, tend to disagree with the value of law enforcement's security capital.

Many tech industry nodes, which rely on technology and preventative security strategies, are not confident in law enforcement's technical ability. In speaking of his experience in working with law enforcement, one network security consultant expressed, "I was not impressed by [the agency] or their second level team, emergency control centers. They didn't understand what I was talking about. Their qualified people are leaving for private contractors to make big bucks." The lack of faith in law enforcement's technical abilities is often derived from comparisons with their private industry equivalents.

The tech industry's economic capital gives them the ability to hire individuals with more technical education. One computer security supervisor uses the example, "If you contract with [a private security company], you get 24 hour support. Some seriously paid technicians." When comparing resources to law enforcement, "The government doesn't have that type of financial support because they don't have paying customers." As a result, assumptions are made by many tech sector security professionals that law enforcement security capital is of little value-added.

Differences in priorities and what is perceived as important can often lead to inter-nodal friction between law enforcement and tech sector nodes. In response to law enforcement's assessment of industry's inability to learn investigations, one network security administrator asks, "Do you need to be a hacker to catch a hacker? Murderer to catch murderers? You need the mindset to recognize the clues even within the IT industry." Another experienced security manager expresses stronger feelings by describing law enforcement's unique investigative skills as "bullshit." From her experience, investigations are in actuality performed by her company. She explains that police investigators merely serve as a middleman and simply relay the prosecutor's evidentiary needs to her security staff. The company security team in turn conducts the investigation and hands law enforcement the requested information to turn in to the judge. She further questions, "What can [law enforcement] bring to the table that businesses can't? What's the value to engage with you other than updates?" referring to security announcements disseminated by law enforcement.

The lack of faith in law enforcement's abilities is cited as a main reason for not reporting criminal activities. One 2006 federal law enforcement agency study conducted in Northern California found the top three reasons for not reporting to law enforcement include: (1) respondents feeling the incident is too small to report (55%), (2) did not feel law enforcement would be interested, and (3) did not think law enforcement could help.[60] One network security professional expresses his lack of confidence in law enforcement's ability, stating, "Government is spending money on investigations and response teams with little to show on that." Despite seemingly incompatible security outlooks, partnerships between law enforcement and tech sector nodes exist at the individual level.

Both law enforcement and private industries recognize the need for expanding network relations in the face of overwhelming cybercrime. Independently, each nodal cluster has inadequate resources and capacity to handle Internet crime. Expanded networks include inter-nodal collaborations between private organizations within the same industry, as well as inter-cluster partnerships with law enforcement and other industries. Security is derived from an arrangement of interdependent relationships.

All nodes in a security network are much stronger when working together and sharing knowledge and resources. No organization, whether law enforcement agency or private company, exists on an island and can handle cybercrime independently. By nature, nodes are interconnected in some fashion. One tech industry security expert from a software company explains, "No one alone can do it all, all the way to the manufacturers of devices." Security is conceptualized holistically and the strength of the overall security network is oftentimes affected by points of weakness or inefficiency.

---

[60] References to survey were asked to be kept confidential.

One point of inefficiency in the criminal justice system in dealing with cybercrime lies within the legal system, particularly with prosecutors.

CRIMINAL JUSTICE CAPACITY AND THE ROLE OF PROSECUTORS

The effectiveness of policing cyberspace can be limited by the capacity of the criminal justice system to process cases. Structural bottlenecks in the criminal justice system can reduce the ability to enforce laws and deter future crime (Pontell, 1982, 1984). System capacity can be diminished when points in the criminal justice system become overburdened. In this regard, limited prosecutorial capacity can reduce the overall criminal justice capacity to handle cyber cases. Similar to white-collar crimes, complex cyber cases are resource intensive and require special prosecutorial knowledge and experience. As a result, the limited number of qualified prosecutors strategically pursues cases to maximize payoffs, serving as criminal justice gatekeepers (Maakestad, Cullen, & Geis, 1988; Smith, Grabosky, & Urbas, 2004; Nhan, 2009). Prosecutorial decision-making is influenced by the sufficiency of evidence, a decision made by individual prosecutors (Smith, Grabosky, & Urbas, 2004: 33; Nhan, 2009). Several elements of cyber cases make prosecution especially difficult, resulting in a significant amount of case avoidance and use of plea bargains.

The complexity of cyber cases require more time and resources compared to traditional street crimes. Extensive time and effort are required to catalog and prepare the vast amount of digital information received from multiple sources for courtroom presentation. One task force prosecutor explains the overwhelming amount of evidence that would be required for a cybercrime case, stating:

> That's how many documents you're going to have for exhibits and you have to figure out each out of those comes from where? You have eBay, you have ISP, you have Yahoo...Some come to you in hard copy paper, some of it is very easy to understand and logical, some of it looks like gibberish, some of it comes to you from email, some comes on a CD or DVD, some come on CD or DVD with a proprietary program that doesn't work on our equipment. Some will send you streaming video you can look at it. There's all these

different ways you can get it. What am I going to need to authenticate this to get the foundation to introduce this at trial?

Each piece of evidence must then be reviewed and reduced to its essential legal elements. Complex cases must ultimately be simplified for the public to understand. Presenting hundreds of pieces of cybercrime evidence can overwhelm lay jurors. The task force prosecutor explains, "You don't want everything. You want to go to trial as succinct and comprehensible for the juror as possible." This is very time consuming and requires in-depth knowledge of multiple forms of technology. He explains:

> If you've never prepared one of these cases for trial, you'll never be prepared for the overwhelming amount of work you have to do for the documents and physical evidence. It's physically taxing to have several hundred exhibits that you have to spread out and you have to look at them and say, ok how are you going to look at them and organize them so it runs smoothly and people understand what it means?

The large amount of time and effort required to prepare cyber evidence is a disincentive for prosecutors to pursue legal action. Moreover, prosecutors are further dissuaded to pursue cybercrime cases by jurisdictional issues associated with the abstract environment (Nhan, 2009).

State and county prosecutors often lack the authority and resources to pursue international investigations. Prosecutors must navigate the complex jurisdictional and bureaucratic space with federal authorities. One task force prosecutor explains:

> When law enforcement goes out of the country, you have to deal with the state department and protocols that no one knows of that can run afoul. Those complications to say nothing of the practical matters of financial wherewithal to go places and to secure evidence that's submissible when it gets back here. If you find a server in Thailand or some place and you need to get a custodian back here, someone whose going to authenticate what it is, it's pretty much beyond practicality.

Compatibility of Desirable Outcomes

Attorneys must negotiate a political landscape that often has economic incentives to allow types of crimes, such as piracy, to persist. Sovereign states have the absolute discretion to create laws and criminalize acts, resulting in a high variation from country to country (Smith, Grabosky, & Urbas, 2004). Russia, for example, has earned a reputation for being lax on enforcing copyright violations and hacking activities. According to U.S. trade negotiator Victoria Espiñel, law enforcement efforts "have not resulted in the kind of robust prosecution and meaningful penalties that would deter the significant increase in piracy that our industry has observed in Russia" (Thomas, 2005). Structural mechanisms in the business world that often undermine legal processes are another disincentive for prosecutors to pursue cybercrime cases.

Dispute resolution business strategies by private industries often bypass the need for legal remedies during cybercrime cases. Prosecutors, who often favor civil remedies over criminal action (Smith, Grabosky, & Urbas, 2004: 37), are often reluctant to pursue cyber cases that they may feel is a waste of time or have no deterrent value. Rational economic decisions override any commitment to justice for companies. One task force prosecutor gives a scenario where a Chinese company during the process of being investigated and charged with copyright violations, can negotiate a settlement while a criminal case is in process. He explains that during the investigation, "You can bet your bottom dollar that Company A which was the original victim is negotiating with the Chinese company and before we get through with the case, they're going to reach an agreement that's going to license these things because it's all about money."

Economic mechanisms can undermine or diminish legal outcomes of victimized individuals. Individual victims are often compensated by credit card companies, resulting in several ramifications. First, investigations and prosecutorial actions can be delayed to prevent an unnecessary allocation of resources to a null case. Second, victim compensation undermines any potential deterrence for future criminals. Moreover, reimbursement can serve as an incentive for cyber criminals, who use it as a neutralization to justify their actions. One task force investigator explains, "It will keep getting worse until the credit card companies stop reimbursing people." Ultimately, this aligns prosecutorial decision-making to with convenience and expeditiousness, rather than meting out justice.

Prosecutors generally accepted cases only when they meet a minimum loss threshold or have special circumstances. The FBI's Internet Complaint Center (IC3) has over 20,000 cases reported monthly and requires a $5,000 minimum loss in order to be considered for investigation (Lourie, 2007). Similar thresholds are set by each task force prosecutorial team. Cases considered for investigation below this minimum loss threshold often require multiple victims to yield higher case clearance rates. Special circumstances are also considered for prosecution.

Task force prosecutors often accept unusual cases that can be used to build knowledge capital and legal precedence. "On occasion though, one of these cases doesn't fit our criteria," explains one task force prosecutor. He questions, "If we do respond to this will it facilitate a growth of an appropriate response in the law enforcement community for this type of situation?" Responses set investigative, legal, and procedural precedence for handling similar situations in the future. However, minimal thresholds are once again required once a case has been normalized.

Atypical cases can build the knowledge capital of the criminal justice community as a whole. One task force prosecutor explains:

> Our philosophy is we want to handle just those cases, overarchingly, that require this kind of resource because if we do all the things that everyone else can handle and one of those cases come along and we're not available for it, it doesn't get done because there's no one else to do it. Our philosophy as a special unit is if you're a special unit then you have to be special and you have to do things that nobody else can do.

Having a focus on unique cyber cases, however, can be a dual-edged sword. On the one hand, specialization can translate into more proficient handling of future cyber cases. However, specialization can further marginalize online crimes as not a "real" crime to other district attorneys. Cases must be pursued by non-task force prosecutors in order to expand the knowledge capital of prosecutors and the capacity of the criminal justice system as a whole. One task force prosecutor explains:

> The average run-of-the-mill ID theft cases [any prosecutor] can handle it. What are people familiar with? Forgery, grand theft; traditional crimes. This represents something new and a little bit [that instills] some apprehension in them. I don't know about this ID theft. Because it's so prominent in the news and law enforcement training circles that people feel like there's something particularly unique and to a certain degree that's correct, but unless you start doing them you'll never get that experience…In that respect, anyone can do them but you have a financial crime case, like ID theft, it's not a case that anybody's going to handle well.

Prosecutors remain constrained by existing structural limitations. The strain of heavy caseloads and limited resources often results in offering plea bargains or dismissing cyber cases altogether.

PLEA BARGAINS, FREE ZONES, **AND** *DISCOUNT JUSTICE*

Plea bargaining is a common prosecutorial strategy used in complex litigation requiring vast resources. Plea bargaining can serve a function to alleviate overwhelmed criminal justice processes. By nature, it is an integral function of the criminal justice system's efficiency. For some, plea bargains serves as the proverbial "grease that helps to lubricate an often frustratingly slow and overburdened justice system" (Love, 2009). However, the overuse plea bargaining in street crime cases has eroded public confidence in the criminal justice system's ability to mete out justice. Perhaps plea bargaining is "the grease that clogs up the arteries of the justice system, and makes that system hardened, calcified, inelastic and diseased- unable to allow justice to flow" (ibid).

Excessive plea bargaining has been controversial. Reignganum (1988) argues that lack of regulation for prosecutorial discretion gives an advantage to prosecutors. Federal judicial reform efforts that set sentencing guidelines and limit judicial discretion have been bypassed by virtually unlimited discretion of prosecutors to negotiate penalties, which creates a disadvantage to defendants who are not in a position to change to more lenient prosecutors (Reinganum, 2000). This prosecutorial advantage has played out in cyber cases.

Plea bargaining is the default strategy used in cybercrime cases to avoid lengthy and costly trials. "Front end" strategies are coupled with minimal punishments to force defendants to accept plea bargains. One task force prosecutor explains:

> If we go to trial it's going to be a very, very expensive trial but in the front end, we charge it completely heavy, so he's looking at thirty to forty counts. So here's the deal, we're going to offer you to plead to two counts and probation with six months in jail. Now that's a steal.

Charging multiple counts does not guarantee a plea bargain, but accused individuals virtually never turn down the offer.

Digital evidence in cyber cases can serve to deter legal defenses and give incentive to the accused to accept plea bargains. Currently, digital evidence in cyber cases is considered by both prosecutors and defenses as nearly infallible. One film industry studio Internet security expert explains, "Whenever we approach the FBI, it's 'here's the entire package of evidence,' not 'something's happening here, help!'" adding, "We have to do our side of the job for the best possible evidence collection." The threat of a strong case and increasing punitive charges by prosecutors further deters defendants from taking the case to trial.

One structural reason for prosecutors desiring to avoid trial litigation is inadequate punitive outcomes. One prosecutor explains, "The problem is when you get a case you know the most that will happen is the guy is going to get probation and minimal time and most you can do is three months, you don't have much bargaining room." The criminal justice system structurally forces both parties to accept plea bargaining by default as the best outcome for both parties. The same prosecutor explains:

> Now we give you a discount at this stage because we don't want to do the extra work it's going to take to contact all the victims, either through search warrant and subpoena all these records, to take the time out to organize the evidence there to use at exhibit at trial. This is an enormously tedious and time consuming task.

Compatibility of Desirable Outcomes 133

One cyber case can potentially cost thousands of dollars and months of litigation. The heavy use of plea bargains and lack of defenses has resulted in very high conviction rates for task force prosecutors, which reinforces a cycle of plea bargaining. One task force prosecutor claims, the defense "won't go to trial," adding, "Essentially, they're going to lose. We have high conviction rates; eighty to ninety percent. If you round it off; you round off numbers we *always* win."

Ironically, the high rates of plea bargains coupled with minimal punishments have deterred any robust defenses from developing. Unlike cases initially using DNA evidence, there has not been any incentive to invest resources into exploring flaws with digital evidence in the courtroom and developing effective defensive strategies. The introduction of DNA evidence into the courtroom initially drew sharp criticism and controversy with the use of statistical likelihoods of DNA matches (Meyers, 2007). Flaws in digital evidence, however, have not been explored in great depth. This may stem from the belief that the binary nature of computer technology is a "magic black box" that is exact and unquestioned without any understanding of how internal mechanisms work (Huey, 2002). One task force district attorney explains the current scenario in the courts:

> In high-tech world the evidence is so irrefutable. Once you make the connection, you got 'em. There is no defense. Just like in gangs. In the early days of gangs and you start putting on gang experts, they're overwhelming, they become gods of the courtroom, you win the case. Eventually, the defense begins to develop their own gang experts and then you got the fight on and you have to be really good. Right now we're in the stage of the defense doesn't have the expertise or the insight. Eventually they will catch up, no doubt about it. This is the way of the future and it's not going to remain in the hands of the prosecution or law enforcement.

One MPAA Internet security expert echoes this opinion, stating, "[The defense] can't refute [the evidence], there's nothing they can do. It's there in black and white." This gives accused individuals great incentive to accepting plea bargains.

There are negative ramifications from the heavy use plea bargaining strategies in cyber cases despite the relatively easy courtroom victories by prosecutors. Plea bargains create an overall reduction in the capacity of the criminal justice system to mete out justice while minimizing any deterrence effects by threat of apprehension and punishment. With increasing minimum thresholds to accept cases, prosecutors are at risk of creating a "free zone", which are the equivalents of legal purgatory where offenders can commit crimes without any criminal consequences. One prosecutor explains:

> What happens is you start to make a *free zone* and everyone realizes it's like drugs with the federal government; unless it's a certain dollar amount or certain quantity, they're not going to touch it. If it's in an area where we don't get to it, [the federal prosecutors] don't get to it; it's like this is where we're free to operate.

The risk of creating free zones also highlights the problem of the general prosecutorial apathy towards cybercrime cases. Instead, cyber cases are deferred to task force prosecutors, who become inundated with large caseloads. This creates a cycle where task force prosecutors are forced to use plea bargaining strategies while general prosecutors do not gain the valuable experience needed to meet the growing demands for cybercrime cases.

Prosecutors have a propensity to avoid cyber cases due to their general lack of experience in dealing with digital evidence. Even for experienced prosecutors, the nature of digital evidence can be difficult of grasp. One task force prosecutor gives an example of a colleague working on a gang case who came to him for assistance with searching a computer for digital photos. The gang prosecutor did not understand the need to image the drive first in order to preserve the integrity of the digital evidence. The task force prosecutor posed the question to the gang prosecutor, "How [are] you [going to] be able to verify when [the pictures] got on there or have any indication of who put them on there?" He adds, "Through the conversation, he says 'Oh I see,' but if he hadn't done that and never had that happen to you, then you'd never know."

The enormous amount of time spent on relatively few cyber cases can give the impression of inefficiency is a major structural disincentive to prosecutors willing to pursue cybercrime cases. Newer

Compatibility of Desirable Outcomes 135

prosecutors, in particular, have no incentive to pursue cybercrime cases which is a good opportunity to gain familiarity with the complexities of digital evidence. Instead, new prosecutors prioritize their tenure around creating a reputation for efficiency. One task force supervisor describes this as a "numbers game." A task force prosecutor expresses that there is a need to train new prosecutors to gain experience in order to normalize cybercrime to be as routine as drunk driving cases. He explains his career was established on trying hundreds of drunken driving cases. He expresses, "There's not a deputy DA around who wouldn't say I wouldn't try a drunk driving case because that's what you cut your teeth on."

New and veteran prosecutors remain apprehensive and focused on more rewarding street crimes without applied experience and general knowledge in cyber cases. A task force prosecutor explains, "Unless you start doing [cyber cases], you'll never get that experience," adding, "People who do economic crime cases, they're used to that, but your average prosecutor is talking about robberies and murders and rapes and the types of crimes that people traditionally think of when they think of felony crimes." Building the general knowledge base to create efficiency in trying cybercrime cases is still a major structural and cultural challenge to prosecutors.

So far, the task force model of specialized prosecutors remains the default method of prosecuting high tech and cyber crimes in California at the state level and below. There is a dramatic increase in high tech and cyber crimes and an acknowledgment of its growing importance. Moreover, cybercrime challenges the current paradigm of crime and punishment. One task force prosecutor stated poignantly, "[Cybercrime is] representative of a developing area of crime that we haven't seen and poses interesting dilemmas as to how to categorize it as a crime, how to investigate it appropriately and also, how to punish it."

CHAPTER SUMMARY

It has been shown that one actor's self-perception of victimization can influence the degree to which it finds law enforcement's security capital (digital forensics) useful. The film industry's perception of crime is marked by clear victimization and by a clear perpetrator (members of release groups). Its desired security outcome to incapacitate and punish these individuals is highly compatible with law enforcement's security capital and successful outcomes. This strong congruence enables high levels of sustained security relations.

In comparison, the tech sector's definitions of success prioritize prevention (network security) over apprehension. This nodal cluster prioritizes uninterrupted business functions and quick restoration in an event of a cyber attack. It has much less utility for digital forensics capabilities offered by law enforcement. Consequently, inter-nodal collaborations are less sustained and utilized more on an *ad hoc* basis. Moreover, the use of law enforcement is often viewed as potentially harmful to a company's public image. Aggressive and conspicuous security tactics do not serve as a deterrent, but can potentially provoke further computer network attacks.

Law enforcement's security capacity, regardless of the degree of usefulness to private industries, is often limited by cultural and structural variables. First, private industries must compete with law enforcement resources with local policing agencies in need of digital forensic services. Oftentimes police loyalty derived from its strong collective solidarity prioritizes policing agencies with street crime cases over corporate victims. Second, prosecutorial priorities and decision-making can limit the system capacity. Prosecutors often rationalize pursuing more fruitful street crime cases over cyber cases that require substantial resources, expertise, and time. These factors are compounded by inadequate laws and general juror apathy.

The next chapter will explore the reasons for legislative and public lack of concern for corporate victims that undermine law enforcement and private industries' ability to secure cyberspace.

CHAPTER SEVEN:
Public Buy-In as Security Stakeholders

The previous chapters examined the structural and cultural make up of each security stakeholder and explored variables in the nodal synapses that affect security collaborations and outcomes. This chapter will marshal these collective findings to suggest that the exclusion of the general public as a key security stakeholder is a primary reason behind the inability of law enforcement and private industries to effectively police cyberspace.

First, the importance of the general public as a security stakeholder will be assessed in the context of public efficacy using the Y2K Millennium Bug as a heuristic model for analysis. Next, the Internet culture will be analyzed to explain the reluctance of public buy-in as security stakeholders. Finally, defensible spaces and new models of security will be explored in a virtual environment using ecological theories and collective efficacy.

THE MISSING LINK: THE GENERAL PUBLIC

The general public represents a sector that has been largely ignored by the public-private discourse in security, which centers on public police and private industries. For example, the Department of Homeland Security (DHS) has underscored the need for public-private cooperation between government agencies and private sector IT users to protect critical infrastructures (Greenemeier, 2004). However, network relations do not extend to the general public as security partners. Instead, the public is generally perceived by law enforcement, state government, and private industries as being outside of the security network framework with no real value in security assets that are contributable to security. Currently, the general public is often perceived as being passive consumers of digital goods, potential victims, and potential lawbreakers. The role of the general public in the security network is determined by how existing security actors perceive and define the public's role. An analysis of the response to the infamous computer programming flaw, the *Y2K Millennium bug*, serves as a good example of the first major national response to a computer crisis. First, it reveals the first large-scale government- industry concerted effort in cybercrime. Second, it is very revealing of the state and industry's perception of and role for the general public in cybercrime.

THE CASE OF THE *Y2K MILLENNIUM BUG*

The Y2K Millennium Bug was theorized to potentially crash computer systems and networks worldwide when internal clocks reset to "00" in the year 2000. Initially, computer programmers intended to save memory by omitting the first two digits of the year in computer programs. These professionals simply did not anticipate their legacy computer codes to still be in use decades later. Computer scientists discovered the flaw and published its existence in the early 1970s before reaching its crescendo of mass public attention during the mid 1990s (Taylor, 1999). The bug was perceived as both a major network security problem by companies and a critical infrastructure emergency by the federal government.[61]

During this crisis, the federal government mobilized the resources of both public (police, emergency services) and private (high-tech companies) institutions in a very coordinated fashion. A *Day One Preparation* program was implemented by the U.S. federal government which carried out "the largest simultaneous mobilization of resources in anticipation of a potential disaster or emergency" ("Y2K Aftermath," 2000: 7). The Y2K Information Coordination Center (ICC) and the Federal Emergency Management Administration (FEMA) established an *ad hoc* communications and reporting network designed to facilitate emergency response from municipal, county, and state agencies. In addition, universal emergency protocols and a clear command structure

---

[61] In 1993, the North American Aerospace Defense Command (NORAD) tested for Y2K compliance by setting their clocks forward to the year 2000 which resulted in the Intercontinental Ballistic Missile (ICBM) alert system crashing.

in a fully staffed command center were established to streamline emergency responses and coordinate resources. Private industries responded accordingly by allocating more resources and communicating incidents with ICC authorities. The concerted effort between government and private industry proved to be effective, but required a large financial investment. The federal government spent $8.5 billion of an estimated $100 billion total spent to avert major problems and disruptions to critical infrastructures ("Y2K Aftermath," 2000: 10). The Y2K crisis has clearly shown that security can effectively be established using public-private collaborations. However, it has also shown that developing a robust and lasting security network requires continuous funding, sustained partnerships, and good communications through strong leadership.

The general public was not included as active security partners as part of the overall security strategy despite the success of the Y2K response. Without this element, monetary investments in security by industry and government cannot be sustained in the long run. The collaboration was dissolved after a successful Y2K operation. The establishment of a more permanent security network requires public participation, which can significantly reduce overall costs and expand the security network exponentially. An analysis of efforts to establish a national anti-terrorism network illustrates the diminishing returns on investments in the current model of security.

DIMINISHING RETURNS ON SECURITY

A post 9/11 anti-terrorism security network has been implemented in North America with coordinated efforts between the military, federal agencies such as the newly created Transportation Security Agency (TSA), and law enforcement at all levels. In addition, security technologies such as surveillance and database systems have been deployed. Despite the massive allocation of resources, "inter-agency conflicts, inefficient technology, [and] lack of intelligence and analytical capacity makes these moves ritualistic and symbolic rather than instrumental and preventative" (Manning, 2006a: 65). Global terrorism has increased sharply in the years following the 9/11 attacks despite sustained funding towards an anti-terrorism network (Glasser, 2005). This indicates that even continuous monetary and personnel investments do not guarantee effective security. Increased spending often results in diminishing returns on security. Linear investments towards the current model of security are often only marginally effective on reducing crime ("Understanding Community Policing," 1994: 5). Kelling et al. (1974), for example, has demonstrated that increasing the number of police officers on patrol have no significant effect on reducing crime rates. Williams III and Wagoner (1995) argue that law enforcement is reactive by nature. Investments in the current paradigm of reactive unilateral policing, such as adding more police officers and investing in crime control technologies, has yielded minimal returns on security.

Proactive policing and crime prevention often require partnerships with the community. Community policing has been shown to be a promising model of security that eases community tensions that has potential to control crime (Gordner, 1995; Trojanowicz & Bucqueroux, 1990; many others). One common thread amongst these security partnerships is the exclusion of or passive role of the general public as security partners. For example, many community policing performance measures and Kelling's et al. (1974: 2) Kansas City patrol experiment only used passive measures of citizen involvement, such as levels of citizen fear of crime, perception of police service, and satisfaction with response time. An effective security network, however, must include the general populace as *active* agents of social control. The principles of community policing can serve as a model for security in cyberspace.

A CASE FOR ACTIVE CITIZEN PARTICIPATION IN CYBER SECURITY: THE CASE OF COMMUNITY POLICING

It has been shown that policing cyberspace requires long-term collaboration and commitments to share resources amongst many security actors. It is unlikely that cybercrime will receive the level of sustained funding and attention in the scale of the Y2K or terrorism in the near future without a catastrophic disaster. Security is simply too costly and overwhelming without the active participation of the general populace. The community policing framework proposes a model of security centered on active community participation and problem solving. It is an ideal model that can be very effective in preventing crime. It is now recognized that "community institutions are the first

Public Buy-In as Security Stakeholders 141

line of defense against disorder and crime" ("Understanding Community Policing," 1994: 5).

In recent decades, community policing has gained widespread adoption from police agencies in the U.S. This movement was spawned by the recognition for the need for crime prevention through community agency. Moreover, it represented a tacit admission that police are no longer capable of being the sole agents of overt social control. In addition, it serves to ameliorate police-community discord that developed as an unintended byproduct of the professional orientation of police impartiality.

At its core, community policing is defined by the U.S. Bureau of Justice Assistance as having two components: community partnership and cooperative problem solving ("Understanding Community Policing," 1994). Effective community policing requires high levels of community interaction for the purpose of building police-citizen rapport. The close relationship can allow citizens to better communicate problems in the community to police. Collaborative security strategies can be tailored towards outcomes based on identified problems.

The public serves a surveillance function and shares security capital in the form of informal social control. This public function is sorely needed in cyberspace, where the public are often apathetic or hostile towards any varieties of formal social control. While there is no universal way to quantitatively measure and evaluate successful community policing outcomes, an examination of one particularly successful case will underscore the need for community involvement.

Jesilow, Meyer, Parsons, and Tegeler (1998) conducted an evaluation of community policing in Santa Ana, California. Specifically, their study looked at the Santa Ana Police Department's implementation of Problem-Oriented Policing (POP). Problem oriented policing is a subset of community policing "that identifies citizens' complaints and lessens them by focusing public and private resources on their solution" using modular police divisions assigned to smaller districts (Jesilow, Meyer, Parsons, & Tegeler, 1998). Using interview data and multivariate analysis, the study found high correlation between the POP program and a significant decrease in citizen complaints on crimes associated with disorder, such as property crimes, drugs and prostitution, and traffic violators. The most significant finding was evidence of a large drop in gang complaints, which was the top priority identified by community members. Active community involvement often involves more than merely reporting crimes to police. Community self-efficacy plays a key role in successful community policing programs. Skogan's (1997: 184) research on community policing finds, "Citizen involvement was expected to go beyond reporting problems to the police; it was anticipated that residents could take personal responsibility for developing solutions to neighborhood problems." In addition, community institutions also played a large role in neighborhood security. Herbert (2006) stresses a normative framework for effective community efficacy is often anchored by public institutions such as schools. Applying this framework to cyber security, one can begin to see the value and importance of active participation by the general public.

Unlike community policing, where there is universal agreement on the need to improve conditions or address specific problems such as gangs and burglaries, crimes committed online do not generally incite a collective will to take action. Instead, the general public is often at odds with the desired security outcomes of businesses and police. This often occurs when the victim of an online crime is a business. Ironically, there is general consensus that stealing from a traditional brick and mortar store is wrong. The misalignment of security sentiments between the general public with law enforcement and private industries suggests there is something inherently different about the Internet environment.

INTERNET CULTURE

The Internet is often perceived as a separate domain disconnected from the physical world. As such, it is often thought to operate under a separate set of rules and norms of behavior. Specifically, the Internet is considered a disembodied "free" space. More importantly, it is widely considered not be "owned" or controlled by any single entity. The Internet was conceived under a *community code* that has permeated today's online collective conscience. Leonard Kleinrock (2004), one of the founding architects of the Internet, outlines the code that governs the Internet as based on "openness," which is characterized by the following principles:

- It serves everyone.
- In many ways, it is an "open" network.
- It provides a means to share works and ideas.
- It is diversifying.
- It is not centralizing.
- It is owned by no one.
- It is always turned on.
- It is empowering.
- It is a publishing machine.
- It offers a means of self-expression.
- It is an innovative machine.
- It is a marketplace of ideas, services, applications, and goods.
- It connects communities of interest.

Initially, the spirit of Internet "freedom" centered on avoiding content limitations, such as open access to the Internet, freedom to access content, and use applications (Powell, 2004). This initial vision has been distorted to mean that crime is acceptable on the Internet.

Any attempts to control, limit, or restrict this open space are seen as affronts to the founding principles of the Internet and should be resisted. This resistance includes subverting any form of law enforcement and external formal controls. Therefore, rule-breaking and even criminal behavior is largely perceived as justified acts of defending the free Internet space. The Internet is considered a last bastion of egalitarian freedom that does not follow the traditional rules and norms of "real" life and should be protected at all cost.

Public attitudes towards online law-breaking often reflect a dichotomous mentality that the Internet is a disembodied space with a separate set of acceptable behaviors. A public survey conducted in Singapore revealed that 94% of respondents felt it is morally wrong to steal a CD from a shop compared to only 43% that felt the same way for illegally downloading a song ("Illegal Downloading and Pirated Media in Singapore," 2006). In another international survey, 38% of respondents from the U.S., United Kingdom, Germany, Italy, France, South Korea, Australia, and Japan felt it was acceptable to download a movie before its theatrical release compared to 72% who felt it was acceptable after a theatrical and DVD release (Morphy, 2004). Online victimization and crime is frequently perceived as being disconnected from real harm.

Illegal behavior is often justified and condoned under the rhetoric of protecting Internet freedom. Examining the language and labels used for online piracy highlights this crime neutralization. Intellectual property theft, for example, is often referred to using less provocative terms such as "file sharing" and "downloading". The word "sharing" conjures Kleinrock's (2004) Internet community code of sharing works and ideas. Moreover, anonymity, which can mask deviance, can be framed in the way that protects the integrity of ideas. The preservation of academic freedom is the main justification for faculty tenures (De George, 2003).

NET NEUTRALITY

One particular source of friction is between the general public and private companies over the issue of *net neutrality*. Net neutrality is "discrimination between the price of transmitting packets based on the identity of either the transmitter or the identity of the receiver, based on the application, or the type of content the packet contains" (Economides, 2008: 209). In other words, net neutrality seeks keeping the Internet free from corporate and governmental interference in the form of creating information hierarchies by limiting or censoring information, bandwidth, modes of communications, and restrictions on equipment. In recent years, Internet Services Providers (ISPs) have been proposing the privatization of information on the Internet, allowing access to certain parts with premium tiered pricing. In other instances, preference and priority may be given to certain applications and web content while limiting access to competing products, services and platforms. Ongoing skirmishes between ISPs, the FCC, and advocacy groups have led to contentious debates over net neutrality (*See* Mark, 2009).[62]

This price discrimination and the commercialization of the Internet violates and undermines the open environment, where universal truth-finding is paramount. For example, China's country-wide firewall ("The Great Firewall") actively monitors and censors political content such as the search strings "Tiananmen Square

---

[62] As of the time of this writing, FCC chairman Julius Genachowski is fighting for legislation to broaden and codify net neutrality rules to mandate non-discrimination requirements for ISPs.

massacre" and "Democracy" (August, 2007). Short term financial benefits for broadband carriers and telecommunications companies are perceived as being at the cost of hindering Darwinian-like competition where the "best" information and content survives (Wu, 2003). There is also debate whether this constitutes reasonable price discrimination or unfair anticompetitive trade practices (Frieden, 2006). Ultimately, net neutrality proponents argue, commercial and political restrictions violate the original intent of the Internet embodied in the community code. This community code, however, is perceived by industry as merely rhetoric and justifications for criminal behavior.

THE MOVIE INDUSTRY AND THE INTERNET COMMUNITY CODE

A major source of friction that prevents incorporating the general public into a larger security role is disagreements on the meaning of the Internet community code. The film industry, in particular, views file-sharing as a crime that is unrelated to the philosophical functions of the Internet. Instead, it is viewed as rhetoric analogous to Sykes and Matza's (1957) techniques of neutralizations (denial of responsibility, harm, victim, injury, and condemning the condemners, and appeals to higher authority) for delinquent and illegal behavior. One MPAA Internet security expert, speaking in the context of Internet piracy, asserts:

> *Free* is a key term when it comes to the Internet. The Internet as the last bastion of freedom, an uncontrollable space to share ideas and information *et cetera,* is bullshit. These pirates are after profit, not freedom. There is always a motive of gain behind the actions of pirates.

For this security expert, the Internet space and physical space theoretically serve the same purpose and should not be differentiated. Therefore, cybercrime and delinquent behavior online should be a treated exactly the same as street crimes. He explains motives behind piracy are unrelated to upholding the Community Code, but instead argues, "It's greed and it's the same thing as any other crime."

To the film industry, the Internet freedom discourse represents a significant threat, embodied in the late former MPAA president Jack Valenti's statement, "You can't compete with free!" (Spring, 2003). This statement is commonly used by the film industry with regards to file sharing, which provides digital content to file sharers at essentially no cost to consumers. This puts the industry at a competitive disadvantage with pirates. Several film industry and MPAA security professionals interviewed embodied this situation with the popular industry phrase, "competing with free". One MPAA Internet security expert sums up the statement as, "You can't compete with free; not free speech, free movies." While argue this is meaningless industry rhetoric,[63] others see this statement as symptomatic of the impact of Internet piracy on changing the current dysfunctional business models.

If price was the sole determining factor in solving or curtailing rampant Internet piracy, in theory, lowering the price just beyond the threshold of the effort it takes to illegally download a song would eliminate piracy. Economic factors, however, do not fully explain Internet piracy. For example, popular rock band Radiohead released an album *In Rainbows* for legal download on their website in 2007. To test the business model for consumer-driven, free-market price points, the album was released without charge to the public. Consumers were asked to name their price for the album, which included zero as an amount. Despite 1.2 million downloads from their official site, over 240,000 users chose to download their album from P2P BitTorrent networks. Moreover, file sharing networks eventually surpassed legal downloads, leading some to conclude that "even *free* can't compete with music piracy" (Gonzalez, 2007). These instances points towards something more than purely economic problem causing the general public to pirate music (ibid).

THE TECH SECTOR AND THE COMMUNITY CODE

The tech sector holds an adversarial view of the general public. A worldview of "us versus them", albeit much less intense than police,

---

[63] Carlo Longino describes the comment as a "cop-out" by industry that is unwilling or unable to change business models to compete with piracy. *See* www.techdirt.com/articles/20070118/183340.shtml.

Public Buy-In as Security Stakeholders 147

has developed between tech companies and the general public when it comes to security efforts. Instead of viewing the public as potential security partners, computer security experts in this industry hold a cynical perception of the general public as being potential attackers. The industry's security goal often stresses *perimeter protection* in order to keep potential malefactors out. One security expert explains, "It's a matter of predicting trends. It's up to us to keep our spears sharp," meaning, being vigilant against potential attackers. Corporate network security is built around a fortress model, where the general public is to be kept outside its walls.

Perceptions of the general public have evolved from nuisances to dangerous threats. One Internet security systems engineer at a large software company explains:

> There is a misnomer about the "innocent hacker" who has no intention of harm or malice. This innocent hacker was just learning and applying his skills to see if he can get into a network and just look around, not intending to damage any files or steal information for personal gain.

It is often difficult to quantify damages to digital data. For the tech sector, even addressing well intentioned *white-hat* hackers comes at a cost. The same security expert explains, "The computer network admin does not know this hacker's intent, so time and effort is used to protect against this person. As a result, all forms of computer crime creates an *IP Tax*, costing everyone money." The enormous resources required for constant security vigilance. Moreover, network administrators cannot go on the offense. One security professional explains his frustration on not being able to use offensive strategies, stating, "Attacking is the portion that's not allowed." The multitudes of vulnerabilities and each company standing alone in defending them all are compounded by the Internet's open infrastructure that invites attackers.

The issue of Internet privacy and anonymity poses a big challenge to certain tech sector companies. Relative anonymity often emboldens Internet malefactors to attack computer networks and makes security and investigations very difficult. Internet anonymity and privacy often creates an environment conducive to crime. One large software company computer security expert explains:

Attribution is our biggest problem. Attribution means placing the action to the person's action. It is the anonymous nature and environment of cyberspace. There are warnings and indication, but it is about being aware.

The issue whether anonymity is good or bad on the Internet is reflective of a longstanding dichotomy between security and openness. Restrictive environments hinder the growth of eCommerce. For example, government restrictions have impeded early growth of eCommerce in China (Stylianou, Robbins, & Jackson, 2004). One security engineer explains this division, stating, "The problem with security is an old one; you can't secure every port and block all outbound data because it will interfere with business functions." The antagonistic relationship between companies and the public means security remains a daunting task for professionals working alone. For some, this is an expensive and losing battle.

Hacker attacks have increased dramatically with the current economic downturn. Cybercrime economy has been described as "booming" for phishing attacks, trojans, and high profile data breaches (Schenck, 2009). Cyber criminals have used schemes that prey on foreclosure victims to panic-stricken retirees. Moreover, employees on the verge of layoffs have used their positions to sell or destroy data (ibid). For example, on January 31, 2009, a logic bomb was set to go off by a laid off employee of Fannie Mae that would have wiped out all data from the company's 4,000 servers (Swanson, 2009).

Botnets, or networks of remotely controlled "zombie" computers, are by far the most dangerous threat to network administrators. Botnets, which are capable of generating spam, committing fraud, and overpowering websites, were identified as the biggest "imminent threat" to security professionals (Singel, 2008). One network security engineer interviewed underscores the seriousness of the threat of botnets. He explains the level of sophistication by organized attackers and the lack of acknowledgement by government and the general public is a dangerous combination. He states:

> There is a big chasm between public consciousness and the reality of computer crime. This extends into the law enforcement community as well. Botnets, or networks of remotely controlled computers used for attacks *et cetera*, are a

major threat which serves as a middleman, making it *very* difficult to find out who's in charge.

The Internet culture of an open environment for sharing information often serves to mask real crime in cyberspace. The open environment is ripe with opportunity for cybercrime. While there is an unwritten code to protect and preserve this openness, there is no code that governs malicious behavior.

Cybercrime is a capitalistic crime of opportunity, even amongst criminals. One movie studio Internet security expert explains a little known current trend:

> In one instance, people are hacking already-hacked systems and stealing their bots. What they do is hack an insecure server, plant a bot, and secure the server from other bot thieves. The result is the creation of a massive botnet. When you have 100,000 computers at your disposal, that's power. You pay me $50,000 or I take down your online gambling site for three days. That's real money.

The real impact of cybercrime is generally not known by the public. Instead, the public oftentimes feels corporate victimization is not a crime, or worse, deserved.

CYBERCRIME AS A VICTIMLESS CRIME

Crimes are often labeled victimless when acts are unlawful but are not perceived to have a real victim or produce real harm. While there may be a social cost, the general public does not acknowledge deviant activities towards corporations on cyberspace as real crimes with real victims. The historic discourse of the seriousness and normative structures of victimless crimes have been studied, such as prostitution (Jenness, 1990; Weitzer, 1991), abortion (Luker, 1984; Kaplan, 1988), homosexuality (Hay, 1996; Brewer, 2003), gambling (Dombrink & Thompson, 1990; Collins, 2003), and drugs (Goode, 1998; many others). Cybercrime often exhibits the same lack of moral outrage, especially when the victim is a corporate entity.

A common thread amongst victimless crimes is the lack of an adverse reaction even when the general public faces the harm of the crime. Sociologist Edwin Lemert (2000) explains this lack of social response as constituting a "compound of acceptance and rejection, frequently manifesting itself as the tacit tolerance of variant social patterns coupled with a nominal or formal disapproval and rejection," resulting in a normalization of deviant behavior. The general public often fails to understand the nature of the crime to make informed judgments or is simply disinterested in the issue altogether from being participants of the deviant acts themselves (Lemert, 2000; Pontell and Rosoff, 2009).

White-collar and corporate crimes are often perceived by the media and general public as being less harmful and do not warrant the level of attention given to violent street crimes. The savings and loans scandals during the 1980s resulted in billions of dollars in taxpayer bailouts of subsidized loans used for risky investments (Calavita, Pontell, & Tillman, 1997). However, top individuals engaging in collective embezzlement through illegal thrifts failed to generate moral outrage. Moreover, crimes committed by elite white-collar criminals, such as Charles Keating and Michael Milken, simply do not have the stigma attached as compared to drug dealers and other street criminals. This suggests a degree of public acceptance or separate standards for elite class deviance originally proposed by Sutherland in 1944.

Ironically, even white-collar crimes that directly cause physically harm to the public do not draw widespread critical attention. Geis (1978) suggested that there may be more victims resulting in death from "corporate condoned violence" than street crimes. Deliberate environmental crime, such as dumping toxic waste into rivers resulting in drinking water contamination resulting in illnesses ranging from birth defects to deaths have only resulted in relatively low public attention and minimal corporate fines (Rosoff, Pontell, and Tillman, 1998; 2008). Rosoff, Pontell and Tillman (1998: 408) explains the lack of moral outrage stemming from the difficulty "visualizing the damage wrought by white-collar offenses," adding, "Television often ignores or downplays corporate crime as well because those crimes lack the dramatic elements that fit the needs of electronic media: clearly defined victims and villains; illegal actions that are easily understood and can be described in quick sound bites."

Public Buy-In as Security Stakeholders 151

There is a body of evidence suggesting that white-collar crimes that is extremely harmful and can be visualized, such as homicide, does rank as more serious and deserving of more punishment than most other forms of crime to the public (Braithwaite, 1982 :738). Nevertheless, public opinion polls have not translated to widespread moral outrage. The lack of legislative and judicial action is indicative of these casual attitudes.

As mentioned, cybercrimes directed towards businesses are generally not considered a serious crime by the general public. Moreover, cyber criminals are not generally perceived as deserving of just deserts justice, but instead, are praised for their actions. One movie studio Internet security expert describes these individuals as "Robin-Hood types" that stand up to greedy corporations. Even more malicious acts, such as the creation and distribution of viruses that interrupt Internet services and destroy information, do not illicit public outrage but are instead perceived as heroic acts of protecting the Internet. One computer chip manufacturer security engineer explains that viruses are sometimes created and distributed to show off technical know-how and defeat security systems.

> It would've been very easy to add code to *Melissa, Code Red, et cetera* to format the hard drive. They haven't done that because they're trying to prove a point. This is *not* how you prove your point by breaking the law.

Cybercrimes share a lot of commonalities with white-collar crime and the perception of being a victimless crime. Ultimately, even widespread harmful viruses are justified as causing no real harm to any persons. Pirates and hackers use these forgiving perceptions to justify their crimes. File sharers often justify that digital information is not literally "stolen" but copied without removing content or property. Moreover, file sharers view their illegal acts as serving a capitalist function of checks and balances to ensure the quality of digital goods and services (Lasica, 2005). For businesses, they key to curtailing cybercrime is not simply by employing the same linear strategy of implementing new technologies and hiring more security personnel. Instead, law enforcement, government, and businesses, face the much more daunting task of changing public attitudes and discourse on cybercrime in order to get the general public to buy-in as security stakeholders.

THE GENERAL PUBLIC AS SECURITY STAKEHOLDERS

It has been discussed that security alliances between public policing and private industries are an important element in building sufficient capital in order to combat cyber and high-tech crimes. While these partnerships have been successful to a certain degree, cyber security resources remain inadequate even with the collective resources of law enforcement and private industries. The crucial missing element is the general public as a security nodal cluster. Two factors contribute to the lack of participation: (1) The failure to include the public in the nodal network as active and important security partners by law enforcement and industries and (2) the lack of public buy-in as security stakeholders.

Private industries' failure to acknowledge and include the general public as security stakeholders does not necessarily mean that both the film and tech industries entirely ignore the public. Rather, each industry determines the capacity to which the general public plays a security role. The general public can participate as active partners with self-motivated agency or as passive recipients of security needing persuasion to obey laws and reprimand illegal behavior. The latter represents private industry's current viewpoints security strategies.

The film industry recognizes the importance of the general public as a long term solution to the piracy problem but fails to give agency to the general public as security partners. This industry designates a passive role for the public. One MPAA security expert explains the film industry's mentally towards the public, stating:

> Public education is the key to curtailing the problem. Right now, the misconception is that pirating movies, software, or music only hurts a big corporation. Furthermore, it is a lot of teenagers who are doing this and going after them are just a bully tactic.

The industry is also cognizant of their contentious relationship with the public. Strong security measures or legal action can trigger public backlash while it was emphasized that inaction can also harm the industry.

Public Buy-In as Security Stakeholders 153

The music industry has suffered immense public backlash by employing aggressive legal strategies. The music industry was the first victim of widespread Internet piracy during the Napster era in the 1990s. Technological security measures were never integrated with music discs, which allowed individuals to easily digitize music and share it across the Internet. Consequently, the RIAA has resorted to legal actions against end-users, a move that has drawn strong public disdain (Nhan, 2008). The film industry is often associated with the recording industry and faces the same harsh criticism.

Efforts by the MPAA to educate the public and draw sympathy have not yielded success but drawn further public contempt. MPAA ads that depict the harm caused to movie set carpenters and other less-glamorous, lower-paid support workers, have been mocked in discussion forums throughout the web. The goal of this strategy is to reorient piracy with the harms associated with traditional street crimes that illicit public outrage. One film studio Internet security expert explains:

> The goal is to instill in the public that it is wrong, there is a real criminal and that social impact of the crime affects them too. There is a misconception that piracy is stealing a few dollars from the rich, but the social impact and ramifications of the losses are enormous. The example was given in that if the movies industry were gone tomorrow, it would impact thousands of lives who are support staff and related businesses that rely on the industry. Not to mention tax revenues.

Despite claims of the widespread impact of piracy on movie studios, record profits in 2007 and 2009 (McClintock, 2009) have equated the attention to piracy as a red herring for corporate greed (Anderson, 2008). However, the approach to security remains public education and not active partnerships.

The film industry believes members of the general public are rational decision-makers that can be deterred through education. One MPAA supervisor asserts, "People only steal if they feel they can get away with it. The goal is to deter through education." He concludes by stating, "It's really about loss prevention." Therefore, security strategies are based on the mentality that digital piracy is theft from a virtual store. In a brick-and-mortar store, security is handled by loss prevention teams and the public is educated through postings and warnings of electronic devices. Therefore, in both virtual and real stores, criminal apprehension and civil actions are remedies for loss prevention. Law enforcement oftentimes shares the same public apathy towards cybercrime. An MPAA Internet security expert explains need resources needed to educate the public as well as police, stating:

> You need different education for different types of people by age and location *et cetera*. There isn't a one-size-fits-all targeting to everyone. We educate and train law enforcement, who also shares the same apathy as the rest of the population. This is because they don't see the "real bad guy" with this and how this can relate to physical harm. They focus more on immediate safety.

Improved security means both increasing public awareness and strengthening ties with law enforcement. Simply educating the public and police in a pedagogical relationship makes it difficult to draw attention to piracy. Instead, the key is getting these two nodal clusters to buy-in as security stakeholders, where losses affect everyone and not just corporate bottom-lines.

The tech sector perceives the public as part of a potential external threat instead of a potential security partner. The public is often not part of a calculated strategy that involves reactive and defensive elements to protecting computer systems instead of acknowledging causal factors for hacking and software piracy. One security expert at a large software company's response typifies this culture, stating, "Today, organizations that really understand the engineered approach use *threat models*. These threat models are about building bridges between all business functions that give an optimal cost/benefit with limited resources; basically focusing on the important issues." These threat models do not incorporate investments in improving conditions and forces that prevent the public from chastising malicious behavior. Until private industries can recognize the public as a potential source of security, the public will continue to perceive hackers and other cyber malefactors as heroes defending the Internet.

THE SOCIOLOGY OF CYBERCRIME

Public attitudes towards piracy, hacking, and other cybercrimes are often reflected by the criminal justice and legal system. General apathy and dismissal of cybercrimes as lesser crimes translate into lighter penalties and fewer law enforcement resources allocated. It has been shown that high-tech crimes task forces are extremely small relative to street crimes. It was also discussed that insufficient judicial resources and structural disincentives create conditions of minimal thresholds and heavy use of plea bargaining strategies. Essentially, public buy-in affects criminal justice and legal buy-in in recognizing high tech and computer crimes as being worthy of attention and resources. An examination of white-collar crime literature reveals some mentalities and mechanisms for these apathetic attitudes towards punishment.

Hagen and Parker (1985) observed that white-collar punishment is not only a function of class position, but of inherent structural mechanisms that facilitate and mask criminal activities. Moreover they found that offenders avoided criminal stigma by being charged violation of a securities act rather than criminal code (ibid: 306). Contextualizing white-collar crime in a just deserts model of crime should result in harsher penalties for white-collar criminals, but the opposite was found to be true (Braithwaite, 1982). Organizational punishment is even more difficult given that penalties are often disbursed amongst shareholders and non-participants.

Socio-legal scholars have argued that punishments for white-collar offenses, despite being potentially more harmful and widespread, simply do not equate to those of street crimes. Reiman (2005: 133) poignantly states, "The simple fact is that the criminal justice system reserves its harshest penalties for its lower-class clients and puts on kid gloves when confronted with a better class of crooks. He points to evidence from federal sentencing served comparing crimes of the poor (robbery, burglary, and auto theft) with crimes of the affluent (fraud, tax law violations and tax fraud, and embezzlement), finding significant differences in sentencing and average time served.

Laws used in prosecuting cybercrime are inadequate. This inadequacy is indicative of the general apathy towards cybercrime. Two areas are cited by subjects interviewed as undermining security and deterrence: (1) inflexibility of current laws and (2) light penalties of cyber laws. The lack of legislative recognition and lack of moral outrage is reflected by the legal system. The light penalties of cyber laws forces task force investigators and prosecutors to apply old laws to cyber cases. One MPAA security supervisor explains the problems with using traditional laws, stating:

> They are still using old laws to convict criminals that don't reflect the true nature of the crime and lump everything. Currently, the state is using two laws to prosecute offenders which are not related to piracy or cybercrime: illegal use of trademarks and true name and address. These are felonies with a maximum of five years imprisonment but realistically offenders get out in one year. The problem lies where the charge does not fit reflect the true nature of the crime and doesn't differentiate a smaller middle user or distributor to a large-scale manufacturing operator.

Inadequate penalties negate any deterrent effect from enforcement. It is widely known by malefactors that cybercrimes are much more difficult to detect and prosecute, giving little disincentive to commit crimes.

One task force federal agent goes as far as to call it an "incentive" to commit cybercrime and fraud. Rational criminals simply take advantage of the low odds of criminal apprehension and punishment. He explains:

> Laws are very behind. Laws need to be more flexible and punitive. There is no deterrence because the penalties are too light. A person who sells drugs or robs a liquor store receives 10 years versus a cyber criminal who gets two or probation. Afterwards, the cyber-criminal has to pay a few thousand dollars as a fine but still has a lot of money left over from the crime, which is worth it. There's almost an incentive to commit a large crime.

CYBER LAWS

Simply increasing the number of cyber laws is not a viable long-term solution. The rapid pace of technological progress can mean an endless rapid cycle of new laws replacing obsolete laws. Cyber-specific laws may not be necessary entirely. Cyber legal expert Susan Brenner (2001) has suggested that when broken down to its core legal elements, it is not necessary to distinguish virtual from non-virtual crimes. She outlines four legal prerequisites for defining and classifying crime: *actus reus*, *mens rea*, attendant circumstances, and harm. She applies this orientation to software piracy, which when redefined, as indistinguishable from common theft:

> *actus reus:* The perpetrator unlawfully took or exercised unlawful control over the property (for example, information or software) of another.
>
> *mens rea*: The perpetrator acted with the purpose of depriving the lawful owner of software or information.
>
> *attendant circumstances:* The perpetrator had no legal right to take or exercise control over the software or information.
>
> *harm:* The victim is deprived of his or her software or information.

When these parts are applied to criminal acts in cyberspace, it was found that separate laws are unnecessary. However, when law enforcement and practitioners were asked whether a separate set of laws were necessary, many opinions differed.

The law enforcement community has mixed opinions on the necessity of laws tailored to cybercrime. One state prosecutor assigned to a task force agreed with Brenner's position in the adequacy of current laws, stating, "Traditional laws are flexible enough to anticipate future crimes," but stresses that penalties were too light. An additional problem with using non-cyber specific laws requires careful framing of traditional laws for successful legal outcomes. According to Smith, Grabosky, and Urbas (2004: 43), choosing the wrong legislative provision when framing charges has resulted in many prosecutors being discouraged from pursing cyber cases. Consequently, a growing number of prosecutors and law enforcement agents have stressed the need for legal reform.

A number of prosecutors and task force members believed the unique nature of the cyber environment justifies cyber-specific laws. One task force federal agent expressed, "We need a set of cyber-laws with more flexibility." Another investigator underscored the need for a separate set of laws with more jurisdictional flexibility. He explains the inefficiency of current laws with this scenario, expressing:

> Yes, we need a set of cyber laws. I'm in California and you're in Georgia. If you steal in Georgia, where is the crime committed? Because the fact is, every pinpoint that it touches is a crime scene. You got to go to each location and generate a report. It is *hugely* inefficient. It's burdensome on the cop and the victim. The jurisdictional problem is *huge*.

However, the solution to cybercrime may not lie in the legal apparatus. It is clear that without sufficient enforcement, legal changes such as increased flexibility and penalties will do very little to deter crime.

Public buy-in as security stakeholders remains the key to sustainable security. Cybercrime will continue outpace the legal system's capacity to process and deter cyber criminals without this element. The current mechanisms for social control, technological solutions by private industry and threat of apprehension by law enforcement, have proven to be insufficient. One film industry Internet security expert with a nihilistic perspective explains the illusion of using technology to solve piracy, stating, "There is copy protection in snake oil." He expresses the profound fallacy of laws created based on technology to stop certain crimes as serving a more instrumental purpose, stating:

> You create a law that enforces a technology that's defeatable. You're setting it up so that people can break the law and you can sue them for it. It doesn't even address the problem. It creates a model where we can litigate our way.

Addressing the problem of cybercrime is much more complex than creating new laws and implementing new technologies. Instead, long-term cyber security requires a reorientation of public mentalities to buy-in as security stakeholders as well as industries and law enforcement to include the public in an active security role. One heuristic model that fits these criteria is based on ecological theories applied to cyberspace.

VIRTUAL NEIGHBORHOODS AND DIGITAL DEFENSIBLE SPACES

French Sociologist Émile Durkheim (1979) explained society in functional arrangements. Social arrangements are derived from an aggregate set of collective social norms conceptualized by the *collective conscience*, or social fabric and collective will of society embodied by norms and mores. Social cohesion in more advanced societies is bound by a functional interdependence of individual by a division of labor (*organic solidarity*). Social forces idle on a homeostatic state between individual roles and the collective will. Disturbances to the functioning of society, such as a national crisis or economic crisis, can function to reinforce social relations (ibid: 321).

This concept of externalities reinforcing the collective will constitutes the theoretical basis for many principles of ecological crime theories. Community enclaves with strong group cohesion are often able to monitor and actively secure demarcated places, or neighborhoods. In stark contrast, Newman (1973: 2) explains, "The anonymous cities we have built, for maximum freedom and multiple choice, may have inadvertently succeeded in severely curtailing many of our previous options. Collective community action, once easy, is now cumbersome." Consequently, these anonymous spaces create opportunities for crime, becoming "spawning grounds of criminal behavior" (ibid: 6). Environments composed of disembodied anonymous identities, such as cyberspace, is often favorable to criminogenic forces.

Jacobs (1961) examines neighborhoods and their abilities to prevent crime through collective efficacy. Three conditions are conducive to security in cities: (1) a clear demarcation between public and private, (2) natural surveillance by "natural proprietors of the street," and (3) continual surveillance by a sufficient population (ibid: 35). Both Newman and Jacobs stressed a normative framework for security, emphasizing physical urban design and private-public relations between police and the citizenry to ultimately create a *defensible space*, or "model for residential environments which inhibits crime by creating the physical expression of a social fabric that defends itself" (Newman, 1973: 3).

Creating this defensible space, in this researcher's opinion, is the ideal solution for exercising social control in cyberspace, which shares many of the same characteristics of a large, anonymous urban city. It is easy to understand why the creation of *digital defensible spaces* (Nhan & Huey, 2008) makes sense when examining the benefits of Newman's original concept. He outlines three conceptual advantages:

1. The problem of indifference is resolved. "An apathetic, detached citizen far too often limits its participation to bitter criticism of police for not accomplishing work which rightly must be undertaken by the citizenry itself" (Newman, 1973: 14).

2. "The regulation of the problem of security, the tradition responsibility of the citizenry, to formally designated authority" (ibid).

3. Security is possible by restricting territory to a single location.

Despite the good fit of this idealistic model, creating an enforceable environment that restricts space and defines territory in cyberspace is difficult. As discussed, the abstract space cannot be defined and limited geographically, as described in urban designers. This is not to say that online communities do not exist. Instead, neighborhoods in cyberspace are defined functionally with many similar characteristics of physical defensible spaces.

There is evidence to suggest that forms of online digital defensible spaces already exist. Early research on Usenet groups[64] reveals that computer-mediated communications can foster a sense of community and support social interaction (Baym, 1995). Regulating behavior online involves a combination of systems that allow for reporting of disruptive behavior and the willingness of community members to take action. Davis (n.d.: 2) explains three conditions needed for regulating online behavior: (1) Crafting norms using rules and guidelines for participation (liken to Newman's restriction of territory), (2) social methods such as implementing reputation systems

---

[64] A message board in a Usenet system for posting messages by topic by different users in different locations.

and removal of anonymity through online profiles, and (3) technical methods for detecting behavior such as banning systems. Similar to reasons discussed in this research, technical solutions are expensive and difficult to design and implement. Like the use of police, Davis adds, the use of moderators is extremely expensive and administratively cumbersome.

Changing public attitudes towards cybercrime is the key impetus to creating defensible spaces online. As mentioned, public buy-in is crucial in establishing a normative framework for security that is efficient and cost-effective. Without universal agreement on what constitutes a crime online, it is difficult to incite active roles in security or reporting illegal behavior. According to Lemert (2000), "ambivalent attitudes" of deviant behavior or crime can result in a situation "in which community tolerance is precariously stabilized just short of a critical point in the tolerance quotient at which collective action is taken." Again, illegal activities such as piracy and hacking are perceived as upholding the Internet code and should be supported. Reversing this behavior, it seems, may be an impossible task. However, one movement on the Internet gives hope for developing a realistic model of security.

THE OPEN SOURCE PARADIGM

One phenomenon that fosters online security through collective action is the *open source* movement. Currently, the paradigm exists as a software development platform in which source code is openly shared for co-development. Open source software (OSS) operates to make software better and less costly (oftentimes free) over privately developed software. To understand the benefits, we first take a look at the tenets of this model. According to Mockus, Fielding, and Herbsleb (2002: 310), these include:

1.) OSS systems are built by potentially large numbers of volunteers. These can also include company support and non-volunteers.
2.) Work is not assigned; people freely choose which work to undertake.
3.) There is no explicit systems level design.
4.) There is no project plan, schedule, or deliverables.

In examining these principles using OSS packages of Mozilla[65] web browsers and Apache[66] web server, Mockus et al. found OSS software to be widely distributed and high quality. This quality is a result of *collective* abilities to identify and fix software glitches and implement features based on the demands of users and testers. With a base of millions of testers, a smaller core of volunteer developers can address vulnerabilities and features desired by users, resulting in much more robust and secure software. This model can have many economic and efficiency advantages over privately produced software, who often hire a limited number testers and developers.

To better understand the fundamentals of OSS, we compare two dichotomous paradigms of computer security: closed models and open models. In a closed model, security is produced by secrecy, such as a combination to a lock. In cryptography for example, this is done by hiding the source code or algorithm, embodied in the catchphrase "security through obscurity." In contrast, OSS is developed in a process of continual peer review or auditing. The source code is open based on the assumption that your "adversary" would already have complete access to your code (Stone, 2004). Consequently, relatively few security "surprises" are discovered.

OSS advocates often refer to the failure of a closed encryption in the 1970s to reinforce their stance on open security. The Digital Encryption Standard (DES), a privately developed cipher encryption algorithm for the U.S. in 1976, was broken soon after release. Hidden weaknesses (both unknown and deliberate) were quickly discovered and exploited. Moreover, DES included secret "backdoor" decryption codes that allowed the government to decipher information. This invasion of privacy provoked strong attacks ("Cracking DES," 1998).

More robust security schemes based on open standards were ultimately adopted for wide use. The open source RSA[67] security algorithm became the standard for data encryption. It was not based on secret codes but factoring extremely large prime numbers. This simple mathematical method required computing-intensive computations that would take computer systems decades to decipher. As computing

---

[65] *See* www.mozilla.org.
[66] *See* www.apache.org.
[67] The RSA encryption public key algorithm was developed in 1977 by Ron Rivest, Adi Shamir, and Leonard Adleman. *See* www.rsa.com.

power increased, the algorithm can be expanded to include more digits, or bits. More advanced security encryption standards have been in use in addition to RSA.

What is perhaps most important aspect of the open source paradigm is the ability for the community to collectively respond to incidents. Since the software was co-produced by the community, it garners a high level of ownership. Therefore, attacks often trigger a community response that quickly fixes the problem (Schneier, 1999). This is akin to Durkheim's (1979) social solidarity of the collective conscience, where the collective responses to external attacks serves to reinforce social solidarity.

To understand the public contempt for media companies and their unwillingness to participate as security partners, we examine the conflict between open-format personal media and closed-format mass media. Consistent with the founding Internet principles, personal media, ranging from home videos to amateur films and projects, is meant to be openly shared on the Internet. User-produced projects are shared and altered by community members, ranging from parodies to inspiring whole new projects and collaborative work under the fair use doctrine under the U.S. Copyright Act.[68] The sharing and co-development of ideas and works on the Internet enriches the user and human experience (Lasica, 2005). This type of media represents the spirit of the Internet and is lauded by the vast majority of Internet users.

In contrast, movie studios are reluctant to share their intellectual property for any type of alteration and only designating them for conditional use specified by end-user agreements. Hollywood

---

[68] The right set forth in Section 107 of the United States Copyright Act, to use copyrighted materials for certain purposes, such as criticism, comment, news reporting, teaching, scholarship, and research. Section 107 sets out four factors to be considered in determining whether or not a particular use is fair: (1) the purpose and character of the use, including whether such use is of commercial nature or is for nonprofit educational purposes; (2) the nature of the copyrighted work; (3) the amount and substantiality of the portion used in relation to the copyrighted work as a whole; and (4) the effect of the use upon the potential market for or value of the copyrighted work. *See* www.library.yale.edu/~llicense/definiti.shtml.

studios often deny even small clips and parts of movies for private use, such as splicing scenes for home movies or school projects. When social media advocate J. D. Lasica (2005: 73) asked the head of Columbia TriStar Home Entertaining Benjamin S. Feingold for permission to splice a few seconds of a movie for a personal video, Feingold replied with "We do have a problem with that. It's Intellectual property. There's blood, sweat and tears behind it. Financial remuneration is required [and] to have people cutting and slicing up your products is not fair." Lasica claims this stifles creative works in the spirit of the Internet and moreover, antagonizes the public to use these works illegally without any sympathy towards the studios.

The open source movement serves as a good model to begin thinking about security in a way that demarcates territory online and harness the collective security potential of the general public. This requires the reorientation of public attitudes that perceives cybercrime as an external threat that triggers rapid and collective responses. Unfortunately, law enforcement and private industries are viewed as part of this external threat, and not as security partners. A lasting solution involves more than simply changing policy, but requires changes in cultural understandings and attitudes. Perhaps one instance where a company has effectively changed cultural perceptions is Apple Incorporated, whose recent success is attributed to more than selling computer and electronics, but selling a sense of collective ownership and loyalty.

Apple has successfully changed the attitudes of its consumers by instilling a unique sense of loyalty. While this may seem like marketing rhetoric, a comparison between Apple products users with their PC counterparts suggests a more significant cultural shift produced by Apple has resulted in reduced crime. According to a NPD consumer research group study, Apple Mac users are three times more likely to pay for music downloads (50%) versus Windows-based PC users (16%) in the U.S. (Marsal, 2007). While no formal study has been conducted and causal connections cannot be made at this point, including the possibility of self-selection bias for Apple users, these numbers do suggest a difference that warrants further investigation.

CHAPTER SUMMARY

It was shown that a robust security network will remain incomplete without the general public's participation as security stakeholders.

Current industry-public relationships are contentious. Corporate victimization does not often illicit public sympathy but often serves to induce further deviant behavior that is condoned and encouraged as a form of resistance. Similar to white-collar crimes, company losses are ultimately passed on the general public.

As in the physical world, collective efficacy may be possible in the virtual world. Newman's (1973) defensible spaces are created by strong community support anchored by police and community institutions working in harmony to protect neighborhoods. While an online environment is decentralized, communities exist online which are capable of exercising forms collective efficacy, which are often found in community message boards. However, securing cyberspace and protecting corporate victims is a much more daunting task that requires greater public buy-in as security stakeholders. One possible model that has been met with a high degree of success is the open source model that incorporates community ownership in a non-hierarchical paradigm analogous to the nodal governance framework. In the final chapter, we use this assessment to explore possible solutions to cyber security in the form of policy and cultural changes.

CHAPTER EIGHT:
Concluding Thoughts and Policy Implications

In the previous chapter, it was shown that public buy-in is a crucial element in establishing sustained cyber security. It was suggested that collective efficacy can be possible in an online environment without geographically-defined territory. However, the key to creating this digital defensible space is through the inclusion of the public as important security stakeholders and not just passive consumers and Internet users; something that has not yet been considered or refused by practitioners and legislators. In this concluding chapter, the purpose of the book and brief summary of findings will be discussed, followed by some observations on research limitations. Next, the contribution of this work for future studies will be considered. Finally, some policy implications will be explored.

THE PURPOSE OF THE BOOK

Cyberspace is a very complex environment that is very difficult to control. Its complexity is derived not only from a technology standpoint, but the new social environment it has created. It has fostered new means of communications and allowed for more access to information than ever before. Its ideology embraces the principles of unfettered information shared openly, discussed, and produced by diverse users. It is an autonomous environment that shapes and is shaped by social relations without external interference. However, the reality of the Internet today is a frontier that has outpaced traditional forms of social control, creating an environment that can facilitate and mask criminal and malicious activity. Traditional ideas of security based on simply reporting crimes to the police, who then take it upon themselves to conduct investigations and apprehend criminals is obsolete. Simply put, there are no islands of security when it comes to cyberspace.

Naturally, this research began with the question, how is cybercrime policed in specifically California? It was quickly discovered that the answer is largely unknown in the published literature. Current studies across disciplines have focused mainly on technological issues of cyber security as well as some theoretical work between police-private industries relations (Wall, 2007). An empirical study specifically of California was needed. Instead of merely providing a descriptive account of what security actors exist in California and their respective roles, this study sought to identify and examine structural, political, economic, and cultural variables that affect cooperation and conflict between actors.

It became apparent that the question of simply how cybercrime is policed in California is a complex question. We essentially ask how a "borderless" abstract environment is policed within the bounds of a politically-defined geographic location. Connecting the physical with the abstract became a major concern for this research. Therefore, instead of using strict geographic limits, such as how community policing is implemented in Santa Ana, California, the study needed theoretical boundaries. A theoretical framework based on functional relations was needed to analyze the nature of multiple congruent complex relationships. It was found that the Nodal Governance theoretical framework was an ideal analytic tool for assessing security in cyberspace. It allows for flexibility with its lesser regard on geographic forms of territory while being robust enough to explore the tangled web of social relations in greater depth.

Relatively little is known about the holistic picture of cyber security. Security discourse often focuses on policing and private industry as an aggregate without taking into account specific industries and other security agents such as state government and the general public. The current discourse often revolves around the "fit" of traditional policing with the Internet environment. Some have suggested that law enforcement's hierarchical command structure and reactive nature is inadequate for cybercrime and requires a paradigm shift (Brenner, 2004b; 2006). Whether this is merely a case of growing pains or a radical change in policing is required, the current mode of policing cybercrime was relatively unknown.

Since the Internet is not localized to a geographic area, territory cannot be easily be enforced by law enforcement. Instead, this abstract space challenges the current paradigm of policing, one that is designed to reinforce boundaries (Huey, 2002). Second, and more importantly, this study attempts to extract structural and cultural forces of individual and aggregate nodes that influence the strength or weakness of security as derivatives to assessing the overall strength of the California security network

SUMMARY

Police have been undergoing a paradigm shift in the past few decades. Modernity and the emergence of the *information society* (Castells, 1996) has shifted police duties from strictly crime control to risk management (Ericson & Haggerty, 1997). Managing greater populations with proportionally fewer resources require offsetting this security deficit. Law enforcement has managed thus far by adopting technology, such as the patrol car with onboard computer systems, geographic information systems (GIS) *et centera*, to further their crime control agendas. In addition, police have formed partnerships with non-law enforcement entities. This ideology is manifested in community policing, a localized security network formed with community agency and active dialogue between citizens and police. This network not only provides increased surveillance but ensured limited resources were efficiently allocated towards community-defined needs. In its ideal form, better public relations are a byproduct of police-community integration.

The community policing model is not only limited to police-citizen relations. Community institutions, such as schools, churches, private businesses and other community security stakeholders also play a significant role in security. This can result in a social network of security capable of collective efficacy (Herbert, 2006). This model is embodied in the nodal governance model of security, a theoretical framework based on Castells' (1996) social network theory. This theory proposes that social relations are built upon a series of interconnected nodes, or structured institutions. Castells' analysis of the growth contemporary urban cities found the development was fostered by information and communications technology. In his understanding of cultural development, information is a commodity that encompasses economic, social, and cultural forces. Power and value are derived from larger networks that are more connected with other nodes, such as metropolitan centers. Consistent with the nodal governance theoretical framework, a new paradigm of security has emerged: one which utilizes the resources of all security actors. Security alliances were formed out of a mutual need in securing Internet space as well as defend against new threats facilitated by the anonymous networked environment. Insufficient resources, limited understandings of the complex environment, and increased losses from victimization, demanded the attention and involvement of law enforcement by both private industry and the general public. In California, these security alliances were forged in the form of a network of five task forces.

Task forces are a strategic model that law enforcement has employed successfully in the past. The task force model serves two purposes: overcoming jurisdictional problems and resource sharing. For example, New York State's Organized Crime Task Force (OCTF), a collaboration of federal, state, and local investigators, has charged over 900 defendants, seized over 500 firearms, and confiscated over $100 million in drugs. According to District Attorney Michael A. Arcuri, "These arrests are another example of separate and distinct enforcement agencies working hand-in-hand to benefit our community and bring justice to those poisoning our neighborhoods with illegal drugs."[69] This success, however, has not come to fruition with cybercrimes.

Unlike the proverbial war on drugs, policing cyberspace has not received significant attention and funding. Several factors can be used to explain this. First, computer crimes are far more complex, requiring not only technical expertise, but the policing of a space that is not bound by politically defined geographic borders. Instead, the demarcation of places are often determined by common interests and enforced through informal social control and limits to information access. This creates major challenges to not only the law enforcement community, but to prosecutors who must contend with jurisdictional matters as well as preparing ephemeral and ubiquitous digital information (Nhan, 2008).

---

[69] *See* www.oag.state.ny.us/press/2006/jul/jul19a_06.html.

Concluding Thoughts and Policy Implications 171

Second, the nature of computer crimes does not fit perfectly with the orientation of traditional policing. Police officers are trained in street crime and successful outcomes are determined by *index crimes* such as arrest rates, clearance rates, and other factors outline in the Uniform Crime Report (UCR).[70] The degree to which law enforcement can be utilized in cybercrime depends on the degree cybercrime resembles traditional street crime. Studies have shown that successful police recruits are a fairly homogenous group that values social services and crime control (Fielding, 1988).

For the film industry cybercrime victims with clearer victimization, nature of losses, and desire for incapacitation and retribution towards offenders, this fits well with law enforcement agendas. This compatible outcome is in contrast to the tech sector, which views merely stopping a current threat is the end goal. This is not without reason; further enforcement attempts can trigger further attacks and victimization. Moreover, the utility of reactive police investigative skills in digital forensics is not as valued compared to preventative network security.

The third reason why cybercrime has not received the attention and funding as street crimes, it is argued in this research, is the lack of public buy-in. Without widespread public support, cyber security will continue to receive minimal investments. This includes political influence and ultimately legal considerations such as harsher penalties. Corporate cyber-victimization in particular, shares the same public apathy as white-collar crimes. Explaining this public apathy will require further research and build upon the work of Lemert (2000), but its effects are clear: task forces remain a low-priority line-item in the California budget without automatic increases in funding. Consequently, task forces remain understaffed with minimum loss thresholds and prosecutors employ plea bargaining strategies, resulting in little to no deterrence for offenders. Moreover, the public has antagonistic feelings towards any forms of formal social control of the Internet, making security an upward battle.

A much larger issue concerning cybercrime is its lack of a clear identity as even a crime. Whether it should be considered an entirely new crime or simply "old wine in new bottles," is debatable (Grabosky, 2001; Brenner, 2004a). Some have even questioned

---

[70] *See* www.fbi.gov/ucr/ucr.htm.

whether there is such a thing as cybercrime due to its abstract form (Brenner, 2001). These unresolved definitional issues make enforcement, laws, and punishment, problematic. The lack of public outrage may be attributed to the ambiguity of computer crimes and lack of public understanding of the harm produced.

According to Hirschi (1986), crime is committed unless restrained by legitimate authority. Part of the difficulty of the enforcement of cybercrime may be explained by public perceptions of the lack of legitimate authority to police the Internet. As explained, the Internet represents a decentralized *free* space, an open forum for the exchange of ideas and information (Kleinrock, 2004). This "information superhighway" is to be defended from external formal social controls, such as government, law enforcement, and corporate entities. As a result, enforcement efforts against hacking and piracy are met with retaliation and intensified crimes that are justified as forms of resistance.

It is suggested that public apathy and antagonism can be overcome by creating a form of community self-efficacy on the Internet. Sampson, Raudenbush, and Earls (1997) define collective efficacy as "social cohesion among neighbors combined with their willingness to intervene on behalf of the common good." This defense of neighborhoods is likened to defensible spaces in urban areas, which has been shown to reduce crime when the community becomes active members of social control (Jacobs, 1961; Newman, 1973). This collective strategy has demonstrated promise as an effective mechanism in community policing efforts (Jesilow, Meyer, Parsons, & Tegeler, 1998). Getting the public to buy-in as security stakeholders, however, will require more research in re-orienting public definitions of security. The question remains, how can we get the public to recognize companies as victims, and more importantly, care enough to take ownership and participate as security stakeholders?

Adding to the problem, many on the side of law enforcement and private industry do not see an active role for the general public, who remain passive consumers in the digital age. Moreover, many subjects interviewed hold a pessimistic view of the future public involvement in policing cyberspace. One task force investigator, frustrated from public and political apathy asserts, "We will never fund cybercrime politically." Consequently, cybercrime remains a marginalized and niche crime despite growing victimization and losses. He continues:

Concluding Thoughts and Policy Implications

Channel five news will never focus on [cybercrime]. There's more money in homicide. We had an $8.1 million [major software company] piracy case...Banks don't make good victims. Technology doesn't make good victims. They're already rich. It's image. Pirating isn't such a crime. It's costly to investigate. It's going take forever to train and very expensive. The problem is public perception. It will never be prioritized.

One thing that the Y2K *Millennium Bug* has taught us is that it takes leadership and a long term financial commitment by all levels of the government. The state serves as a powerful node within any given security network, serving as a communications and resource broker. This is especially important in future cyber emergencies to protect critical infrastructures, with NATO assessing cyber warfare as being equivalent to a "missile attack" (Johnson, 2008).

RESEARCH LIMITATIONS

The scope and exploratory nature of this research limits the generalizability of findings beyond the State of California. It is intended to give a holistic snapshot of cyber security efforts in California. However, because cybercrime is connected internationally, general security implications beyond the scope of California are frequently expressed by subjects interviewed. Until comparative mapping exercises are conducted in other locations, initial findings remain largely limited to California. Despite the limited scope of the research, it does provide a framework for future comparative studies.

One area that was largely not addressed by this study is the role of federal agencies such as the FBI. Federal agencies typically address national and international jurisdictions and tend to focus on issues related to national security and infrastructure protection. This was due to two primary reasons: First, the FBI was wary of an outside researcher inquiring about relations with other law enforcement agencies and the general public. Second, the scope of the research would have been too large to obtain a national sample. It must be noted that access was eventually granted by the FBI, but too late to pursue for further data collection. However, issues of cybercrime deemed *terrorism* in nature were off-limits. Future research will address comparisons between federal and state policing of cybercrime. Federal and international implications can be made despite limiting the scope of this research to the task force network in California. While the task forces are based in California, its members include federal agents that have been involved in national and international cases. The task forces have on numerous occasions collaborated with international agencies. In cases of film piracy, there is some latitude for assessing piracy nationally and internationally. The MPAA and MPA deal with piracy on national and international levels. In addition, it was discussed that California is a high tech hub and has the largest concentration of illegal piracy activity in the United States.

It was determined that a quantitative study was not possible at the time of this writing. First, there are simply too few investigators to develop a sufficient sample size for hypothesis testing. Second, there was simply too little known about the policing of cybercrime in California to formulation appropriate research questions and assumptions. There are few empirical on policing cyberspace, requiring an exploratory approach. As more information becomes available, future research can quantify findings to compare with equivalent national and international samples. Continued qualitative comparisons can also be performed using nodal mapping exercises in other locations. Despite a growing body of literature, empirical criminological and sociological examinations of cybercrime are in great need to help guide policy.

SOME THOUGHTS ON POLICY

Based on information collected in this exploratory work, a few very preliminary considerations can be made. These thoughts on policy are centered on developing long-term solutions.

1. Policymakers must rethink cybercrime as not being a marginalized crime-type. Considering cybercrimes as a priority equivalent to street crimes and funding it accordingly can have an immediate impact. Sustained funding and prioritization can give private industries faith that nodal relations will not change with the social and political atmosphere. One computer chip manufacturer network security expert explains government support must not be

"dictated by society's pendulum and the political landscape," and to "get out of knee-jerk reactions." Another security professional asserts, "We must take the 'e' away from everything. It's not e-crime, it's just crime."

2. Recruitment and training of law enforcement personnel must include more emphasis in computer crimes as being a "real" crime. This should include significantly more technical skills training and education, as well as actively recruiting candidates with technical backgrounds. This will undoubtedly be met with strong resistance by the established police culture which continues to emphasize street crimes and will depend on strong political will to implement changes over time. As Internet technologies become more ubiquitous, demands for Ericson and Haggerty's (1997) *knowledge workers* capable of understanding, processing, and collecting digital information, will greatly increase.

3. Private industries should increase sharing security capital with law enforcement. Private industries should perceive monetary and training donations to law enforcement as investments. Moreover, specialized policing units, which provide services that prevent losses, should be considered an integral part of the company and incorporated into security budgets. For example, a one-time $50,000 donation was given to a task force from a large software company that was saved $8.1 million. One OES assistant asserts, "One million dollars to [a large company] is nothing. Task forces have not been getting donations. We received $50,000 from [one software company]. It's like a penny for them." Moreover, equipment and technical training are not provided to law enforcement at no cost by all companies with the exception of the MPAA, which does provide occasional free training. While ethical concerns may arise, funding and resources will remain critical.[71]

---

[71] It must be noted that structural barriers also limits law enforcement's ability to receive equipment. According to one task force supervisor interviewed, several months are required to get equipment donations

4. Structural and cultural impediments must be eliminated by law enforcement to allow for more integrative collaborations. Law enforcement must be willing to share investigations with companies. The task forces have shown that law enforcement is capable of learning highly complex technical skills. It must be reciprocated that industry professionals can also learn to preserve evidentiary chains and gain investigative experience. This can potentially reduce underreporting and build inter-nodal trust.

5. Invest in human capital and relationship building over technology. It is clear that fighting cybercrime depends largely on human relations. Investments in developing a unified database are expensive and do not have much utility in real-world applications. Inter-nodal connections still rely heavily on trust-based networks developed through interaction and "vouching" for individuals. Active relationship-building coordinators with enough resources can create, expand, and strengthen security networks.

6. Most importantly, recognition and incentives must be given to the general public to participate as security stakeholders. This is a very complex issue that will require further research into specifics on how to achieve this. The open source development movement can serve as a heuristic model to change business and enforcement practices that align to the public's interest.

LESSONS LEARNED, GENERAL AREAS OF SPECIALIZED POLICING, AND PRIVATE-PUBLIC POLICING PARTNERSHIPS FOR FUTURE RESEARCH

The Internet challenges our current thinking of crime and social control. Some perceive cybercrime as a manifestation of old crimes on a new medium (Grabosky, 2001; Brenner, 2001; Wall, 2004; Huey,

---

approved. Large amounts of paperwork and time is required by investigators with large caseloads. This often results in receiving outdated equipment that may no longer be needed.

Concluding Thoughts and Policy Implications 177

2001), while others have categorized it as a new form of crime or not even a crime at all. How society and the criminal justice and legal system perceive this crime will determine how it will respond to it. One county prosecutor interviewed in this research explains, "[Cybercrime is] representative of a developing area of crime that we haven't seen and poses interesting dilemmas as to how to categorize it as a crime, how to investigate it appropriately and also, how to punish it." Further research is required to determine what factors contribute to degree to which society and the criminal justice system are willing to address and dedicate resources to this growing problem. However, academics must also be willing to give attention to cybercrime.

Further research is only possible with greater academic buy-in. The marginalization of cybercrime is also reflected in much of academia in the social sciences. Developing understandings in this area is critical to creating effective policies and strategies to combat the growing problem. Currently, much of cybercrime research in criminology and other social sciences are deferred to non-mainstream journals and outlets. Cyber-specific journals, while rich in information, are not disseminated in wider audiences, but instead perceived of as a niche crime. More prestigious journals often shun cybercrimes in favor of more traditional crime, or designate the occasional special issues. Unfortunately, monetary losses in white-collar and cybercrime far exceed that of street crimes and warrant more academic, political, enforcement, and public attention. This research has given valuable insight into not only how cybercrime is policed in California, but why it is performed in a particular way. Access to all five task forces, as well as technically-oriented individuals from the MPAA and tech companies, is very rare.

An interdisciplinary approach is required for understanding the complexity of cybercrime and behavior in the complex environment. It is clear that cybercrime is not a separate domain independent from social, political, and economic forces. This is reflected in academic studies of policing cybercrime, where it spans multiple disciplines ranging from computer science and economics to sociology and criminology.

Through this research, it became apparent that the main limitations of policing cyberspace have less to do with technical education, but with larger political and social issues found in all crime. When framed in the context of white-collar and corporate crime, it becomes easier to understand why complex crimes are largely marginalized by the criminal justice system but by society as a whole. However, as the number of victims and economic impact grows, an increasing number of legislators are acknowledging its political importance. One promising sign is the framing of cybercrime in the context of critical infrastructure protection, national security and terrorism. The Obama administration in particular, has given cybercrime much needed attention. Cybercrime is already considered a clear and present danger but is only emerging in the consciousness of political, commercial, academic, and other social spheres of study.

This research has contributed to the growing literature on nodal governance and social mapping using the very important and timely issue of cybercrime. The empirical mapping gave insight into each security actor's function, culture, and security assets from the perspectives of each nodal set. How each actor interfaces reveals power dynamics and inter-nodal structural, political, economic, and cultural mechanisms. Moreover, a study of how this California network situates within the larger context of a national security and the country-level security network should be considered in future research. In addition, international comparisons of policing cyberspace are areas in need of exploration. Sociopolitical and economic variables that facilitate or hinder public and governmental buy-in as security stakeholders should be explored.

Digital defensible spaces are perhaps the area that is most suitable for empirical testing. This can be accomplished by measuring responses to deviant behavior in virtual community enclaves, such as message boards and online chat rooms. It is suspected that collective efficacy can be very strong in an online environment when members define and take ownership of virtual territories. While there are research studies related to the behavior of online learning and problem-solving in peer-controlled forums (Zhang & Peck, 2003), it is not known of any studies conducted on measuring collective efficacy in the context of crime in the online environment.

The scope of this research encompasses a larger contribution to the research body on specialized policing and private-public policing relations. The 9/11 terrorist attacks have accelerated the need for more complete security, resulting in the emergence of a "private security industry" (Wakefield, 2003). Post 9/11 controversies concerning private security forces have reopened the discourse on the ethics of private security (Scahill, 2005). This highlights a particular area of

Concluding Thoughts and Policy Implications 179

research that needs further exploration: the negative ramifications of private and hybrid policing of cybercrime. There has been increasing interest in cybercrime the criminological field despite the need for more funding for cybercrime research. Growing interest in cyber research has been evident from the increased number of special sections and groups within criminological and sociological associations. The goal is to eliminate the distinction between cybercrime and crime, which can allow better entry into higher tiered journals. Overcoming marginalization as a niche paradigm is perhaps the biggest challenge facing the small number of dedicated cyber-criminology researchers. It is especially important in the development of cyber research to acknowledge the blurred distinction between what is cybercrime and what is crime and that ultimately, there may not be a separate category. In the meantime, this research serves as a good platform to explore this emerging complex crime.

References

Adomi, E. E. & Igun, S. E. (2008). Combating cyber crime in Nigeria. *The Electronic Library*, (26)5.

Aiken, M., Vanjani, M., Ray, B., & Martin, J. (2003). College student Internet use. *Campus-wide information systems.* (20)5, 182-185.

Airoldi, E. & Malin, B. (2004). *Data mining challenges for electronic safety: The case of fraudulent intent detection in e-mails.* Proceedings of the Workshop on Privacy and Security Aspects of Data Mining in conjunction with the IEEE International Conference on Data Mining, Brighton, England. Pp. 55-77.

Anderson, N. (2008). What piracy crisis? MPAA touts record box office for 2007. *Ars Technica.* Retrieved on March 8, 2008 from arstechnica.com/news.ars/post/20080305-for-movie-biz-tales-of-piracy-and-record-profits.html.

Anderson, R. (2001). Why information security is hard: An economic perspective. Proceedings from the 17th Annual Computer Security Applications Conference, 2001. December 10-14, 2001, 358-365.

Armstrong, H. and Russo, P. (2004). Electronic forensics education needs of law enforcement. *Proceedings of the Eighth Colloquium on Information Systems Security Education.* West Point Military Academy, West Point, NY.

Arora, A., Telang, R. & Xu, H. (2003). Timing disclosure of software vulnerability for optimal social welfare. *Workshop on Economics and Information Security*, May 13-15, 2004.

August, O. (2007, October 23). The Great Firewall: China's misguided – and futile – attempt to control what happens online. *Wired Magazine.* Retrieved on April 11, 2008 from http://www.wired.com/politics/security/magazine/15-11/ff_chinafirewall.

Baldor, L. C. (2009, May 29). Obama announces U.S. cyber security plan. *Associated Press*. Retrieved on November 1, 2009 from www.msnbc.msn.com/id/30998004/ns/technology_and_science-security.

Bayley, D. H. (2006). *Changing the guard: Developing democratic police abroad*. New York: Oxford University Press.

Bayley, D. H. & Shearing, C. D. (2001). The new structure of policing: Description, conceptualization, and research agenda. National Institute of Justice Research Report, July. Retrieved on July 24, 2007 from www.ncjrs.gov/pdffiles1/nij/187083.pdf.

Bayley, D. H. & Shearing, C. D. (2006). The future of policing in Tim Newburn's (ed.) *Policing: Key readings* (pp. 715-732). Portland: Willan Publishing.

Baym, N. K. (1995). The emergence of community in computer-mediated communication. In Jones, S. G. (Ed.), *CyberSociety: Computer-Mediated Communication and Community* (pp. 138–163). Thousand Oaks, CA: Sage.

Becker, H. S. (1996). The epistemology of qualitative research in Jessor, R., Colby, A., and Shweder R. A. (Eds.) *Enthnography and Human Development: Context and Meaning in Social Inquiry* (pp. 53-71). Chicago: University of Chicago Press.

Benson, M. L., Maakestad, W. J., Cullen, F. T., & Geis, G. (1988). District attorneys and corporate crime: Surveying the prosecutorial gatekeepers. *Criminology*. 26(3), 505-518.

Biddle, P., England, P., Peinado, M., & Willman, B. (2002). *The darknet and the future of content distribution*. Microsoft Corporation: 2002 ACM Workshop on Digital Rights Management. Retrieved on December 2, 2006 from www.crypto.stanford.edu/DRM2002/prog.html.

Bittner, E. (1995). *The quasi-military organization of the police* in Kappeler, V. E. (Ed.) The police and society. Prospect Heights, IL: Waveland Press.

Bobb, M. J., Epstein, M. H., Miller, N. H., & Abascal, M. A. (1996). Five years later: A report to the Los Angeles Police Commission on the Los Angeles Police Department's Implantation of Independent Commission Recommendations.

Bopp, W. (1977). *O.W. Wilson and the search for a police profession*. Port Washington, NY: Kennikat Press.

References

Bort, J. (2007, July 6). How big is the botnet problem? *Network World.* Retrieved on March 29, 2008 from library.osu.edu/sites/guides/apagd.php#newsarticle.
Bowles, S. & Gintis, H. (2002). Social capital and community governance. *The Economic Journal.* (112), F419-F436.
Branigan, S., Burch, H., Cheswick, B., & Wojcik, F. (2001). What can you do with a traceroute? *IEEE Internet Computing Online.* Retrieved on March 4, 2008 from ieeexplore.ieee.org/iel5/ 4236/20709/00957902.pdf?tp=&isnumber=&arnumber=957902.
Bratus, S. (2007). What hackers learn that the rest of us don't: Notes on hacker curriculum. *IEEE Security & Privacy.* (5)4, 72-75.
Brenner, S. W. (2001). Cybercrime investigation and prosecution: The role of penal and procedural law. *Murdoch University Journal of E Law.* (8)2.
Brenner, S. W. (2001b). Is there such thing as "virtual crime"? *California Criminal Law Review.* (4)1.
Brenner, S. W. (2004a). Cybercrime metrics: Old wine, new bottles? *Virginia Journal of Law and Technology.* (9)13.
Brenner, S. W. (2004b). Toward a criminal law for cyberspace: A new model of law enforcement? *Rutgers Technology and Law Journal.* (30).
Brenner, S. W. (2007). Private-public sector cooperation in combating cybercrime: In search of a model. *Journal of International Commercial Law and Technology,* 2(2).
Brenner, S. W. & Clark, L. L. (2006). Distributed security: Preventing cybercrime. *John Marshall Journal of Computer and Information Law.*
Brewer, P. R. (2003). The shifting foundations of public opinion about gay rights. The *Journal of Politics.* (65)4, 1208-1220.
Broache, A. (2008, February 8). Report: Microsoft aided $900 million in piracy bust. *CNet News Blog.* Retrieved on February 15, 2008 from www.news.com/8301-10784_3-9867873-7.html.
Bryman, A. (1999). The debate about quantitative and qualitative research. In Bryman, A. & Burgess, R. G. (Eds.) *Qualitative Research Volume 1* (pp. 35-69). Thousand Oaks, CA: Sage Publications.
Bureau of Justice Assistance (1994). *Understanding community policing: A framework for action.* Bureau of Justice Assistance Response Center, NCJ 148457, August. Retrieved on August 16, 2007 from www.ncjrs.gov/pdffiles/commp.pdf.

Burris, S., (2004). Governance, microgovernance and health. *Temple Law Review.* (77), 335-362.

Burris, S., Drahos, P., & Shearing, C. D. (2005). Nodal governance. *Australian Journal of Legal Philosophy.* (30), 30-58.

Calavita, K. & Pontell, H. N. (1994). The State and white-collar crime: Saving the savings and loans. *Law & Society Review.* (28)2, 297-324.

Calavita, K., Pontell, H. N. & Tillman, R. H. (1997). *Big money crime: Fraud and politics in the savings and loan crisis.* Berkeley: University of California Press.

Calhoun, C. (1992). The infrastructure of modernity: Indirect social relationships, information technology and social integration. In Haferkamp, H. & Smelser, N. (Eds.), *Social Change and Modernity* (pp. 205-236). Berkeley: University of California Press.

Carey, L. (2009, July 29). Can PTSD affect victims of identity theft: Psychologists say yes. *Associated Content.* Retrieved on November 21, 2009 from www.associatedcontent.com/article/ 2002924/can_ptsd_affect_victims_of_identity.html.

Casey, E. (2004). *Digital evidence and computer crime: Forensic science, computers and the Internet, 2nd Edition.* San Diego, CA: Academic Press.

Castañeda, F., Sezer E. C., & Xu, J. (2004). WORM vs. WORM: Preliminary study of an active counter-attach mechanism. *Proceedings of the 2004 ACM Workshop on Rapid Malcode,* Washington, DC (pp. 83-93). New York: ACM Press.

Castells, M. (1996). *The information age: Economy, society and culture, vol. I: The Rise of the Network Society* 2nd Ed. Maiden, MA: Blackwell Publishers Inc.

Chu, J. (2001). *Law enforcement information technology: A managerial, operational, and practitioner guide.* Boca Raton: CRC Press.

Chun, S. (2009, November 6). Cyber attacks demand strong public-private response. *Roll Call.* Retrieved on November 8, 2009 from www.rollcall.com/news/40346-1.html.

Coffman, K. G. & Odlyzko, A. M. (2001). Internet growth: Is there a "Moore's law" for data traffic? In Abello, J., Pardalos, P. M., & Resende, M. G. C. (Eds.) *Handbook of massive data sets,* Kluwer, (pp. 47-93). Retrieved on November 2, 2009 from www.dtc.umn.edu/~odlyzko/doc/internet.moore.pdf.

References

Collins, P. (2003). *Gambling and the public interest.* Westport, CT: Praeger Publishers.
Combating high-tech crime in California: The task force approach (1997). Report by Ohlhausen Research Inc. for the California High-Tech Task Force Committee. Retrieved on June 13, 2008 from www.jciac.org/docs/art-HTC.pdf.
Condry, I. (2004). Cultures of music piracy: An ethnographic comparison of the US and Japan. *International Journal of Cultural Studies.* (7)3, 343-363.
Corbett, R. & Marx, G. T. (1991). Critique: No soul in the new machine: Technofallacies in the electronic monitoring movement. *Justice Quarterly.* 8(3), 399-414.
Coren, M. (2005, January 31). Digital evidence: Today's fingerprints: Electronic world increasingly being used to solve crimes. *CNN Law Center.* Retrieved on March 5, 2008 from www.cnn.com/2005/LAW/01/28/digital.evidence/index.html.
Cosley, D., Frankowski, D., Kiesler, S., Terveen, L. & Riedle, J. (2005). How oversight improves member-maintained communities. *Proceedings of the Conference on Computer-Human Interfaces 2005*, Portland, OR, (pp. 11-20).
Cracking DES: Secrets of encryption research, wiretap politics, and chip design (1998). Electronic Frontier Foundation. Sebastopol, CA: O'Reilly and Associates.
Crank, J. P. & Longworthy, R. (1992). An institutional perspective of policing. *The Journal of Criminal Law and Criminology.* 83(2). 338-363.
Cullen, F. T., Hartman, J. L., & Jonson, C. L. (2008). Bad guys: Why the public supports punishing white-collar offenders. *Crime, Law and Social Change.* (51)1: 31-44.
Davis, J. P. (n. d.). The experience of 'bad' behavior in online social spaces: A survey of online users. *Social Computing Group, Microsoft Research.* Retrieved on April 13, 2008 from research.microsoft.com/scg/papers/Bad%20Behavior%20Survey.pdf.
De George, R. T. (2003). Ethics, academic freedom and academic tenure. *Journal of Academic Ethics.* (1)1, 11-25.
Dekker, M. (1997). Security of the Internet. *The Froehlich/Kent Encyclopedia of Telecommunications.* (15), 231-255.
Dodge, M. & Kitchin, R. (2001). *Mapping cyberspace.* New York: Routledge.

Doheny-Farina, S. (1996). *The wired neighborhood.* New Haven, CT: Yale University Press.

Dombrink, J. & Thompson, W. N. (1990). *The last resort: Success and failure in campaigns for casinos.* Reno, NV: University of Nevada Press.

Drahos, P. (2004). Intellectual property and pharmaceutical markets: A nodal governance approach. *Temple Law Review.* 77(2), 401-424.

Dupont, B. (1999). *Policing the Information Age: Technological errors of the past in perspective.* Paper presented at the History of Crime, Policing and Punishment Conference at the Australian institute of Criminology in conjunction with Charles Sturt University. Canberra, December 9-10.

Dupont, B. (2006). Power struggles in the field of security: Implications for democratic transformation. In Wood, J. & Dupont, B. (Eds.) *Democracy, Society and the Governance of Security* (pp. 86-110). New York: Cambridge University Press.

Durkheim, E. (1979). *Suicide: A study in sociology* (Simpson, G., Ed. Spaulding, J. A. and Simpson, G., Trans.). New York: The Free Press. (Original Work Published 1897).

Economides, N. (2008). "Net neutrality," Non-discrimination and digital distribution of content through the Internet. *I/S: A Journal of Law and Policy for the Information Society.* (4)2, 209-233.

Edwards, J. E., Thomas, M. D., Rosenfeld, P., & Booth-Kewley, S. (1996). *How to conduct organizational surveys: A Step-by-Step Guide.* Thousand Oaks, CA: Sage Publications.

Ericson, R. V. & Haggerty, K. D. (1997). *Policing the risk society.* Buffalo, NY: University of Toronto Press.

Ernesto (2009, April 6). X-Men lead downloaded over a million times. *TorrentFreak.* Retrieved on December 2, 2009 from torrentfreak.com/x-men-leak-downloaded-over-a-million-times-090406/.

Espiner, T. (2007, December 14). Cracking open the cybercrime economy. *ZDNet.* Retrieved on April 21, 2008 from news.zdnet.com/2100-1009_22-6222896.html.

Faulk, C.J. et al. (2004). Forensic examination of digital evidence: A Guide for law enforcement. *National Institute of Justice Special Report.* Retrieved on March 16, 2008 from www.ncjrs.gov/pdffiles1/nij/199408.pdf.

Fielding, N. G. (1988). *Joining forces: Police training, socialization, and occupational competence.* London: Routledge.

References

Fisher, S. (1998, September 14). L.A.'s capital for software counterfeits – Los Angeles, California. *Los Angeles Business Journal*.

Flyvbjerg, B. (2006). Five misunderstandings about case-study research. *Qualitative Inquiry*. (12)2, 219-245.

Foley, L., Gordon, S., & ITRC Staff (2007). Identity theft: The aftermath 2007. Identity Theft Resource Center. Retrieved on November 21, 2009 from www.idtheftcenter.org/artman2/uploads/1/Aftermath_2007_20080529v2_1.pdf.

Foley, L., Foley, J., Hoffman, S. K., McGinley, T. G., Barney, K., Nelson, C., Pontell, H. N., & Tosouni, A. (2005). *Identity Theft: The Aftermath 2004*. Identity Theft Resource Center. Retrieved on June 25, 2007, from www.idtheftcenter.org/artman2/uploads/1/The_Aftermath_2004_1.pdf

Forst, B. & Manning, P. K. (1999). *The privatization of police: Two views*. Washington, D.C.: Georgetown University Press.

Foucault, M. (1979). *Discipline and punish: The birth of the prison*. New York: Vintage Books.

Frieden, R. (2006). *Net neutrality or bias?: Handicapping the odds for a tiered and branded Internet*. Retrieved on April 11, 2008 from papers.ssrn.com/sol3/papers.cfm?abstract_id=893649.

Furnell, S. M. (2001). The problem of categorizing cybercrime and cybercriminals. Paper presented at the Second Annual Australian Information Warfare and Security Conference, November 29-30, 2001.

Gamiz Jr., M. (2008). Private security industry grows as pay rate stays flat. *The Morning Call*. Retrieved on June 23, 2008 from www.mcall.com/business/local/outlook/all-security-030908,0,2413617.story.

Gantz, J. F., Reinsel, D., Chute, C., Schlichting, W., McArthur, J., Minton, S., Xheneti, I., Toncheva, A., & Manfrediz, A. (2007). The expanding digital universe: A forecast of worldwide information growth through 2010. IDC white paper sponsored by EMC retrieved on June 9, 2007 from www.emc.com/about/destination/digital_universe/

Garofalo, J. & McLeod, M. (1989). The structure and operations of neighborhood watch programs in the United States. *Crime and Delinquency*. (35)3, 326-344.

Gausnell, S. G. & Stoll, A. E. (2007). Overcoming objections to digital evidence. Paper presented at the FDCC 2007 Winter Meeting. Scottsdale, Arizona, February 28-March 3, 2007.

Geller, W. A. & Morris, N. (1992). Relations between federal and local police. *Crime and Justice.* (15), 231-348.

Genov, N. (2004). Transformation and anomie: Problems of quality of life in Bulgaria. *Social Indicators Research.* (43)1-2, 197-209.

Glaser, B. G. & Strauss, A. L. (1967). *The discovery of grounded theory: Strategies for qualitative research.* Chicago: Aldine Publishing Company.

Glasser, S. B. (2005, April 27). U.S. Figures Show Sharp Global Rise in Terrorism. *The Washington Post*, pp. A1.

Goldstock, R., Marcus, M., Thacher II, T. D., & Jacobs, J. B. (1990). *Corruption and racketeering in the New York City construction industry: The final report of the New York State Organized Crime Task Force.* New York: New York University Press.

Gonzalez, N. (2007, October 17). Even free can't compete with music piracy. *Tech Crunch.* Retrieved on April 6, 2008 from www.techcrunch.com/2007/10/17/even-free-cant-compete-with-music-piracy.

Goode, E. (1998). *Between politics and reason: The drug legalization debate.* New York: St. Martin's Press.

Gordner, G. W. (1995). Community policing: Elements and effects. *Police Forum.* (5)3, 1-8.

Government Accountability Office (GAO)(2007, June). Cybercrime: Public and private entities face challenges in addressing cyber threats. *United States Government Accountability Office Report to Congressional Requesters GAO-07-705.* Washington, D.C.: U.S. Government Printing Office.

Grabosky, P. N. (2001). Virtual criminality: Old wine in new bottles? *Social and Legal Studies*, (10)2: 243-249.

Grabosky, P. N. (2007). *Master's series in criminology: Electronic crime.* Upper Saddle River, NJ: Pearson, Prentice Hall.

Greenberg, A. (2007, October 16). Free? Steal it anyway. *Forbes.* Retrieved on April 7, 2008 from www.forbes.com/2007/10/16/radiohead-download-piracy-tech-internet-cx_ag_1016techradiohead.html.

Greene, J. R. (2004). Community policing and organization change. In Wesley G. Skogan's (Ed.) *Community Policing (Can It Work?)* (pp. 30-53). Belmont, CA: Wadsworth/Thomsom Learning.

References

Greene, T. C. (2001, March 6). Amazon division hacked, thousands of CCs exposed: Door wide open for 4 months. *The Register*. Retrieved on August, 16, 2007 from www.theregister.co.uk/2001/03/06/amazon_division_hacked_thousands/.

Greenemeier, L. (2004, April 19). Homeland security needs public-private cooperation. *Information Week*. Retrieved on April 3, 2008 from www.informationweek.com/news/management/showArticle.jhtml;jsessionid=HZOGWCUCB3BUOQSNDLPCKHSCJUNN2JVN?articleID=18902167&_requestid=547216.

Hi-tech crime 'is big business.' (2007, September 17). *BBC News*. Retrieved on March 29, 2008 from news.bbc.co.uk/2/hi/technology/6998068.stm.

Hafner, K. & Markoff, J. (1991). *Cyberpunk: Outlaws and hackers on the computer frontier*. New York: Simon & Schuster.

Hagan, J. & Parker, P. (1985). White-Collar crime and punishment: The class structure and legal sanctioning of securities violations. *American Sociological Review*. (50)3, 302-316.

Hammersley, M. (1996). The relationship between qualitative and quantitative research: Paradigm loyalty versus methodological electicism. In Richardson, J. T. E. (Ed.) *Handbook of Qualitative Research Methods for Psychology and the Social Sciences*. Malden, MA: Blackwell Publishing.

Harrison, A. (2006, March 13). *The Pirate Bay: here to stay? Wired News*. Retrieved on December 2, 2006, from www.wired.com/news/technology/0,70358-0.html.

Hauben, M. & Hauben, R. (1997). *Netizens: On the history and impact of Usenet and the Internet*. Los Alamitos, CA: IEEE Computer Society Press.

Hay, H. (1996). *Radically gay: Gay liberation in the words of its founder*. (Roscoe, W., Ed.). Boston: Beacon Press.

Hendry, A. (2008, January 24). Piracy busts bigger than Ben Hur: Victorian police shut down Australia's largest ever piracy operation. *Computer World*. Retrieved on February 11, 2008, from www.computerworld.com.au/index.php/id;324368563.

Herbert, S. (1998). Police Subculture Reconsidered. *Criminology*. (36)2, 343-370.

Herbert, S. (2006). *Citizens, Cops and Power: Recognizing the Limits of Community*. Chicago: University of Chicago Press.

Higgins, G. E., Fell, B. D., & Wilson, A. L. (2007). Low self-control and social learning in understanding students' intentions to pirate movies in the United States. *Social Science Computer Review.* (25)3, 339-357.

Hirschi, T. (1986). On the compatibility of rational choice and social control theories of crime. In Cornish, D. B. & Clarke, R. V. (Eds.) *The Reasoning Criminal: Rational Choice Perspectives on Offending.* New York: Springer-Verlag.

Hoath, P. & Mulhall, T. (1998). Hacking: Motivation and deterrence, part 1. *Computer Fraud and Security.* (1998)4, 16-19.

Holt, T. (2005, November). Beyond the bedroom hacker? Examining hacker social organization with multiple data sources. *Paper presented at the meeting of the American Society of Criminology,* Royal York, Toronto.

Howe, J. (2005, January). The shadow Internet. *Wired Magazine.* (13)1. Retrieved on October 3, 2006, from www.wired.com/wired /archive/13.01/topsite.html.

Huey, L. J. (2002). Policing the abstract: Some observations on policing cyberspace. *Canadian Journal of Criminology.* 44(3), 243-255.

Husted, B. W. (2000). The impact of national culture on software piracy. *Journal of Business Ethics.* (26)3, 197-211.

Internet Crime Report January 1, 2006 – December 31, 2006. National White Collar Crime Center and the Federal Bureau of Investigation. The Internet Crime Complaint Center (IC3). Retrieved on April 1, 2008, from www.ic3.gov/media /annualreports.aspx.

IP Academy (2006). *Illegal downloading and pirated media in Singapore: Consumer awareness, Motivations and Attitudes.* Retrieved on February 22, 2008 from www.ipacademy.com.sg /site/ipa_cws/resource/executive%20summaries/Exec_Sum_Illegal .pdf.

Jacobs, J. (1961). *The death and life of great American cities.* New York: Random House Inc.

Jenness, V. (1990). From sex as sin to sex as work: COYOTE and the reorganization of prostitution as a social problem. *Social Problems.* (37)3, 403-420.

Jesilow, P., Meyer, J., Parsons, D., & Tegeler, W. (1998). Evaluating problem-oriented policing: A quasi-experiment. *Policing: An International Journal of Police Strategies and Management.* (21)3, 449-464.

Jesilow, P., Pontell, H. N., & Geis, G. (1993). *Prescription for profit: How doctors defraud Medicaid.* Berkeley: University of California Press.

Jick, T. D. (1979). Mixing qualitative and quantitative methods: Triangulation in action. *Administrative Science Quarterly.* (24)4, 602-611.

Johansson, T. D. (2000). Visualization in cybergeography: Reconsidering cartography's concept of visualization in current user-centric cyber-geographic cosmologies.

Johnson, B. (2008, March 6). NATO says cyber warfare poses as great a threat as a missile attack. *The Guardian.* Retrieved on May 15, 2008 from www.guardian.co.uk/technology/2008/mar/06 /hitechcrime.uksecurity.

Johnson, C. (2004, July 10). Task force found way to top of Enron. *The Washington Post.* Retrieved on March 17, 2008 from www.washingtonpost.com/wp-dyn/articles/A39847-2004Jul9.html.

Johnson, K. (2006, May 5). Law enforcement agencies find it difficult to require degrees. *USA Today.* Retrieved on August 8, 2007 from www.officer.com/article/article.jsp?siteSection=4&id=32666.

Johnston, L. (2006). Transnational security governance. In Wood, J. and Dupont, B. (Eds.) *Democracy, Society and the Governance of Security* (pp. 33-51). New York: Cambridge University Press.

Johnson, R. B. & Onwuegbuzie, A. J. (2004). Mixed methods research: A research paradigm whose time has come. *Educational Researcher.* (33)7, 14-26.

Joint Committee on Taxation, Senate Committee on Finance (2003). *Report of the Investigation of Enron Corporation and Related Entities Regarding Federal Tax and Compensation Issues, and Policy Recommendations, Volume 1: Report.* 108th Congress First Session, JCS-3-03. Retrieved April 24, 2008, from www.house.gov/jct/s-3-03-vol1.pdf.

Joseph, N. & Alex, N. (1972). The uniform: A sociological perspective. *The American Journal of Sociology.* 77(4). 719-730.

Kahan, D. M. (2002). Reciprocity, collective action and community policing. *California Law Review.* (90)5, 1513-1539.

Kane, J. & Wall, A. (2006). *The 2005 National Public Survey on White Collar Crime.* National White Collar Crime Center. Retrieved on August 16, 2007, from www.nw3c.org/research/docs/national_public_household_survey.pdf.

Kappeler, V. E., Sluder, R. D., & Alpert, G. P. (2006). Breeding Deviant conformity: Police ideology and culture. In Kappeler, V. E. (ed.), *The Police and Society 3rd Edition.* Long Grove, IL: Waveland Press.

Kaufman, C., Perlman, R., & Speciner, M. (2002). *Network Security: Private Communication in a Public World, 2nd ed.* Upper Saddle River, NJ: Prentice Hall.

Kaplan, J. (1988). Abortion as a vice crime: A "what if" story. *Law and Contemporary Problems.* (51)1, 151-179.

Kelling, G., & Moore, M. (1988). *From political to reform to community: The evolving strategy of police.* In Greene, J. & Mastrofski, S. (Eds.), Community Policing: Rhetoric or Reality? (pp. 1-26). New York: Praeger.

Kelling, G., & Moore, M. (2005). The evolving strategy of policing. In Newburn, T. (Ed.) *Policing: Key Readings* (pp. 88-108). Portland, OR: Willan Publishing.

Kelling, G. L., Pate, T., Dieckman, D., & Brown, C. E. (1974). *The Kansas City preventive patrol experiment: A summary report.* Washington D.C.: The Police Foundation. Retrieved on April 3, 2008 from www.policefoundation.org/pdf/kcppe.pdf.

Kleinrock, L. (2004). The Internet rules of engagement: Then and now. *Technology and Society.* (24), 193-207.

Klockers, C. B. (1988). The rhetoric of community policing. In Klockers, C. B. & Mastrofsk, S. D. (Eds.) *Community Policing: Rhetoric or Reality.* New York: Praeger.

Knapp, W., Monserrat, J., Sprizzo, J, Thomas, F.A., & Vance, C. (1972). *The Knapp Commission Report on Police Corruption.* New York: George Braziller.

Kornblum, J. (2002). Preservation of fragile digital evidence by first responders. *Digital Forensics Workshop,* August 8, 2002. Retrieved on March 13, 2008 from http://www.e-fense.com/helix/Docs/Jesse_Kornblum.pdf.

Kravets, D. (2009, November 18). It's alive! Hollywood claims Pirate Bay tracker lives. *Wired.* Retrieved on November 20, 2009 from www.wired.com/threatlevel/2009/11/open-bit-torrent.

References

Krazit, T. (2009, December 24). DDoS attack hobbles sites, including Amazon. CNET. Retrieved on December 25, 2009 from www.cnn.com/2009/TECH/12/24/cnet.ddos.attack/index.html.
Krebs, B. (2005, December 13). Tech group blasts federal leadership on cyber-security. *The Washington Post.* Retrieved on June 18, 2008 from www.washingtonpost.com/wp-dyn/content/article/2005/12/13/AR2005121301294.html.
Kshetri, N. (2005). Pattern of global cyber war and crime: A conceptual framework. *Journal of International Management.* (11), 541-562.
Kshetri, N. (2007). Barriers to e-commerce and competitive business models in developing countries: A case study. *Electronic Commerce Research and Applications.* (6), 443-452.
Kvale, S. (1994). Ten standard objections to qualitative research interviews. *Journal of Phenomenological Psychology.* (25)2, 147-173.
Lasica, J. D. (2005). *Darknet: Hollywood's war against the digital generation.* New Jersey: Wiley and Sons.
Leamer, E. E. & Storper, M. (2001). The economic geography of the Internet Age. *Journal of International Business Studies.* (32), 4.
Leggett, H. (2009, July 10). The next hacking frontier: Your brain? *Wired.* Retrieved on November 3, 2009 from www.cnn.com/2009/TECH/07/10/mind.hacking/index.html.
Lemert, E. M. (2000). Rules, deviance, and social control theory. In Lemert, C. C. & Winter, M. F. (Eds.), *Crime and Deviance: Essays and Innovations of Edwin M. Lemert.* Lanham, MD: Rowman and Littlefield.
Lenhart, A. & Madden, M. (2007). Social networking website and teens: An overview. Pew Internet Project Data Memo. Retrieved on August 12, 2007 from www.pewinternet.org/pdfs/PIP_SNS_Data_Memo_Jan_2007.pdf.
Lenk, K. (1997). The challenge of cyberspatial forms of human interaction to territorial governance and policing. In Loader, B. D. (Ed.) *The Governance of Cyberspace: Politics, Technology and Global Restructuring* (pp. 126-135). New York: Routledge.
Lessig, L. (2005). *Free culture: The nature and future of creativity.* New York: Penguin Books.
Levy, S. (2001). *Hackers: Heroes of the Computing Revolution.* New York: Penguin Books.

References

Leyden, J. (2004, May 18). UK police lack e-crime savvy officers. *The Register*. Retrieved on March 2, 2008 from www.theregister.co.uk/2004/05/18/police_e-skills_crisis/.

Licklider, J.C.R. & Taylor, R. W. (1968). The computer as a communication device. *Science and Technology*. (1968) April, 21-41.

Lofland, J. & Lofland, L. H. (1995). *Analyzing Social Settings: A Guide to Qualitative Observation and Analysis 3rd Edition*. Belmont, CA: Wadsworth Publishing.

Lonsway, K., Moore, M., Harrington, P., Smeal, E., & Spillar, K. (2003). *Hiring and retaining more women: The advantages to law enforcement agencies*. National Center for Women and Policing Online Publication. Retrieved on August 8, 2007 from www.womenandpolicing.org/pdf/NewAdvantagesReport.pdf

Lourie, A. (2007). *United States House of Representatives Committee on the Judiciary Subcommittee on Crime, Terrorism, and Homeland Security*. Concerning "Privacy and Cybercrime Enforcement Act of 2007." Retrieved on December 16, 2009 from www.usdoj.gov/criminal/cybercrime/LourieTestimony121807.pdf.

Love, D. (2009, June 12). Opinion: Plea bargains in the criminal McJustice system. *News One*. Retrieved on December 3, 2009 from newsone.com/nation/opinion-plea-bargains-in-the-criminal-mcjustice-system/.

Lui, Q., Safavi-Naini, R., & Sheppard, N. P., (2003). *Digital rights management for content distribution*. Proceedings of the Australasian information security workshop conference on ACSW frontiers 2003, Adelaide, Australia. (34), 49-58.

Luker, K. (1984). *Abortion and the politics of motherhood*. Berkeley: University of California Press.

Lyon, D. (1997). Cyberspace sociality: Controversies over computer-mediated relationships. In Loader, B. D. (Ed.) *The Governance of Cyberspace: Politics, Technology and Global Restructuring* (pp. 23-37). New York: Routledge.

Maclean, S. (2005, July 21). Internet criminals are stronger than ever. *Business Edge*. Retrieved on March 15, 2008 from www.businessedge.ca/article.cfm/newsID/10118.cfm.

Madden, M. & Rainie, L. (2005). Music and video downloading moves beyond P2P. Pew Internet Project Data Memo. Retrieved on August 12, 2007 from www.pewinternet.org/pdfs/PIP_Filesharing_March05.pdf.

References

Manning, P. K. (1988). Community policing as a drama of control. In Green, J. R. & Mastrofski, S. D. (Eds.) *Community Policing* (27-45). New York: Praeger.

Manning, P. K. (2006a). *Two case studies of American anti-terrorism.* In Wood, J. and Dupont, B. (Eds.) Democracy, Society and the Governance of Security (pp. 52-85). New York: Cambridge University Press.

Manning, P. K. (2006b). *The police: Mandate, strategies, and appearances.* In Kappeler, V. E. (ed.) The Police and Society 3rd Edition. Long Grove, IL: Waveland Press.

Mark, R. (2009, November 20). NYC considers net neutrality resolution. eWeek. Retrieved on November 21, 2009 from www.eweek.com/c/a/Government-IT/NYC-Considers-Net-Neutrality-Resolution-150577/.

Marsal, K. (2007, December 19). Mac Users Much More Likely than PC Users to Pay for Music – NPD. *Apple Insider.* Retrieved on April 13, 2008 from www.appleinsider.com/articles/07/12/19/mac_users_much_more_likely_than_pc_users_to_pay_for_music_npd.html.

Marx, G. T. (1997). Some conceptual issues in the study of borders and surveillance. In Zureik, E. & Salter, M. B. (Eds.) *Global Surveillance and Policing: Borders, Security, Identity* (pp. 11-35). Portland: Willan Publishing.

McCarthy, I. P., Rakotobe-Joel,T., & Frizelle, G. (2000). Complex systems theory: Implications and promises for manufacturing organizations. *International Journal of Manufacturing Technology and Management.* (2)1-7, 559-579.

McCarty, B. (2003). Automated identity theft. *Security & Privacy, IEEE.* (1)5, 89-92.

McClintock, P. (2009, August 31). Summer sets box office record: 2009 is highest-grossing summer ever. Variety. Retrieved on September 3, 2009 from www.variety.com/article/VR1118007956.html?categoryid=3717&cs=1&nid=2563.

McCone, J. A., et al. (1965). Violence in the city: An end or a beginning? *The Governor's Commission on the Los Angeles Riots.* Retrieved on November 13, 2009 from www.usc.edu/libraries/archives/cityinstress/mccone/contents.html.

McLeod, K. (2005). *Freedom of expression®: Overzealous copyright bozos and other enemies of creativity.* New York: Doubleday.

McMillan, R. (2008, January 14). Nashville laptop theft may cost $1 million. *Infoworld.* Retrieved on June 19, 2008 from www.infoworld.com/article/08/01/14/Nashville-laptop-theft-may-cost-1-million-dollars_1.html.

Mercuri, R. T. & Neumann, P. G. (2003). Security by obscurity. *Communications of the ACM.* (46)11, 160.

Meyers, L. (2007). The problem with DNA: Forensic evidence increasingly includes genetic fingerprinting, but researchers worry that juries may put too much stock in the results. *Monitor on Psychology.* (38)6.

Mintz, J. (2008, February 7). Microsoft helps nab $900M piracy ring. The Associated Press. Retrieved on February 27, 2008 from www.examiner.com/a-1208462~Microsoft_Helps_Nab__900M _Piracy_Ring.html?cid=sec-promo.

Mockus, A., Fielding, R. T., & Herbsleb, J. D. (2002). Two case studies of open source software development: Apache and Mozilla. *ACM Transactions on Software Engineering and Methodology.* (11)3, 309-346.

Moore, M. H. & Trojanowicz, R. C. (1989). Corporate strategies for policing. *Perspectives on Policing: A Publication of the National Institute of Justice, U.S. Department of Justice, and the Program in Criminal Justice Policy and Management, John F. Kennedy School of Government, Harvard University.* (6).

Morphy, E. (2004). MPAA steps up fight against piracy. *Newsfactor.com.* Retrieved on October 24, 2007 from www.newsfactor.com/story.xhtml?story_title=MPAA-Steps-Up-Fight-Against-Piracy&story_id=25800.

Morse, J. M. (1994). Qualitative research: Fact or fantasy? In Morse, J. M. (Ed.), *Critical Issues in Qualitative Research Methods.* Thousand Oaks, CA: Sage Publications.

Muncaster, P. (2005). Police fail to cope with e-crime: Firms expected to improve their own security. *Computing.* Retrieved on August 14, 2007 from www.computing.co.uk/itweek/news/2085853 /police-fail-cope-crime.

National White Collar Crime Center (NW3C) and Bureau of Justice Assistance (BJA) (2008). *2008 Internet Crime Report.* Retrieved on November 13, 2009 from www.ic3.gov/media/annualreport/ 2008_IC3Report.pdf.

Newman, O. (1973). *Defensible spaces: Crime prevention through urban design.* New York: Macmillan.

Nhan, J. (2008). *"It's like printing money": Piracy on the Internet.* In Schmallager F. & Pittaro M. (Eds.), Crimes of the Internet (pp. 356-383). Upper Saddle River, NJ: Prentice Hall.

Nhan, J. (2009). Criminal justice firewalls: Prosecutorial decision-making in cyber and high-tech crime cases. In Jaishankar, K. (ed.) *International Perspectives on Crime and Justice.* Cambridge: Cambridge Scholars Publishing.

Nhan, J. & Bachmann, M. (2010). Developments in cyber criminology. In Maguire, M. & Okada, D. (Eds.) *Critical Issues of Crime and Criminal Justice: Thoughts, Policy and Practice.* Thousand Oaks, CA: Sage.

Nhan, J. & Huey, L. J. (2008). Policing through nodes, clusters and bandwidth: The role of network relations in the prevention of and response to high-technology crimes. In Leman-Langlois, S. (Ed.) *Techno-Crime: Technology, Crime, and Social Control.* Portland: Willan.

Parker, D. B. (1983). *Fighting computer crime.* New York: Scribners.

Penalties for white collar crime: Hearings before the Subcommittee on Crime and Drugs of the Committee on the Judiciary United States Senate, 107th Congress, 2nd Session (2002). J-107-87.

Pew Internet & American Life Project Surveys, March 2000-April 2009. Pew Internet & American Life Project. Retrieved on December 4, 2009 from www.pewinternet.org/Static-Pages/Trend-Data/Internet-Adoption.aspx.

Pisani, J. (2006, October 2). Spy vs. spy: Corporate espionage. *Business Week.* Retrieved on March 22, 2008 from www.businessweek.com/technology/content/sep2006/tc20060929_557426.htm.

Pleyte, M. (2003). White collar crime in the twenty-first century. *UC Davis Business Law Journal.* (4)1. Retrieved on October 21, 2007 from http://blj.ucdavis.edu/article/514/.

Plummer, L. C. (1999). Community policing: Thriving because it works. *Police Quarterly.* (2)1, 96-102.

Pontell, H. N. (1982). System capacity and criminal justice: Theoretical and substantive considerations. In Pepinsky, H. E. (ed.), *Rethinking Criminology* (pp. 131-143). Beverly Hills: Sage Publications.

Pontell, H. N. (1984). *A capacity to punish: The ecology of crime and punishment.* Bloomington: Indiana University Press.

Pontell, H. N. & Calavita, K. (1993). White-collar crime in the savings and loan scandal. *Annals of the American Academy of Political and Social Science.* (525), 31-45.

Pontell, H. N. (2002). 'Pleased to meet you...won't you guess my name?': Reducing identity fraud in the Australian tax system. Paper presented at the Centre for Tax System Integrity, The Australian National University. *"Identity Fraud and Illegal Tobacco: An Absence of Integrity,"* Sponsored by the Australian Taxation Office. October 29, 2002.

Pontell, H. N. & Rosoff, S. M. (2009). White-collar delinquency. *Crime, Law and Social Change.* (51)1, 147-162.

Powell, M. K. (2004). Preserving Internet freedom: Guiding principles for the industry. Speech presentation at the Silicon Flatirons Symposium on "The Digital Broadband Migration: Toward a Regulatory Regime for the Internet Age" University of Colorado School of Law. Boulder, Colorado, February 8, 2004.

Preece, J. (2000). *Online communities: Designing usability, supporting sociability.* New York: John Wiley & Sons Inc.

Preece, J. (2004). *Etiquette online: From nice to necessary.* Communications of the ACM. Special Issue: Human-Computer Etiquette: Managing Expectations with Intentional Agents. (47)4, 56-61.

Rainie, L., Fox, S., Horrigan, J., Fallows, D., Lenhard, A, Madden, M., Cornfield, M., & Carter-Sykes, C. (2005). A decade of adoption: How the Internet has woven itself into American life. Pew Internet and American Life Project. Retrieved on August 12, 2007 from www.pewinternet.org/PPF/r/148/report_display.asp.

Ramsbrock, D., Berthier, R. & Cukier, M. (2007). Profiling attacker behavior following SSH compromises. *Proceedings from the 37th Annual IEEE/IFIP International Conference on Dependable Systems and Networks* (Pp. 119-124).

Reaves, B. A. & Hickman, M. J. (2004). Law enforcement management and administrative statistics, 2000: Data for individual state and local agencies with 100 or more officers. *Bureau of Justice Statistics*, March NCJ 203350. Retrieved on March 17, 2008 from www.ojp.usdoj.gov/bjs/pub/pdf/lemas00.pdf.

Reiman, J. (2005). *The rich get richer and the poor get prison: Ideology, class, and criminal justice, 7th edition.* Boston: Allyn and Bacon.

References

Reinganum, J. F. (1988). Plea bargaining and prosecutorial discretion. *The American Economic Review.* (78)4, 714-728.

Reinganum, J. F. (2000). Sentencing guidelines, judicial discretion, and plea bargaining. *RAND Journal of Economics.* (31)1, 62-81.

Richardson, R. (2008). CSI computer crime & security survey. *Computer Security Institute.* Retrieved on September 30, 2009 from www.gocsi.com.

Ritter, N. (2006). Digital evidence: How law enforcement can level the playing field with criminals. *National Institute of Justice Journal.* (254), NCJ 214116. Retrieved on April 24, 2008 from www.ojp.usdoj.gov/nij/journals/254/digital_evidence.html.

Riordan, T. (2008, February 18). Princeton researchers envision a more secure Internet. *EQuad News.* Retrieved on June 18, 2008, from www.princeton.edu/main/news/archive/S20/31/02148/index.xml?section=science.

Rosoff, S. M., Pontell, H. N., & Tillman, R. (1998). *Profit without honor: White-collar crime and the looting of America.* Upper Saddle River, NJ: Prentice Hall.

Rosoff, S. M., Pontell, H. N., & Tillman, R. (2007). *Profit without honor: White-collar crime and the looting of America 4th edition.* Upper Saddle River, NJ: Prentice Hall.

Sampson, R. J., Raudenbush, S. W., & Earls, F. (1997). Neighborhoods and violent crime: A multilevel study of collective efficacy. *Science.* (277), 918-924.

Sandoval, G. (2007, August 2). Reports: BitTorrent index suprnova.org to rise again. *CNET News Blog.* Retrieved on August 18, 2007 from news.com.com/8301-10784_3-9754292-7.html.

Scahill, J. (2005, September 21). Blackwater down. *The Nation.* Retrieved on May 16, 2008 from www.thenation.com/doc/20051010/scahill.

Schenck, S. (2009, January 29). Hacker business booming during recession: Phishing, malware, and data breaches for profit are on the rise while the rest of the economy struggles. Obsessable. Retrieved on March 31, 2009 from www.obsessable.com/news/2009/01/29/hacker-business-booming-during-recession/.

Schurr, A. (2006, August 14). When it's time to bring in the feds. *Network World.* Retrieved March 11, 2008 from www.networkworld.com/news/2006/081406-security-feds.html.

Schneier, B. (1999). Open source and security. *Crypto-Gram Newsletter*. Retrieved on May 20, 2008, from www.schneier.com/crypto-gram-9909.html.
Shearing, C. D. (2006). Reflections on the refusal to acknowledge private government. In Wood, J. and Dupont, B. (Eds.) *Democracy, Society and the Governance of Security* (pp. 11-32). New York: Cambridge University Press.
Shearing, C. D. and Stenning, P. C. (1981). Modern private security: Its growth and implications. *Crime and Justice.* (3), 193-245.
Shearing, C. D. & Wood, J. (2003). Nodal governance, democracy, and the new 'denizens.' *Journal of Law and Society.* (30)3, 400-419.
Shultz, E. E. & Shumway, R. (2001). *Incident response: A strategic guide to handling system and network security breaches.* Indianapolis: New Riders.
Sims, R. R., Cheng, H. K., & Teegen, H. (1996). Toward a profile of student software piraters. *Journal of Business Ethics.* (15)8, 839-849.
Singel, R. (2008, April 9). Zombie computers decried as imminent national threat. *Wired.* Retrieved on April 9, 2008 from http://blog.wired.com/27bstroke6/2008/04/zombie-computer.html.
Singer, M. (2002, April 19). Feds bust Silicon Valley software piracy ring. Internet News. Retrieved on October 31, 2009 from www.internetnews.com/dev-news/article.php/1013121/Feds+Bust+Silicon+Valley+Software+Piracy+Ring.htm.
Siwek, S. E. (2006). The true cost of motion picture piracy to the U.S. economy. *Institute for Policy Innovation Report #186.* Retrieved on March 16, 2008 from www.ipi.org/ipi%5CIPIPublications.nsf/PublicationLookupFullTextPDF/293C69E7D5055FA4862571F800168459/$File/CostOfPiracy.pdf?OpenElement.
Siwek, S. E. (2007). The true cost of copyright industry piracy to the U. S. economy. *Institute for Policy Innovation, IPI Report No. 189.* Retrieved on April 21, 2008 from www.ipi.org/ipi%5CIPIPublications.nsf/PublicationLookupFullTextPDF/02DA0B4B44F2AE9286257369005ACB57/$File/CopyrightPiracy.pdf?OpenElement.
Skogan, W. G. & Hartnett, S. M. (1997). *Community policing, Chicago Style.* New York: Oxford University Press.

References

Skogan, W. G. (2004). Representing the community in community policing. In Skogan, W. G. (Ed.) *Community Policing (Can It Work?)*. Belmont, CA: Wadsworth/Thomsom Learning, 57-75.

Skolnick, J. H. (1966). *Justice without trial: Law enforcement in democratic society*. New York: Wiley.

Skolnick, J. H. (1994). *Sketch of the policeman's working personality 3rd edition*. New York: Wiley.

Skolnick, J. H. & Fyfe, J. J. (1993). *Above the law: Police and the excessive use of force*. New York: The Free Press.

Smith, R. G., Grabosky, P., & Urbas, G. (2004). *Cyber criminals on trial*. New York: Cambridge University Press.

Sommer, P. (1998). Digital footprints: Assessing computer evidence. *Criminal Law Review Special Edition*. December 1998, 61-78.

Spring, T. (2003, May 22). Three minutes with Jack Valenti: The MPAA's main man tells his tactics for fighting piracy (and sometimes the tech industry) and selling movies. *PC World*. Retrieved on June 17, 2008 from www.pcworld.com/article/id,110698-page,1/article.html.

Statement of Gilbert Geis. White-collar crime hearings before House Subcommittee on Crime. 95th Congress, 2nd session, 1, (1978).

Strader, J. K. (2006). *Understanding white collar crime*. LexisNexis/Matthew Bender.

Strauss, A. & Corbin, J. M. (1990). *Basics of qualitative research: Grounded theory procedures and techniques*. Thousand Oaks, CA: Sage Publications.

Stenger, R. (2001, August 13). FBI Nabs Four in $10 Million Software Piracy Bust. *CNN Sci-Tech*. Retrieved on March 13, 2008 from archives.cnn.com/2001/TECH/industry/08/13/microsoft.software.

Stone, M. (2004, February 13). Is open source secure? *O'Reilly Linux DevCenter*. Retrieved on April 12, 2008 from www.oreillynet.com/linux/blog/2004/02/is_open_source_secure.html.

Straub, D. W. & Welke, R. J. (1998). Coping with system risk: Security planning models for management decision making. *MIS Quarterly*. (22)4, 441-469.

Stylianou, A. C., Robbins, S. S., & Jackson, P. (2004). Perceptions and attitudes about ecommerce development in china: An exploratory study. In Hunter, G. and Tan, F. (Eds.), *Advanced Topics in Global Information Management, Volume 3* (pp. 295-311). Hershey, PA: Idea Group Publishing.

Sutherland, E. H. (1939). White-collar criminality. *American Sociological Review.* 5(1), 1-12.
Sutherland, E. H. (1944). Is "white-collar crime" crime? *American Sociological Review.* (10)2, 132-139.
Swanson, E. (2009, February 2). Fannie Mae logic bomb attack 'Tip of the iceberg'. Cenzic. Retrieved on December 10, 2009 from blog.cenzic.com/public/item/225397.
Sykes, G. M. and Matza, D. (1957). Techniques of neutralization: A theory of delinquency. *American Sociological Review.* (22)6, 664-670.
Tanenbaum, A. S. (2003). *Computer networks, 4th Edition.* Upper Saddle River, NJ: Prentice Hall.
Taylor, C. (1999, January 18). The history and hype: Computer scientists may disarm the Y2K bomb in time, but that doesn't mean they didn't screw up along the way. *Time.* Retrieved on April 2, 2008 from www.time.com/time/teach/glenfall99/y2k.pdf.
Thomas, J. (2005). Intellectual Property Theft in Russia Increasing Dramatically: U.S. Officials Warns of "Rampant Piracy and Counterfeiting." *U.S. Department of State USINFO.* Retrieved on October 24, 2007 from usinfo.state.gov/ei/Archive/2005/May/19-415943.html.
Thompson, W. C. (1995). Subjective Interpretation, Laboratory Error and the Value of DNA Evidence: Three Case Studies. *Genetica.* (96)1-2, 153-168.
Thompson, W.C., Ford, S., Doom, T., Raymer M., & Krane, D. E. (2003). Evaluating forensic DNA evidence: Essential elements of a competent defense review. *Champion.* (24).
Toward a Safer and More Secure Cyberspace (2007). Report by the Committee on Improving Cybersecurity Research in the United States Computer Science and Telecommunications Board Division on Engineering and Physical Sciences. National Research Council and National Academy of Engineering of the National Academies. Goodman, S. E. and Lin, H. S. (Eds.). Washington, D.C.: National Academies Press.
Townsend, J. J., Riz, D. & Schaffer, D. (2004). *Building portals, intranets, and corporate web sites using Microsoft servers.* Boston: Addison-Wesley Professional.
Trojanowicz, R. & Bucqueroux, B. (1990). *Community policing.* Cincinnati, OH: Anderson Publishing.

References

Uchida, C. D. (1997). The development of the American police: An historical overview. In Dunham, R. G. and Alpert, G. P. (Eds.) *Critical Issues in Policing: Contemporary Readings* 3rd ed. Prospect Heights, IL: Waveland Press.

United States Department of Justice, Bureau of Justice Assistance (2004). *Understanding community policing: A framework for action.* Washington, D. C.: U.S. Government Printing Office. Retrieved on April 3, 2008 from www.ncjrs.gov/pdffiles/commp.pdf.

United States Governmental Accountability Office (2006). *Internet infrastructure: DHS faces challenges in developing a joint public/private recovery plan.* GAO Report to Congressional Requestors GAO-06-672. Retrieved on August 10, 2007 from www.gao.gov/new.items/d06672.pdf.

United States Senate, Special Committee on the Year 2000 Technology Problem (2000). *Y2K aftermath: Crisis averted final committee report.* Washington, D.C.: U.S. Government Printing Office.

United States White House Executive Report (2003). *The national strategy to secure cyberspace.* Washington D.C.: U.S. Government Printing Office. Retrieved on April 7, 2008 from www.whitehouse.gov/pcipb/cyberspace_strategy.pdf.

U.S. Department of Justice, Federal Bureau of Investigation (1989). *White collar crime: A report to the public.* Washington, D.C.: Government Printing Office.

Van Maanen, J. (1975). Police socialization: A Longitudinal examination of job attitudes in an urban police department. *Administrative Science Quarterly.* (20), 207-227.

Vollmer, A. & Schneider, A. (1917). The school for police as planned at Berkeley. *Journal of the American Institute of Criminal Law and Criminology.* (7)6, 877-898.

Walker, S. (1984). "Broken windows" and fractured history: The use and misuse of history in recent police patrol analysis. *Justice Quarterly.* (1)1, 75-90.

Walker, S. & Katz, C. M. (2002). The police in America: An introduction. New York: McGraw-Hill.

Wall, D. S. (2004). What are Cybercrimes? *Criminal Justice Matters.* (58)1, 20-21.

Wall, D. S. (2006). *The Internet as a conduit for criminal activity.* In Pattavina, A. (ed.) information technology and the criminal justice system (pp. 77-93). Thousand Oaks, CA: Sage Publications.

Wall, D. S. (2007). Policing cybercrimes: Situating the public police in networks of security within cyberspace. *Police Practice and Research.* (8)2, 183-205.

Wall, D. S. (2008). Cybercrime, media and insecurity: The shaping of public perceptions of cybercrime. *International Review of Law, Computers and Technology.* 22(1-2), 45-63.

Wasserman, S. & Faust, K. (1994). *Social network analysis.* Cambridge: Cambridge University Press.

West-Brown, M. J., Stikvoort, D., Kossakowski, K. P., Killcrece, G., Ruelfle, R., & Zajicek, M. (2003). Handbook for computer security response teams (CSIRTs), 2nd Edition. Carnegie Mellon Software Engineering Institute. Retrieved on December 2, 2009 from www.cert.org/archive/pdf/csirt-handbook.pdf.

Williams, H. E. (1997). *Investigating white-collar crime: Embezzlement and financial fraud.* Springfield, IL: Charles C. Thomas Publisher.

Wilson, J. Q. (1968). *Varieties of police behavior: The management of law and order in eight communities.* Cambridge, MA: Harvard University Press.

Wilson, M. I. & Corey, K. E. (2000). *Information tectonics: Space, place and technology in an electronic age.* New York: John Wiley & Sons.

Wakefield, A. (2003). *Selling security: The private policing of public space.* Cullompton, UK: Willan.

Ward, M. (2004). Hackers exploit windows patches: Malicious hackers and vandals are lazy and wait for Microsoft to issue patches before they produce tools to work out how to exploit loopholes in windows, say experts. *BBC News.* Retrieved on March 15, 2008 from news.bbc.co.uk/1/hi/technology/3485972.stm.

Walker, S. (1983). Racial minority and female employment in policing: the implications of "glacial" change. *Crime and Delinquency.* (31), 555-572.

Webster, J. A. (1973). *The realities of police work.* Dubuque, IA: Kendall-Hunt Publishing.

Weitzer, R. (1991). Prostitutes' rights in the United States: Failure of a movement. *The Sociological Quarterly.* (32)1, 23-41.

White, M. D. (2008). Identifying good cops early: Predicting recruit performance in the academy. *Police Quarterly.* (11)1, 27-49.

References

Williams III, F. P. & Wagoner, C. P. (1995). Making the police proactive: An impossible task for improbable reasons. In Kappeler, V. E. (Ed.), *The police and society: Touchstone readings* (pp. 365-374). Prospect Heights, IL: Waveland Press.

Wilson, J. Q. (1968). *Varieties of police behavior: The management of law and order in eight communities.* Cambridge, MA: Harvard University Press.

Wood, J. (2006). Research and innovation in the field of security. In Wood, J. and Dupont, B. (Eds.) *Democracy, society and the governance of security* (pp. 217-240). New York: Cambridge University Press.

Wood, J. (2006b). Dark networks and the place of the police. In Flemming, J. and Wood, J (Eds.) *Fighting crime together: The challenges of policing and the security networks.* Sydney: University of New South Wales Press.

Wood, J. & Shearing, C. (2006). *Security and nodal governance.* Paper presented at the Temple University Beasley School of Law October 25, 2006, Philadelphia. Retrieved on March 18, 2008 from www.law.temple.edu/pdfs/Faculty/woodpaper.pdf.

Wood, J. & Shearing, C. (2007). *Imagining security.* Portland, OR: Willan Publishing.

Wright, B. (2004). Internet break-ins: New legal liability. *Computer Law & Security Report.* (20)3, 171-174.

Wu, T. (2003). Network neutrality, broadband discrimination. *Journal of Telecommunications and High Technology Law.* (2), 141-179.

Young, T. (2007, March 9). Cybercrime must be a priority: Independent peer says laws that cannot be enforced are useless. *Computing.* Retrieved on August 16, 2007, from www.computing.co.uk/computing/news/2185135/lord-erroll-cubercrime-needs.

Zhang, K. & Peck, K. L. (2003). The effects of peer-controlled or moderated online collaboration on group problem-solving and related attitudes. *Canadian Journal of Learning and Technology.* (29)3, 93-112.

Zhao, J. & Thurman, Q. C. (2004). *The Nature of Community Policing Innovations* in Thurman, Q. C. and Zhao, J. (Eds.) Contemporary policing: Controversies, challenges, and solutions: An anthology. Los Angeles: Roxbury Publishing Company.

Index

Access to data, 37
Asia, 34, 96
Bad guys, 29, 101-102, 109, 115, 124
Borders, 7, 27, 57, 168
California, 6, 10-11, 13, 15, 26, 28-29, 32-35, 37-39, 44-49, 51, 53-54, 56-57, 59-60, 62-64, 71, 74-76, 87-91, 94, 97, 99, 105, 112, 134, 141, 157, 166-169, 171-172, 175-176
Capital, 9, 10, 21-24, 26, 31, 54-55, 61, 63, 65-66, 75, 77, 82-83, 86-87, 95, 98-100, 105, 107-108, 110, 112-113, 117, 122-125, 129-130, 135, 141, 151, 173-174
Collective efficacy, 170
Computer security, 2, 6, 25, 34-35, 47, 60, 63, 95, 113-114, 125, 146-147, 161
Critical infrastructure, 105, 138, 175
Defensible space, 159, 165
Educational background, 80
FBI, 3, 6, 27, 61, 70, 83, 95, 125-126, 129, 131, 171
Forensic, 10, 46, 61, 69, 77, 78, 135

Forensics, 108
Freedom, 102-103, 143, 145, 158
Geeks, 82
Hackers, 3, 6, 12, 95, !13, 147, 151, 154
Identity theft, 6, 7, 28-29, 59, 182, 193
Information society, 17, 20, 167
Inter-nodal, 10, 22, 40, 51, 54, 56, 75, 83, 92-94, 105, 107-108, 116, 123, 125-126, 135, 174, 176
Interview, 11, 28, 36, 38-40, 50-54, 56, 73, 141
IRB, 38
Legal, 4, 10-13, 27-29, 32, 35, 40-41, 47, 49, 60, 62-63, 68, 77, 98, 102, 104, 110, 112, 114-116, 124, 126-129, 131, 133, 146, 152, 154-157, 169, 174
Mapping, 10, 13, 54-56, 67, 74-75, 171-172, 176
Measures of success, 18, 20, 75, 108-109, 111
MPAA, 33, 47-48, 81, 96, 99, 102, 111-113, 116-118, 133, 145, 152-153, 155, 172-173, 175, 179

Nodal governance, 9-10, 13, 15, 21-22, 25, 32, 52, 54, 56, 59-60, 62, 75, 93, 99-100, 164, 167-168, 176, 184
OES, 11, 29, 37-38, 44, 46, 49-50, 60, 64, 76, 88-94, 173
Plea bargain, 11, 28, 131
Police culture, 79, 122
Prosecutor, 66, 71, 77, 82, 124-125, 127-135, 157, 174
Qualitative, 35, 51
RIAA, 102, 152
Risk, 3, 7, 9, 15, 19-20, 60, 88, 97, 110, 114, 120, 133, 167
Sample Guide Questions, 40-43
Sample size, 48-50, 172
Sarbanes Oxley, 39
Steering committee, 36, 41, 44, 46, 48-50, 63-64, 83, 88, 90, 92
System capacity, 11, 13, 16, 32, 105, 135
Task force, 9
trust, 2, 8, 17-18, 27, 64, 85, 92, 116, 118, 123, 174
Victimization, 7, 12, 29, 60, 95, 107-108, 113, 135, 143, 149, 164, 168-170
Warez, 103